Unqualified Education

A Practical Guide to Learning at Home
Age 11 – 18

About the Authors

Unqualified Education is the sequel to *One-to-One, A Practical Guide to Learning at Home Age 0 – 11*, which was first published in 2001, and quickly became the top-selling resource book for home-educating families in the UK and Europe.

One-to-One shows how the basics of education – reading, writing, arithmetic, etc. – can be covered without compromising the essence of childhood, and Unqualified Education explains how the principle of learning for enjoyment can be extended into the field of secondary education.

The majority of the book is written by Gareth Lewis, who has taught mathematics and science in state and private schools in the UK, and has worked as a private tutor for children with special needs. For the past twelve years he has home educated his three children with his wife, Lin.

Bethan, Wendy, and Samuel Lewis have contributed extensively to the book by providing the illustrations, taking responsibility for the literature, cooking, and crafts sections, and editing and proofreading the text.

The family moved to Brittany, France, in 1994, where they have a smallholding from which they operate an independent publishing company, Nezert Books.

Gareth is the editor of the Freedom-in-Education website and the Freedom-in-Education newsletter.

Unqualified Education

A Practical Guide to Learning At Home
Age 11 – 18

Gareth Lewis

Illustrations
Bethan, Wendy and Samuel Lewis

Nezert Books
Nezert, 22160 Duault, France

First Published 2003
Reprinted 2004

Published by Nezert Books
Nezert, 22160 Duault, France

Copyright © 2003 Nezert Books

British Library Cataloguing-in-Publication Data
A catalogue record for this book is available from the British Library
ISBN: 0952270579

Contents

Preface

All the problems that exist in our school system arise from a basic misunderstanding about the nature of education.

Everything that is done in school is based on the assumption that it is possible to teach things to people – which is not the case: people learn things because they want to learn them and not because someone else has decided that they should.

When a parent or teacher has grasped this simple fact, their whole attitude to education changes. The object becomes to place as many interesting and stimulating experiences in the path of the child as possible, to be prepared to answer questions, and to make as wide a variety of information and resources available as conditions allow.

A set curriculum, tests and exams, a rigid timetable and a stifling environment are all obstacles to the path of real education.

The purpose of this book is to suggest a means by which young people can explore and develop their own interests, learn at their own pace, and set their own goals and targets – and thereby make a good start in the process of becoming educated.

Parents sometimes worry that if their children are not taught to accept the confines and restrictions of the current school system they will be unable to deal with the realities of modern life, but, if anything, the opposite is true: a system that concentrates on examinations and qualifications instead of upon education itself, is not of any lasting use to the people who work their way through it. It does not provide them with the knowledge, the skills, or the drive that they need in order to make a success of their lives; instead, by teaching people to conform, it makes it more difficult for them to do what they believe to be right and it makes it harder for them to be innovative, entrepreneurial, inventive and creative in later life.

Real education is as vital and as useful as it has ever been. Unfortunately, children today are offered a mirage of education; they are told that spending up to twenty years of their lives in school and university will give them an education – but it does not. The typical university graduate is often one-dimensional, lacking in initiative and unable to fend for themselves.

Parents, children and young people are faced with a situation in which they have to take responsibility for their own education – a daunting but immensely enjoyable task.

"We must not believe the many who say that only free people should be educated, but we should rather believe the philosophers who say that only the educated are free."

Epictetus

Introduction

Since writing **One-to-One**, *A Practical Guide to Learning at Home, Age 0 –11*, I have been accused of being both too extremely anti-school and too supportive of parents who do send their children to school. Surprisingly, perhaps, both of these accusations have been made by home-education groups.

In reality, I do not see myself as having any fixed opinion about schools: if a school is capable of treating a child with more kindness and consideration than they would receive elsewhere, then that must be a good thing and should be encouraged. On the other hand, when schools oppress children and make them unhappy, this also should be pointed out: no one should cling to an ideological attachment to something that isn't working. My analysis is that, in the vast majority of cases, schools are not working and that people should be looking for alternatives.

However, this book is not about criticising the school system, it is about explaining that people do have a choice.

> "Thank goodness I was never sent to school; it would have rubbed off some of the originality."
>
> *Beatrix Potter*

My own children, who are now twenty-one, seventeen and fifteen-years-old, have only been to school for short periods of time. For most of their lives, they have learnt at home, with my wife, Lin, and myself.

It has been a rewarding experience for all of us. We have never allowed our agenda to be set by people from outside – we have not followed a curriculum, nor have our children wanted to do exams.

Education has taken place for all of us. Our children are self-taught artists who have illustrated this book (they have also edited and proof-read the text). Our writing skills, language skills, computer skills and knowledge of history, geography and science is increasing all the time. The sections on cooking and gardening reflect the skills that we have acquired in these areas – skills that none of us had twenty years ago.

Our children have also benefited from their involvement in our other projects. They helped while I built a house in Brittany; they were fully involved in the creation and performances of our touring marionette theatre (which supported us for a while when we moved to France) and they now help in our publishing business. I believe that they have enjoyed a more natural form of education than that provided by the current education system and I am convinced that young people in general would benefit from a similar education – one that is not centred around examinations, qualifications and being told what to do, but which gives them the freedom to develop their own talents in their own way.

Ouch! Where am I? I seem to be in the future!

The Importance of Education

It is easy to forget that universal schooling has only been available in most industrialised countries for about one hundred years. Before that, people were in little doubt as to the value of education – the ability to read and write set someone apart from the rest of their community; it meant that they could write and receive letters, understand official forms, and even read books. Those people whose studies had allowed them to learn foreign languages, to study the classics, read works of literature, and delve into the mysteries of history, science, and philosophy, automatically became the leaders of society.

Ironically, the introduction of mass schooling has tended to erode the value of education: in people's minds, it has become inextricably linked with going to school and those people who do not like school (which seems to be a large proportion of the population) lose interest in the whole idea of education, both for themselves and as something that they can value in others.

This should not be taken as a sign that education has lost its intrinsic value, or that there are some people who are simply incapable of appreciating the virtues of education, it is rather a sign that schools have lost their way and that instead of firing their students with an enthusiasm for learning, they are actually having the opposite effect.

> "The mind is not a pitcher to be filled, but a fire to be lighted."
>
> *Plutarch*

Qualifications

One of the reasons behind the decline in the value placed upon education, is that schools link education to qualifications. In the early days of schooling, pupils attended school until they had learnt to read and write, and then most of them left – to work on the family farm, to help in the home, or to take up an apprenticeship. In these circumstances the school was not required to award qualifications. Now that work patterns have changed, pupils are not allowed to join the workforce at the age of twelve or thirteen, but are expected to stay at school. Schools have responded to this by setting examinations and awarding qualifications that, theoretically at least, determine whether a student can go on to university or get a particular job.

This is inevitably detrimental to the cause of education. Education has always been, and always will be, a statement of the individuality of each human being. Just as no two artists ever paint exactly the same picture, no two people will ever have exactly the same view of the world – the better educated they are, the more confidence they will have to stick to their own view, because it is more likely to be based upon carefully thought-through arguments, backed up by facts.

Aaagh!

Qualifications, on the other hand, require uniformity: only those people who give the expected answers are allowed to pass the tests that are required for any particular award.

Qualifications do have their value in selecting people for employment, etc., but it is a serious mistake to try to associate them with the process of education. It would have been much better for all concerned – parents, children, and teachers – if the two things could have been kept completely separate.

Home-Based Education

The reason that this book focuses upon learning at home is not because schools are intrinsically incapable of providing an education, but because the patterns built up over the past fifty years make it very difficult for anyone involved in them to behave in a humane and sensible manner.

The home, on the other hand, offers a better educational environment than ever before; books are plentiful, people have access to well-stocked libraries, and the internet makes information from around the world readily available. Learning at home is not something new – people have been doing it for thousands of years and it has always had the advantage of allowing people to study the things that interest them at their own pace and in their own way.

Learning at home has the added advantage of allowing parents and children, brothers and sisters, grandparents and grandchildren, to work together in a constructive way that does not involve older people taking on the role of 'teachers' and younger people the role of 'pupils', but instead allows people of different ages and different generations to share their experiences, their skills and their knowledge with each other, and at the same time explore new ideas and new subjects that none of them have tackled before.

This book is not about trying to persuade people to leave school but is making the point that, whereas schools may be able to offer qualifications, they do not offer an education: it is still up to you to get that for yourself.

Problems with School

Parents should only send their children to school when they are sure that it is doing them good. If parents had been more rigorous in this respect in the past, it is unlikely that any of the problems that are now endemic within the school system would have been able to develop.

As it is, many schools *do* now have serious problems and parents are not being fair to their children if they send them into dangerous or unpleasant situations. If a child is being affected by any of the following it is difficult to see how continuing to send them to school can be justified:

- **Bullying:** The hierarchical nature of schools makes bullying an intrinsic part of school life. Pupils bully each other but this is only a reflection of the way in which they are themselves being bullied by the school staff. Some of the worst bullying has always taken place in some of the most prestigious schools, where pupils are put under extreme pressure to do what they are told.

- **Drugs:** It is not normal for young people to take drugs without the knowledge of their parents and families: this is a problem associated with schools, directly caused by the way in which they isolate children from their families.

- **Cigarettes and Alcohol:** As with drugs, schools create the conditions that cause children to start smoking cigarettes and drinking excessive amounts of alcohol.

- **Crime:** Schools contribute to the sense of alienation that allows some young people to view breaking the law as excusable.

- **Underachievement:** Schools are responsible for making some people think that they are of below-average ability; this discourages them and makes them lose interest in education.

- **Low educational standards:** A fixed curriculum and continual testing inevitably leads to a decline in educational standards. Many children are intensely bored by the work that they do at school.

The Alien in My Desk: Part 2

Good Schools

In theory, there is no reason why schools should cause all these problems. There *are* isolated examples of good schools and they tend to share the following characteristics:

- The absence of a fixed curriculum.
- Wise teachers who put the needs of the students before predetermined school policies and who have an enthusiasm for their subjects.
- Freedom from tests and exams.
- Good resources.
- Involvement of people from all sections of the community.
- No compulsion.

When these conditions are met, a school can provide a very positive and dynamic learning environment: students encourage and inspire each other and at the same time make use of the skill and expertise of the staff.

The fact that a school does not compel pupils to sit tests and exams, does not mean that it cannot help those pupils who want specific qualifications to prepare for the relevant examinations. The most important thing is that students should not feel that they are being forced to do things against their will.

Educational research confirms what most people would believe to be true in any case: happy children learn better than unhappy children. It shows that children are happier in small schools than in big schools, that there needs to be a strong bond of respect between pupils and teachers and that the more involved a school is with the local community – and the more involved parents are with the school – the better.

Of course, people can be unhappy even in good schools and it is probably impossible to create an educational institution that would suit everyone, but it is still surprising that not more effort is made to make schools of this sort available to every child.

Bad Schools

Unfortunately, it is all too easy to list the points that go to make a bad school, because most of us have experienced them for ourselves:

- A fixed curriculum.
- Teachers who put predetermined school policies before the needs of the students.
- Frequent tests and exams.
- Poor resources.
- Isolation from the wider community.
- Compulsion to attend school; compulsion to behave in a certain way; compulsion to attend specific lessons.

From a purely abstract perspective, there may appear to be nothing wrong with schools that are run on these principles, but, in practice, they do not work.

Young people who attend secondary schools are old enough to form their own opinions about the 'education' that they are receiving. They feel that they are entitled to expect to receive something very worthwhile in exchange for the time that they are made to spend at school and it does not take them long to realise that, in most cases, this expectation is not going to be fulfilled.

Young people's perception of school is that it is they who have to make all the sacrifices, but that they get none of the benefits. They sacrifice their time and their liberty, and in return are cooped up for years in dingy classrooms where they are made to learn irrelevant things parrot-fashion only to be awarded qualifications which are, at best, of dubious value and which are frequently of no use at all.

Schools of this sort may have a veneer of gentility but they are essentially run on compulsion. Pupils are only treated with a measure of civility provided they do exactly what they are told to do, when they are told to do it; they have to start and stop work according to the ringing of bells, they are not allowed to go outside when they want to, have breaks when they want to, speak when they want to or go home when they want to. They are not allowed to study the things that interest them nor do the things that they want to do. This is not education, and it is confusing to describe it as such.

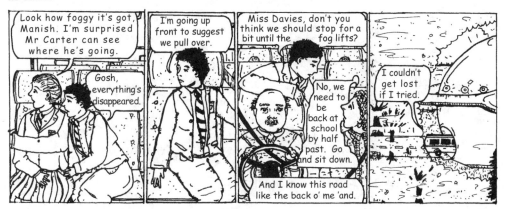

7

How Can They Have Got it so Wrong?

Even if schools were educationally successful, the social problems for which they are responsible – which include bullying, drug abuse, and crime – would make it difficult to understand why society has tolerated them for so long.

The reason is that the history of schools is inextricably linked to the changes that have taken place in working practices over the past two or three hundred years.

Prior to the Industrial Revolution, schools only played a small, specialised role within the overall structure of education. For example, grammar schools trained young men from aristocratic families to become the administrators that kept the machinery of government functioning; the way that these schools were run, and the material that they taught, hardly changed from the days of the Roman Empire up to the middle of the nineteenth century.

Another example is the primary school movement that arose during the Reformation; somehow ordinary people across Europe managed to find premises and employ teachers to teach their children to read and write. This freed them of their dependence upon the ruling, educated elite and opened the door to political change and social reform.

It is important to note that in neither of these examples were schools used to teach all children everything that they needed to know. In the Roman world, only a few people went to school – engineers, artisans, farmers and the people who were responsible for looking after the home all learnt their skills in the real world, usually from members of their family. When primary schools were first introduced, children only attended them for a few mornings per week, until they had learnt to read; this was because they had full lives outside of school from which they could only be spared for the minimum time required to learn the rudiments of reading and writing.

In fact there has never been a time, until now, when mass schooling has been used as a way to educate everyone. It is the extended family that has always been the principal provider of education in every country of the world, throughout history, and, by and large, the extended family has done a much better job than an institution like school could ever hope to do.

> "Experience is the best teacher"
> *English Proverb*

Panel 1: This is funny. We seem to be in some sort o' tunnel, but there isn't a tunnel on this road.

Panel 2: Be quiet a minute, everyone. Does anyone remember there being a tunnel on the way here? — Don't say we're lost. — That's typical.

Panel 3: The- the engine's stalled. We've come to a standstill. I- I don't like this, Miss Davies. — Don't panic, Carter. I can hear voices outside. I'll wind down the window and find out what's going on.

Panel 4: Hi there! Welcome aboard!

How Schools Took Over

The traditional system of families caring for and educating their own children started to break down when parents were required to go to work in places that were not deemed fit for children.

This is essentially the story of the Industrial Revolution. Before the introduction of factories, children could divide their time between the home, the garden, the fields and the workshops. They were welcome everywhere, were useful (to a certain extent) everywhere and were learning everywhere.

Once one, or both, parents had to go to work in a factory, there was no longer a role for their children and something had to be found for them to do.

It is not surprising that people turned to schools. Schools were seen to be doing good – they were teaching children to read and write, which was an indisputably good thing. It therefore seemed reasonable to suggest that children should spend more time at school and learn more things.

Unfortunately no one took into account the things that the children would not be learning by not being in the home, in the garden, in the fields and in the workshops.

This process began in earnest just over one hundred years ago – even at the beginning of the twentieth century the United Kingdom did not have a complete primary school system and it was only halfway through the century that secondary education became compulsory.

Over this period the amount of time parents are expected to spend at work has steadily increased and the amount of time that children are required to spend in school has grown accordingly.

Inevitably, less time with their parents means more problems for children, and school can do nothing to compensate for this. The past hundred years have seen the emergence of youth crime, drug abuse, falling educational standards and increasing family break-up as people lose the ability to maintain a normal family life.

Are schools to blame? Not really. They do the best job that they can in the circumstances, but until the focal point of each child's life is firmly rooted back in their own family, they are always going to fail.

Alternatives to the Traditional School

It is easy for people to become so concerned with the problems that exist in their local schools that they lose sight of the fact that they do have options.

Home-Based Education

The simplest and most effective solution to all school-related problems is to stop going to school.

Much of this book is dedicated to the practical aspects of learning at home. It is something that is within the scope of all families and no one should ever think that they are not able to educate themselves or that they are not fit to be their children's teacher.

Supporting Children at School

Parents play an important role in helping their children at school by giving them their unquestioning support.

For example:

- Be prepared to visit the school and talk to teachers with whom your child does not have a good relationship.
- Be prepared to question excessive or pointless homework assignments.
- Do not force your child to go into school on days that they do not want to.
- Make time to be with your child – especially on days when they are off school.
- Maintain a good relationship with the school: support school activities, fund-raising, etc.
- Do things with your child that have nothing to do with school: cooking, gardening, craft projects, etc.
- Make sure that your child knows that you will love them just the same, and think just as highly of them, whether they do well, or badly, in their schoolwork.

'Alternative' Schools

There are schools that try to provide an alternative to mainstream schools. These have to be judged upon their individual merits.

Alternative schools are best when they are making a serious effort to get away from the idea of school being the place where parents leave their children to be educated. Schools that allow parents to attend and take part in lessons, that encourage part-time and flexi-schooling and that are well integrated with the local community are therefore preferable to those that have conventional classes and which give parents and children very little say in how things are organised.

An Alternative Curriculum

A problem can arise with 'alternative' schools from the very fact that they try to teach a more enlightened curriculum than their state school counterparts.

It is easy for a slightly eccentric curriculum to develop, which may be neither interesting nor of much use in the outside world.

Rudolf Steiner foresaw this danger when he started the first Waldorf school and he insisted that pupils in his school should have covered the same material as those that went to state schools at certain key ages – such as at the transition from primary school to secondary school.

This pragmatic approach may have contributed to the long-term success that sets Waldorf education apart from many other alternative education initiatives of the last century.

Moving Between Schools

People spend up to fourteen years in school; this is a very long time and becomes tedious even when the schools concerned are liberal, caring and flexible. When the school system is oppressive and rigid, it becomes suffocating. It therefore makes sense to move between schools, or in and out of school, over the course of that period.

This ties in well with the idea that people should be responsible for their own education from the very beginning. Instead of expecting the school system to provide a complete education, parents and children can pick appropriate schools at appropriate times to meet their specific requirements.

Home-Based Learning

In most developed countries, parents are under a legal obligation to ensure that their children receive a good education. This obligation is technically discharged by sending a child to school, but few people – when they are being really honest – would say that schools *do* provide a good education. Thus whether a child goes to school or not, their real education has to take place in and around the home.

There are two sides to home-based learning: the work that a young person is able to do on their own and the work that they do with the help of other people, usually their parents.

It is this second side that causes the most difficulty. Many parents do not think that they are capable of teaching their own children and, consequently, believe that they have no choice but to rely upon professional schoolteachers.

Are Parents Capable of Teaching?

If parents were so intimidated by the memory of the genius of their own teachers that they felt that they could never achieve such a standard themselves, then perhaps they could be excused for doubting their own ability to teach, (although a good teacher should inspire their pupils rather than make them feel inadequate). In most cases, however, the precise opposite is true: people feel incapable of teaching mainly because the years they spent at school were such a waste of time. They remember hardly anything that they did and know that they would not be able to repeat for their child all the lessons that they themselves sat through in the classroom.

When viewed from a logical perspective this is not such a great disadvantage as it first appears: if school lessons are so ineffective as to leave such a small impression, then it is perhaps best that they are not repeated, and if the methods used by the teachers failed to make them respected and their opinions valued, then it is perhaps preferable not to expose another generation of children to a similar situation.

It may be precisely because they don't think that they already know everything, that a parent could make the best possible teacher for their child.

What makes a good teacher?

If one accepts that the teacher's role is to inspire their pupils, then it follows that they cannot begin to do their job properly until they win their pupils' respect, and this can only be done by acting with honesty and integrity.

In addition, a good teacher has time for their pupils, listens to the ideas and questions they put forward and tries to provide honest answers; they are prepared to say when they do not know something; they are always kind and considerate and never victimise or humiliate a pupil. Above all, a good teacher makes a pupil feel special. Parents are capable of all these things – the amount of academic or intellectual knowledge that they possess is of only secondary importance.

> "There is no rank in natural knowledge of equal dignity and importance with that of being a good parent."
>
> *Benjamin Franklin*

How to teach

Surprisingly, humility plays a large role in good teaching: none of us are as clever as we would like to imagine, and it is usually when we are holding forth on a subject on which we believe ourselves to be an expert that we are making the biggest fools of ourselves.

Teaching needs redefining, especially when it takes place in the home; rather than it being a parent instructing a child, it calls for a degree of cooperation and working together. The parent should be able to bring a wealth of experience to the situation which provides balance and a sense of perspective, and perhaps this makes them the 'teacher'. Their child brings the enthusiasm that you have when finding out about something for the first time and perhaps this makes them the 'pupil'. It is a powerful combination and it means that parents and children are capable of achieving great things when they work together.

It is quality rather than quantity that is important in this relationship. Parents have many demands upon their time and are unlikely to be able to stay at home with their children all day, every day and this must be compensated for by making the most of the time that they *can* spend together. In practice, home-based learning usually involves a combination of a young person learning with the help of their parents, and learning on their own.

Self-Education

Far from being a problem, the fact that young people who do not go to school have to take at least some responsibility for their own education has many advantages.

- **Efficiency:** When you decide for yourself that you want to read a particular book, or find out about a particular subject, you will do it much more efficiently than when you do it because you have been told to.
- **Enjoyable:** By definition, self-education is enjoyable – if you don't want to do something, you don't have to.
- **Greater Flexibility:** Working on one's own gives ultimate flexibility: as soon as you decide to do something, you can do it, you don't have to wait for a group of other people.
- **More Integrated:** When you educate yourself, you avoid the problems that arise from having different teachers for different subjects; you do not have unconnected areas of knowledge in your head, but instead integrate everything that you learn with everything that you already know, as you go along.
- **Creates Good Habits:** There never comes a time when you have learnt all that there is to know or when learning ceases to be a source of pleasure. If you develop an interest in knowledge and learning when you are young, it will stay with you for life.
- **Preparation for Life:** Taking responsibility for your own education develops those qualities, such as independence, initiative, resourcefulness and self-confidence, that will enable you to succeed in later life.
- **Produces Good Citizens:** For their continued well-being, countries require citizens who are capable of thinking things through for themselves and who are prepared to stand up for the things in which they believe. These are precisely the qualities that are undermined by typical school-based learning, but which are likely to be developed by someone who takes responsibility for their own education.

> "All men who have turned out worth anything have had the chief hand in their own education."
>
> *Sir Walter Scott*

Exams, Qualifications and the Purpose of Education

Schools are run on the premise that education and qualifications are one and the same thing – if a school or university awards a qualification to someone, then that is proof that they are educated. This is damaging to everyone concerned: the pupils who are awarded the qualifications believe themselves to be well educated, which they almost certainly are not; pupils who fail to get qualifications are made to feel stupid and inadequate, which they obviously cannot be; teachers are deprived of the chance to do their job properly; and society as a whole suffers as educational standards go into decline.

The truth is that qualifications and education are almost mutually exclusive. Education requires freedom and flexibility and people have to be at liberty to study those things that interest them and to make up their own minds about whether or not they are achieving the goals that they set themselves – none of this is possible when their main objective is to pass an exam and gain a qualification.

Examinations

Examinations and tests have become such a universal feature of the modern 'education' system, that it is easy to lose sight of the fact that, until recently, they were used very sparingly in most developed countries.

Almost everyone acknowledges that examinations are a very poor way of assessing people's abilities – if they measure anything at all, it is simply whether or not someone is good at sitting examinations, but they are not accurate even in this, as people can get good marks one day and bad marks the next, when sitting virtually identical tests; and people also acknowledge that they interfere with the process of education, but schools are trapped in a cycle that makes their use more or less inevitable.

At one time, only wealthy people could afford to send their children to secondary schools and because people who had been to secondary school could read and write better than most other people, had some understanding of languages, and had at least

been introduced to classical literature and culture, they were the only ones eligible to work in administrative positions and to take a place in 'polite' society. In this way, schools helped to maintain the divisions that existed in society and ensured that poor people found it difficult to escape from manual labour and from employment that required no education.

The past hundred years have seen the gradual introduction of state-funded secondary schools, and compulsory education for everyone. In these circumstances it was no longer possible for secondary schools to base their entry requirements simply on the wealth and social standing of a child's parents. Examinations provided the obvious solution. At first they were only used to select 'scholarship' students – pupils from poor backgrounds who were allowed to attend grammar schools – but the system was soon extended so that grammar schools selected all their pupils on the basis of test results. Once the idea of examinations had been accepted, it was not long before leaving certificates were replaced by qualifications awarded by bodies independent of the schools themselves. Universities then followed the lead set by schools and started to select students on the basis of how well they had done in school examinations.

Because the status of a school depends on how many of its students go to university, they have put more and more effort into ensuring that their pupils do well in examinations, with the result that their original purpose – real education – appears to have been almost forgotten.

Examinations in Imperial China

Examinations are not altogether new – the imperial government of China routinely made use of nationwide examinations in order to select candidates for the civil service. Passing this exam became an obsession in certain sections of society and it was not uncommon for unsuccessful candidates to commit suicide.

The system produced stable government but it also led to the development of a huge bureaucracy that crippled the country through its lack of initiative, its inability to make decisions and its greed. This system of government repeatedly drove ancient China into a state of paralysis from which it only escaped through revolution or military defeat.

The problem is made worse by the fact that people have lost sight of the purpose of qualifications. In particular, they have forgotten that it is not possible to devise a qualification that proves that someone is educated: for example, you might be able to demonstrate that someone has read one of Shakespeare's plays, but you could never determine whether or not they had enjoyed reading it and whether or not their life has been enriched by the experience. The same applies to everything that is worthwhile in the realm of knowledge – music, art, literature, philosophy, science, and even, surprisingly perhaps, mathematics. Education is about self-development and only the individual concerned knows whether or not they have succeeded. It is not only presumptuous, but positively harmful, when teachers, university professors and government officials try to devise qualifications that imply that certain people have achieved a good level of education.

Qualifications vs. Education

The only valid role for qualifications is in the field of employment: we expect those people who are recognised as being skilled at a certain job to be able to devise a selection procedure, a training programme, and a final qualification that ensures that the rest of the population can be fairly confident that everyone doing that job is competent and trustworthy. In some professions, such as that of airline pilots, it is critically important that everyone involved should be well qualified but in many other jobs there is no reason why people should be required to have a qualification. In either event there is no definitive link between qualifications and education.

There are some positions in society that we all wish *could* be filled by well-educated people: the world would undoubtedly be a happier place if the political leaders were cultured and statesmanlike, caring only for the best interests of humanity as a whole, and in the same way we wish that judges, doctors, teachers and other people in authority could have a higher level of understanding than people in more mundane jobs. This is unlikely to happen, however, when advancement is based principally upon people's ability to pass examinations.

A school/university system that resorts to examining and assessing its students is compromised in its ability to provide an education. It therefore makes sense for individuals to opt out of it, to educate themselves, and then to opt back in if they decide that they want a particular qualification in order to do a particular job.

Secondary Education

Secondary education presents a different set of problems from primary education. Almost everyone agrees that children should be taught to read and write, which is the principal purpose of primary education, and differ only on how it should be done. In the case of secondary education, however, there is not even consensus on what should be taught or why children are being compelled to learn it.

Compulsory secondary education was introduced into most industrialised countries over the course of the twentieth century as a response to changing patterns of work. There were less jobs available for young people and, in order to deal with the problem, governments raised the school leaving age. Thus the idea of making children stay on at school came first, and discussions about what they should do in these schools came afterwards. This was clearly a recipe for disaster.

- **Education:** If the purpose of secondary education is to introduce young people to the world of learning – literature, languages, art, mathematics, science, history, philosophy – then the worst possible way to do it is through compulsion. These are things that need to be aspired towards; people need to be given time to discover their own desire to explore the world of knowledge. It is entirely inappropriate to force it upon young people simply because you cannot offer them a proper role in society. Not surprisingly, the main effect of including this sort of material in the school curriculum has been to alienate many people from it for the rest of their lives.

- **Training for Work:** The best way to learn how to do a job is through practical experience – the closer a training scheme is to the work itself, the more effective it proves to be. That is the reason why apprenticeships, in which a young person works with a skilled craftsperson over a number of years, are so successful in producing highly-skilled workers. Schools are almost as far removed from a real-life situation as it is possible to be and it is not surprising that 'training' gained at school proves virtually useless in the outside world. Given the number of years spent at school, the extent to which they fail to equip people to do real work is scandalous.

Teenagers

It is not the fault of young people that there is no role for them in society and it is not their fault that they are not allowed to work, and that the 'education' they are offered is uninspired and demeaning.

The years covered by secondary education should be a special time in a person's life; it is when they grow from being a child into an adult, and they are entitled to expect the best that society can offer to guide them through this transition. Instead, they are often marginalized and segregated from the rest of society. They are denied almost any opportunity to voice their concerns about the 'education' to which they are subjected and they are not allowed to make any complaint about the way they are being treated.

In these circumstances it is hardly surprising that they become prey to problems such as drug abuse, smoking, drinking, crime, etc., but these should not be seen as 'teenage' problems – they are society's problems and teenagers are the more or less helpless victims. It would be in everyone's interest to find a way of treating teenagers with a proper amount of respect and dignity.

Parents and Teenagers

In an ideal world perhaps everyone would adopt a positive and supportive attitude towards teenagers, but, in practice, just one single adult making the effort to treat them as a human being can make all the difference in a young person's life. In most cases, the person most able to do this is their parent.

This involves the parent talking to their child, making time to be with them, and being committed to doing meaningful activities with them. If a young person does not want to go to school, this will probably involve spending a few hours per day studying together; if they do go to school, it could involve doing something like cooking or gardening together in the evenings. In either event, it requires that a parent makes a conscious decision to be as available to their child when they are a teenager as they were when they were younger. If they do this, they will discover that the little child of their memories has not metamorphosed into a teenage monster, but is still the same sensitive, caring, loving person that they always were, only that they are now a little older and wiser and, consequently, a little more enjoyable to be with.

Academic Work

The fact that academic subjects such as literature, languages, science, history and geography have become associated with doing well at school, has made it easy to lose sight of the fact that people only studied these subjects in the first place because they were enjoyable.

Many of the things that are now considered worthwhile but disagreeable or difficult, started out purely as a source of entertainment or inspiration. This obviously applies to Shakespeare's plays, the classics of Greek and Roman literature and to great novels, but it is also true of a surprisingly large amount of other academic material; historians, scientists and geographers have written books, performed experiments, and put forward new ideas because they have had a passion for what they do, and it is impossible to grasp the significance of their work without sharing their enthusiasm.

Part of the reason why schools fail to communicate this enthusiasm is because they have introduced examinations and assessment into the process of education. For example, when a modern student studies the work of Isaac Newton, they are not simply trying to understand what Isaac Newton was saying, how he arrived at his conclusions, and whether or not he was correct, they are trying to work out what questions the examiner will ask about Isaac Newton, what answers the examiner will expect and what is the 'accepted opinion' about Isaac Newton. The result is that even though the student has theoretically studied the work of Isaac Newton (and may have a certificate to that effect), what they have really studied is the views and prejudices of the people who set the school examinations. In this way schools succeed in making the most exciting things tedious and uninteresting.

The simplest way to circumvent this problem is to not go to schools that teach in this way, and if you study at home not to use school books or follow a school curriculum. Instead, take the time-honoured approach of studying things that interest you; expect to be entertained, moved, and informed when you read a book; study things in depth; don't be afraid to read classic authors and to consult original texts; and view your education as something of which you are in control and which is going to enrich your life.

Practical Work

Even though academic work has the potential to be of interest to everyone (and everyone has the potential to be interested in academic work), it does not follow that everyone should be made to do academic work. Compulsory secondary education was not introduced to improve academic standards, it was introduced because there were no jobs for young people to do. This represents just about the worst possible reason for forcing people into education – "You've got to go to school, because we have got nothing useful for you to do" – and it is not surprising that it causes people to resent everything to do with schools and with the education system. Everyone, young people included, needs to feel that their work is valued and that they are useful.

The problem can be solved by parents making the home, instead of their workplace, the centre of their lives. An active home provides a young person with a wealth of practical activities, which not only keep them fully occupied but also help them to develop into a multi-faceted, mature adult. These activities can include such things as looking after younger brothers and sisters, caring for elderly relatives, cooking and preparing meals, cleaning and maintenance, growing fruit and vegetables, painting and decorating, needlework, woodworking, maintaining vehicles, using a computer, electrical repairs, plumbing, and a host of other activities.

Schools try to provide some of these activities with the aid of gardening lessons, cooking lessons, etc. but these efforts often serve to highlight the extent of the problem: the only way to learn to cook is to cook meals for your family, and to then sit down and enjoy the food that you have prepared; you learn gardening by growing vegetables that you then cook when you are preparing meals for your family, etc. All these activities are interrelated and young people need to be at home, participating in the running of a home, in order to acquire the practical skills that are necessary for life.

When pursued properly, these activities do not compete with an academic education, they stimulate and augment it: in order to improve your cooking you have to read recipes, you have to be able to convert between imperial and metric measurements, you become inspired to search the internet for new ideas, you have to understand the properties of yeast, the effect of heat, etc., etc., and the same applies in every other area of practical activity.

Paid Work

Young people find themselves growing up in a world that places enormous importance on money, and the things that money can buy, and this puts them in a difficult situation – in order to lead independent lives they need money, but they are given very few opportunities to earn money from satisfying, or even honest, work.

This is not a simple problem, but has arisen over the past few hundred years as a result of a succession of changes in the way in which people live. Prior to the beginning of the Industrial Revolution money was not as important as it is now: people produced most of the things they needed, and, furthermore, children worked with their parents from a young age and had an automatic share in the family's resources. When factories and mines were first developed, children accompanied their parents to work in the traditional manner, but they were found to be an encumbrance and also an embarrassment. Stories of children toiling underground in coal mines, or being injured in the cotton mills, outraged public opinion and reforms were introduced that placed strict limitations upon the exploitation of child labour.

These reforms may have been well intentioned, but they fell far short of what was required. The problem was not that children were in the workplace, it was that the workplace was not fit for children. The effect of the legislation was to separate children from their parents, and to condemn them to be inadequately cared for in poor schools, and has given rise to the current situation in which young people are still largely cut off from activities that would allow them to fulfil a meaningful role in society.

The solution may be for individual families to turn back the clock and to work together at practical activities, in the traditional manner. This could be anything from building, gardening, cooking, crafts, woodwork, electronics, pottery, painting, or mechanics right through to things like writing or research that may be closely linked to academic work.

If you become good at these activities, opportunities are bound to arise for earning money from them. This money can be shared out on terms that reflect the relative contributions made by different members of the family, and even if it is not enough to meet all the family's needs, it still represents a step towards a more sensible system in which work and family life are integrated with each other. This represents a powerful advantage that home-based education has over school-based education.

Careers Advice

Some people, for whatever reason, seem to be clear from a young age that they want to have a particular career. When this is the case, it makes sense for them to get the necessary qualifications as quickly as possible, and to start working in their chosen field as soon as they can. If they don't like it, they have no one to blame for pushing them into it, and the drive that enabled them to succeed in one field will help them to change direction and succeed in another.

Other people have no particular idea about what job they want to do and, when this is the case, it is a mistake for them to rush into anything. The question that they are being confronted with is essentially: "What do you want to do with your life?" and if the answer is along the lines of : "I don't know what I want to do but I'm studying science at school, so I'll be a doctor."; "I don't know what I want to do but my parents want me to go to university to study ..., so I will, to please them."; "I don't know what I want to do, but I've been offered a job at ..., so I may as well do it."; etc., they would be better advised *not* to rush into anything.

Before anyone dedicates their precious time and their unique abilities to a particular career, they should be sure that they are doing it because they want to. Nothing is more depressing than being in a job that you don't like, or doing something that you don't agree with and having to say to yourself: "I'm only doing this to please so and so."; or "I'm only doing this because I couldn't think of anything better to do."

Too often, one comes across people caught up in organisations, doing inexplicable and inexcusable things and, when challenged, their reason is that they are only "doing their job" – as though they never had any choice about the job that they were going to do.

The world would certainly be a better place if everyone could say "I'm doing this job because I want to, I enjoy it, I believe that it is worthwhile, and if there is anything wrong with the way that it is being done, I will fix it."

Therefore, if you are not completely sure about the career that you intend to follow, why not carry on with your education, try to get a better understanding of what is going on, support yourself with the skills that you do have, and see what happens?

Further Education

The First Universities

The first universities were not financed by governments and they did not have permanent members of staff. They did not award degrees, they did not offer courses and there was no fixed term of study.

They arose spontaneously when scholars started to gather together in a particular town. These scholars met in inns and taverns, talked to each other, discussed ideas, exchanged books, and hired rooms to deliver lectures. The town established a reputation for being a centre of learning, new students were drawn to it, learned men visited it and chose to reside there and, gradually, a loose-knit university structure developed.

These institutions acted as a catalyst for change, they challenged established religious and scientific dogmas and played a key role in both the Renaissance and the Reformation. They provided the intellectual motivation that led to a political and religious revolution.

Most people associate the term 'further education' with university and college courses, but, just as school is now probably one of the worst places to go in order to get a primary or secondary education, universities are no longer the best places to go in search of further education.

The reason for this is mainly to do with qualifications: students enrol on a course, and at the end of that course are assessed by their teachers and awarded a degree or certificate according to whether or not they have succeeded in pleasing those teachers. In fact, the situation is even worse than this because universities have external monitoring which means that students have not only to please their own teachers, but also teachers from other universities or institutions. The effect of this system is to produce uniformity: only those students who give the accepted answers, in the accepted way, are awarded their degrees, and only those students who are awarded degrees can themselves go on to become university teachers. In this way, it does not take long for a university to become dull and lacking in originality.

This may not be a problem when it comes to being trained to do a specific job (and this is the role towards which universities now appear to be gravitating), but it will not help you to fulfil the thirst for knowledge and the quest for understanding that is the hallmark of a human being.

Unqualified Education

Hopefully, there comes a point in a person's life when they no longer want to be told what to do and what to think by someone else, and from this time onwards they become fully responsible for their own education. Life itself becomes the teacher, and only the individual concerned is able to judge whether or not it has been a success.

The objective of this education is to develop those qualities that have long been regarded as the attributes of the truly learned person – things such as integrity, honesty, impartiality, objectivity, courage, fortitude, creativity, originality, and compassion.

From ancient times, the story of the life of King Crœsus has been cited as an example from which people could learn:

King Crœsus

As the result of a series of successful military campaigns and well-struck alliances, King Crœsus managed to build up a substantial empire in the area that is now part of Turkey. His court became renowned throughout the ancient Mediterranean world for its wealth and opulence (hence the phrase 'as rich as Crœsus'), and he enjoyed an unrivalled reputation amongst the monarchs of his time for the power and military might that he had at his disposal.

When Solon, the Athenian philosopher and lawmaker, visited his court, Crœsus took the opportunity to ask him whom he considered the happiest man that he had ever met. Solon considered for a moment and answered "Tellus of Athens."

Crœsus was a little surprised, and asked whom Solon considered to be the second most happy person that he had ever met. Solon answered, "The brothers Cleobis and Bito."

Crœsus was even more astonished, and pointed out to Solon the luxury with which they were surrounded. He demanded that Solon agree that the person who was in control of such wealth and power must surely be happy and that he, Croesus, must be the happiest person that Solon had ever met.

Solon answered that he was unable to comment upon Crœsus' state of happiness

Continued over page

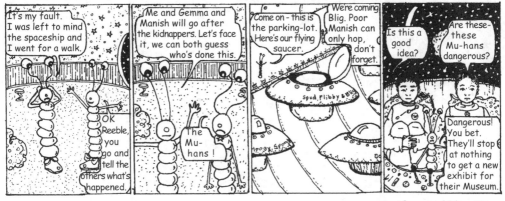

because it is only at the moment of death that it is possible to determine whether or not someone is truly happy.

The years passed and Crœsus' fortunes changed dramatically. His kingdom was invaded and his armies defeated by Cyrus, the Persian King. Crœsus was captured and condemned to death by burning. He was in a state of complete despair and had not spoken a single word since his capture but, when the fire was lit and he could feel the heat of the flames, Solon's words came back to him and, with a deep groan, he uttered Solon's name three times.

At this point there was a clap of thunder and a torrential downpour of rain, which extinguished the fire. Cyrus commanded that Crœsus be cut free and brought before him. Crœsus related to him the conversation that he had had with Solon, and how he had recalled it at the moment that he believed he was about to die.

He explained that those things that he had considered so important up until a few weeks before – servants, wealth, power, etc. – had ceased to be of any interest to him at all, but that he now regretted many other things that he had left undone in the course of his life. He no longer considered himself to be, or to have ever been, the happiest man alive.

Cyrus was so touched by this story that he spared his life and Crœsus lived to became one of the Persian king's most trusted advisers.

Romeo and Juliet *words taken from the play by William Shakespeare.*

In Verona there lived two rival families - the Capulets and Montagues. Three times the quiet of the streets had been disrupted with their fighting and death was now the forfeit for disturbing the peace again. Romeo, a Montague, had married the young daughter of the Capulets and was resolved not to fight any members of her family. Even when Tybalt, Juliet's cousin, challenges him to a duel, Romeo refuses to retaliate.

Subjects Covered by this Book

Education has to be a balance between practical skills and theoretical knowledge. The main purpose of this book is to suggest how that balance may be struck:

Literature

Great works of literature have, until recently, always been the cornerstone of every system of education. Cultures mark their progress through the writings of outstanding individuals. We learn about ancient Greece by reading Homer and Plato, we learn about Rome by reading Livy and Plutarch, we learn about English culture by reading Shakespeare, Jane Austen, Charles Dickens, etc.

The fact that modern schools shy away from studying these great authors in depth is evidence that they are not really in the business of education.

History

History teaches more lessons than any other subject – just about anything and everything that human beings are capable of, is contained in the study of history. It is also by far the most interesting subject because it is, in essence, the story of millions and millions of lives, each one of which would take a lifetime of study to fully comprehend. In some ways, all other academic subjects are included within history: subjects such as chemistry, physics, biology and mathematics only exist in the form that they do because of the work of people who lived in the past.

Gardening

An understanding of Nature is essential to any understanding of life - and Nature is not something that can be studied from books – it has to be experienced. Anyone growing up in an urban environment is dangerously estranged from the world of Nature, and gardening is the simplest and most direct way of establishing a relationship with the natural world. It is therefore essential that young people should have the chance to manage their own gardens.

Gardening also has the advantage of being the most practical of all activities as it allows someone to grow their own food.

Cooking

The ability to cook is a basic skill that everyone needs to have. An education that does not teach people how to cook is not really an education at all.

Art and Crafts

The ability to make things is one of the characteristics that sets human beings apart from the rest of Nature. Learning how to create items that are both beautiful and useful should be one of the cornerstones of any programme of education.

Unfortunately, art and crafts do not lend themselves to being taught within the confines of a school timetable and this is an area that everyone has to take responsibility for themselves, whether they go to school or not.

Geography

Geography makes a good starting point for 'academic' work. It involves things that are of interest to everyone: countries, cities, rivers, the peoples of the Earth, etc. It can be studied by drawing maps and reading atlases, and stimulates thought and discussion.

Science

There are two sides to science: on the one hand there is the effort to understand life and the universe through the use of logic and reasoning, and on the other there is the commercial exploitation of scientific ideas. A good education should help people to unravel these two strands.

Languages

In previous centuries educated people could read classic works of literature in their original language. In present times, standards have slipped and the best that most people aim for is to be able to ask directions or to order a meal in a foreign language. However, we have not become more stupid than our forefathers and there is no reason why we should not all be able to learn two or three languages to a reasonable degree of proficiency.

Mathematics

In some ways mathematics represents the purest form of knowledge and it has to be pursued with respect and with diligence if it is to be understood. A certain degree of experience of life is required to really understand the beauty of mathematics. It may be possible to teach children to do simple algebra and trigonometry but how can they be expected to grasp the philosophical implications?

If the ancient Greeks reserved the study of mathematics for adults, then why do we force it upon children? This is another of the mysteries of our education system.

Modern technology

One of the surprising things about learning at home and self-education is that it is the most effective way of keeping up with new technology.

In schools, the pupils are generally better at using new technology than their teachers, which illustrates the point that to be up to date with technology there is no choice but to be self-motivated and committed to a process of lifelong learning.

Music

One of the tragedies of our culture is that even though we pride ourselves on our wealth and achievements, we don't spend time on those activities that have always done the most to enrich human life – music being the prime example.

Everyone has the potential to play at least one musical instrument well – all that is required is practice.

Continued on page 32

Sonnet 55

Not marble, nor the gilded monuments
Of princes, shall outlive this powerful rhyme:
But you shall shine more bright in these contents
Than unswept stone, besmear'd with sluttish time.
When wasteful war shall statues overturn,
And broils root out the work of masonry,
Nor Mars his sword, nor war's quick fire shall burn
The living record of your memory.
'Gainst death and all-oblivious enmity
Shall you pace forth; your praise shall still find room,
Even in the eyes of all posterity
That wear this world out to the ending doom.
    So, till the judgement that your self arise,
    You live in this, and dwell in lovers' eyes.

Shakespeare

Literature

Contents:

Literature

My own educational background is in the sciences: my university career did not involve reading any great works of literature – we read scientific papers published in technical journals. Prior to that, I had not been a great reader and it is only since having children of my own that I have come to appreciate the value of good literature.

It began with reading children's books. Some books were patently so much better than others; they were more enjoyable to read, held my children's attention and made a deeper impression upon them, and I slowly came to appreciate the difference between good books and not-so-good books.

Good literature is well written and touches the reader in such a way that a connexion is made between reader and author. This connexion can bridge all gaps – time, race, culture and age.

The natural starting point is with traditional stories - myths and legends that have been passed down from generation to generation for hundreds or thousands of years. They are a fount of wisdom and understanding that cannot be gained from any other source, and it is a terrible pity that young people today seldom get a chance to hear or read them in their original form. Fairy stories in particular should not simply be reserved for small children. When told properly they raise the basic issues that confront young people as they are growing up: "Should one marry for love or for convenience?", "In one's career, should one follow one's conscience or one's desire for wealth and status?", etc. These stories appeal equally to boys and to girls and in some senses provide a complete and challenging education in themselves.

Using traditional stories as a bench mark for what is, and what is not, good literature, it is possible to proceed to other books.

"What we become depends on what we read after all the professors have finished with us. The greatest university of all is the collection of books."

Thomas Carlyle

Continued from page 29

The advantages of being well read

There are some very real advantages to reading well-written books: reading is the best way of increasing the range of one's vocabulary and it is by reading well-written prose that one becomes familiar with the rules of grammar - far more so than by studying grammar itself. Consequently, a well-read person is more articulate than someone who does not read: they have more words at their disposal and are able to say the things that they want to say, in the way that they want to say them.

A more subtle advantage of being well read is the way in which it connects you to the culture in which you live. Until you have read the major works of world literature for yourself, you tend to be unaware of how often they are referred to by people on the radio, on the television, by people writing in the papers and magazines, by books and by ordinary people trying to express significant ideas.

What makes a book a classic?

In the short term, people never agree about which books are good and which are not, but common sense asserts itself in a remarkably short space of time. Poor books tend to disappear from view after a few years, no matter how much praise they receive on their appearance, and few books retain their popularity for more than a few decades. It seems as though mankind *does* have some kind of collective wisdom that allows it to select and cherish really worthwhile works of literature.

A few books and a few writers have proved themselves to have a lasting appeal and any sensible education should involve reading them. However, it is important to remember that these books have survived not because they are considered to be worthy but because people have enjoyed them. To read them without enjoying them, is to miss the point.

> "Books are the legacies that a great genius leaves to mankind, which are delivered down from generation to generation as presents to the posterity of those who are yet unborn."
>
> *Joseph Addison*

33

Literature and School

The reason why classic literature does not automatically spring to mind as being a source of enjoyment and entertainment may have something to do with schools.

The school curriculum was originally based upon those things that were recognised as making someone well educated, cultured and sharp-witted. This naturally included a study of classic literature.

Unfortunately no one took into account that people would come to loathe the things that they did at school. Instead of giving people an introduction to the world of books, schools have succeeded in creating the idea that good books, especially those that were written a long time ago, are in some way difficult or uninteresting - not worth the effort and probably beyond the comprehension of an ordinary person.

Everything that could be done wrong has been done wrong:

- You are made to read bits and pieces of a book in set lesson times, instead of reading it through from start to finish.

- You sometimes have to read a book in a classroom that is full of chaos.

- You may be *made* to read while a teacher demands 'total silence' in the room.

- You may be made to read aloud even when you don't want to.

- You may be made fun of for enjoying a book.

- Books are often started but not finished.

- You sometimes have to use books that have not been cared for, which contain graffiti and which are in poor condition.

- You are given tests and exams about books.

Fortunately, in spite of everything, people still regard books as one of the treasures of our civilisation. They are still enjoyed by millions of people and it is possible for young people to develop a love of books whether or not they go to school.

Literature in the Home

For a young person to discover the pleasure of a good book they have to acknowledge that although, at school, books sometimes represent a form of torture, everywhere else they are a source of pleasure. This is made easier by the fact that schools no longer dedicate much time to studying good books.

Reading aloud

The key to success lies in reading aloud: parents read aloud to their very young children and there is no reason why people should not continue to read books to each other indefinitely. The common sense approach is to progress from picture books to story books; from story books to children's literature; and from children's literature to adult literature.

Reading aloud is fun because it gives people a chance to indulge that part of themselves that likes to act and perform. It is an interactive activity in which the audience response is as important as the reading itself.

People traditionally read stories at bedtime but you can read aloud at any time that members of the family are gathered together: when you are drawing, painting, sewing, knitting, washing-up, etc.

Reading a book aloud is a very different experience from reading it in one's head: you are forced to go at a slower pace; you cannot skip things that you find boring; you can only read when you have gathered your audience together in one place, which usually means you can only read one or two chapters at a time; and of course you can discuss it with the people you are reading to, or who are reading it to you. This enables you to get to know the book much better than if you were reading it to yourself.

It must also be remembered that many people do not like to read - either because they have had traumatic experiences at school, or because it is something to which they have not yet been attracted. They are still, however, capable of appreciating good literature. Reading aloud to them gives you a chance to enjoy yourself, and them a chance to become intimately acquainted with books, without being subjected to unwelcome pressure to read for themselves.

Recommended Books

The following pages contain a list of recommended books. The criteria used in their selection is how well they adapt to being read aloud. The list is based on our own experiences, and even if some of the titles seem intimidating we have found that these are the books that are the most enjoyable and the most stimulating.

Books that Have a Universal Appeal

There are some common characteristics that give these books a universal appeal:

- **Being well written:** Poorly-written books do not stand up to being read aloud. The person reading the book is tempted to make fun of the poor writing, which can be amusing for a while, but eventually everyone feels that they are wasting their time by reading second-rate material.

- **They Contain an Element of Truth:** A good book establishes a connection between the author and the reader. The person reading the book must feel that they are being spoken to directly by the author and that the author is revealing something true about themselves.

- **They have a Good Story:** A good story does not always have a happy ending but it has to be finished off properly and it has to make sense.

The majority of the greatest works of world literature were not originally written in the English language. However, some of them are so good that they are worth reading even in their translated form.

Shakespeare has to take the pre-eminent position because he is the only English-speaking writer whose work would win automatic inclusion in any collection of world literature.

Modern Books

It is difficult to find modern books that match the warmth and the perception of books written in previous times. Perhaps this has something to do with the commercialisation of the world of publishing and the way that it interrelates with the academics who make the judgements about what is good and what is bad in the field of literature. It is possible that there is good literature being written today, going largely unnoticed because it fails to comply with the demands of the modern book trade.

In terms of education, there is no reason why this should be seen as a problem. People who learn to appreciate good books through reading classics will be able to search out good modern literature for themselves, if they so wish.

Old Books

Sometimes, people are a little apprehensive of books written a long time ago. They worry that such books may be uninteresting and hard to understand, but nothing could be further from the truth. One of the most remarkable things about old books is the way in which they teach you that people are the same now as they have always been.

Furthermore, by reading a lot of books, one becomes aware that some stand out, even amongst the classics. An example of this is the Bible – you do not have to be a Christian in order to be overawed by the simplicity and beauty of the New Testament; Homer's Odyssey is, in a different way, another such book; and an equivalent from India is the Ramayana.

Some of these books, or stories, have survived for thousands of years, being retold to each new generation; some have given rise to great religions. Whatever the case, and whatever their origins, these books deserve to be given pride of place in any educational programme. To be ignorant of books that have had such a monumental effect upon human life, is to be ignorant indeed.

It is not out of disrespect for these books that they have been included in the literature section, but rather it is out of great respect for the sense and discrimination of children and young people. All you have to do is read these books and you will experience their special qualities for yourself.

37

Charles Dickens (1812 - 1870)

Charles Dickens was a novelist, playwright, social reformer, magazine editor, public speaker and the father of ten children. He was extraordinarily energetic and between 1836 and his death in 1870 he wrote fifteen novels, numerous short stories, thirteen plays, hundreds of speeches and over fourteen thousand letters.

He had a difficult childhood. His father was beset by financial worries, and when Charles was just twelve years old, was arrested and imprisoned for debt. Charles was sent to work in a factory and the memory of the months spent pasting labels on bottles of boot blacking, haunted him for the rest of his life. After a year he left and in 1827 was engaged as a law clerk and began to write articles for a morning newspaper. His engaging style and remarkable powers of observation soon won him a following in literary circles and, at the age of twenty-four, he was engaged to write accompanying text for a series of comic engravings.

Not content to act as a mere copywriter, Dickens was soon asking the illustrator to provide pictures to fit his text. The resulting story, Pickwick Papers, quickly started to attract national attention.

"No words can express the secret agony of my soul as I … felt my early hopes of growing up to be a learned and distinguished man crushed in my breast."
Charles Dickens - remembering his experiences of factory work.

Pickwick Papers

Mr Pickwick is the hero of Pickwick Papers. He is a loveable, bespectacled old man whose unworldliness leads him into many comical situations. It was Dickens' introduction of Samuel Weller, Mr Pickwick's resourceful manservant, that led to Pickwick Papers becoming a publishing sensation. Sales rocketed and by the end of the year had reached 40,000 for each monthly instalment; Pickwick merchandise was on sale everywhere; five theatrical adaptations appeared even before the book was completed; and crowds attended the stagecoaches that delivered the next instalment to each town. At first Mr Pickwick was a figure of fun, but in the course of the story he changes into a great-hearted hero. By the time the loosely-connected series of adventures had been rounded off, Dickens was established as the supreme writer of his day. Critics sneered at his lack of formal learning and his journalistic style, but the public adored him and greeted each successive work with unbounded enthusiasm.

Nicholas Nickleby

Nicholas Nickleby was Dickens' third novel. Like Pickwick Papers, it does not have a carefully-constructed plot but is a series of rambling adventures full of humour and *joie de vivre.*

Nicholas and Kate Nickleby are forced to make their own way in the world when their father dies a bankrupt. Kate finds employment as a sempstress and Nicholas travels to Yorkshire and becomes a teacher at Dotheboys Hall.

Like much of Dickens' early work, Nicholas Nickleby is in the style of a traditional fairytale, with a beautiful heroine, a handsome hero, an evil villain, and a gloriously happy ending. It is one of his most delightful stories.

Martin Chuzzlewit

In 1842 Dickens visited the United States, and the following year the first instalments of Martin Chuzzlewit appeared. Its brilliant style and unforgettable characters immediately earned it a place amongst Dickens' comic masterpieces, even though the scenes set in the New World met with a mixed reception from American readers. In this extract one of Dickens' most famous characters, Mr Pecksniff, is introduced:

"It has been remarked that Mr Pecksniff was a moral man. So he was. Perhaps there never was a more moral man than Mr Pecksniff: especially in his conversation and correspondence. He was a most exemplary man: fuller of virtuous precept than a copy-book. Some people likened him to a direction-post, which is always telling the way to a place, and never goes there: but these were his enemies; the shadows cast by his brightness; that was all. His very throat was moral. You saw a good deal of it. You looked over a very low fence of white cravat, and there it lay, a valley between two jutting heights of collar, serene and whiskerless before you. It seemed to say, on the part of Mr Pecksniff, 'There is no deception, ladies and gentlemen, all is peace, a holy calm pervades me.' So did his hair, just grizzled with an iron-gray, which was all brushed off his forehead, and stood bolt upright, so lightly drooped in kindred action with his heavy eyelids. So did his person, which was sleek though free from corpulency. So did his manner, which was soft and oily. In a word, even his plain black suit, and state of widower, and dangling double eye-glass, all tended to the same purpose, and cried aloud, 'Behold the moral Pecksniff!' "

Martin Chuzzlewit, Chapter 2

Bleak House

"London. Michaelmas Term lately over, and the Lord Chancellor sitting in Lincoln's Inn Hall. Implacable November weather. As much mud in the streets, as if the waters had but newly retired from the face of the earth, and it would not be wonderful to meet a Megalosaurus, forty feet long or so, waddling like an elephantine lizard up Holborn Hill. Smoke lowering down from chimney-pots, making a soft black drizzle, with flakes of soot in it as big as full-grown snow-flakes - gone into mourning, one might imagine, for the death of the sun. Dogs, undistinguishable in mire. Horses, scarcely better; splashed to their very blinkers. Foot passengers, jostling one another's umbrellas, in a general infection of ill-temper, and losing their foot-hold at street-corners, where tens of thousands of other foot passengers have been slipping and sliding since the day broke (if this day ever broke), adding new deposits to the crust upon crust of mud, sticking at those points tenaciously to the pavement, and accumulating at compound interest."

Bleak House, Chapter 1

This is the opening of Bleak House, one of the greatest of Dickens' later novels. The humour and buoyancy of his earlier works is not so apparent here, but the descriptions of Victorian London – its slums and great houses, and of the beautiful, unspoilt countryside with which it was surrounded, are unrivalled in their vividness.

Unusually, the narrator is female: Esther Summerson's modesty and sweetness of character endear her to everyone about her and she is one of the most realistic of Dickens' heroines. Dickens' plots are famously complicated but Bleak House has few of the blind alleys and untied ends that are a feature of his other works. In the course of the story, links are discovered between the richest and the poorest characters and it has been called one of the first examples of the detective story.

Esther and Caddy Jellyby - Bleak House
"She would not sit down, but stood by the fire, dipping her inky finger in the eggcup, which contained vinegar, and smearing it over the inky stains on her face, frowning the whole while and looking very gloomy."

Little Dorrit

In this novel Dickens attacks the infamous debtors' gaols, in which his own father had been briefly imprisoned, and government bureaucracy in the form of the Circumlocution Office, a vast institution whose aim in life is to prevent anything from being done.

Set against this background are the hero, the diffident, kind-hearted Arthur Clennam, and the heroine, Little Dorrit. Her father has been an inmate of the debtors' prison for over twenty years and she toils to support him and her feckless brother and sister with uncomplaining devotion. When Arthur Clennam returns home after an absence of many years he finds her working for his mother. She arouses his pity and he begins to take an interest in her:

"Now that he had an opportunity of observing her, Arthur found that her diminutive figure, small features, and slight spare dress, gave her the appearance of being much younger than she was. A woman, probably of not less than two-and-twenty, she might have been passed in the street for little more than half that age. Not that her face was very youthful, for in truth there was more consideration and care in it than naturally belonged to her utmost years; but she was so little and light, so noiseless and shy, and appeared so conscious of being out of place:... that she had all the manner and much of the appearance of a subdued child. Little Dorrit let herself out to do needlework. At so much a day - or at so little - from eight to eight, Little Dorrit was to be hired. Punctual to the moment, Little Dorrit appeared; punctual to the moment, Little Dorrit vanished. What became of Little Dorrit between the two eights, was a mystery."

Little Dorrit, Chapter 5

A Christmas Carol

Dickens wrote a series of Christmas stories, but none were so popular as a A Christmas Carol. It is the story of Ebenezer Scrooge, an old miser who is changed for-ever when three spirits show him the past, the present and the future. He understands the worthlessness of wealth, and promises, henceforth, to honour Christmas and to be a good friend and benefactor to one and all.

"Once upon a time - of all the good days in the year, on Christmas Eve - old Scrooge sat busy in his counting-house. It was cold, bleak, biting weather; foggy withal; and he could hear the people in the court outside go wheezing up and down, beating their hands upon their breasts, and stamping their feet upon the pavement stones to warm them. The City clocks had only just gone three, but it was quite dark already - it had not been light all day - and candles were flaring in the windows of the neighbouring offices, like ruddy smears upon the palpable brown air...

'A merry Christmas, uncle! God save you!' cried a cheerful voice. It was the voice of Scrooge's nephew, who came upon him so quickly that this was the first intimation he had of his approach.

'Bah!' said Scrooge. 'Humbug!' "

A Christmas Carol, Chapter 1

A Tale of Two Cities

A Tale of Two Cities was written during a difficult phase of Dickens' life. He was more famous than ever, but he had separated from his wife and had recently performed the first of the gruelling public reading tours which were eventually to undermine his health.

The story is set in the time of the French Revolution and the action moves between Paris and London - the two cities of the title. The atmosphere is brooding and there is almost none of Dickens' usual comedy to lighten the sense of impending doom. The hero, Sydney Carton, is a dissolute but noble-hearted barrister who falls in love with the beautiful Lucie Manette. She does not return his affection and Carton sacrifices himself to ensure her happiness in Dickens' most harrowing ending.

Lucie Manette faints into the arms of Sydney Carton, after learning of the death sentence passed on her husband.

Great Expectations

In Great Expectations, Dickens made extensive use of his childhood memories and the first chapters, recounted by the young Philip Pirrip, or Pip, convey the innocence and frequent bewilderment with which a child views the world. The plot is tightly constructed and the writing particularly brilliant. Pip's 'great expectations' take him from his childhood home in rural Kent to London and, finally, back to the countryside again. In the course of these travels he learns to distrust wealth and fame and comes to love the simple things that he first appreciated as a child.

"One night, I was sitting in the chimney corner with my slate, expending great efforts on the production of a letter to Joe… With an alphabet on the hearth at my feet for reference, I contrived in an hour or two to print and smear this epistle:

'MI DEEr JO i opE U r krWItE wEll i opE i sHAL soN B HABELL 4 2 TEEDGE U JO AN THEN wE sHOrl b sO GLOdd AN wEn i M PRENGTD *(apprenticed)* 2 U JO woT larX AN BLEvE ME INF xn PIP.'

There was no indispensable necessity for my communicating with Joe by letter, inasmuch as he sat beside me and we were alone. But I delivered this written communication (slate and all) with my own hand, and Joe received it as a miracle of erudition.

'I say, Pip, old chap!' cried Joe, opening his blue eyes wide, 'what a scholar you are! An't you?'

'I should like to be,' said I, glancing at the slate as he held it: with a misgiving that the writing was rather hilly.

'Why, here's a J,' said Joe, 'and a O equal to anything! Here's a J and a O, Pip, and a J-O, Joe.'

I had never heard Joe read aloud to any greater extent than this monosyllable, and I had observed at church last Sunday when I accidentally held our Prayer-Book upside down, that it seemed to suit his convenience quite as well as if it had been all right.

Wishing to embrace the present occasion of finding out whether in teaching Joe I should have to begin quite at the beginning, I said, 'Ah! But read the rest, Joe.'

'The rest, eh, Pip?' said Joe, looking at it with a slowly searching eye, 'One, two, three. Why, here's three Js, and three Os, and three J-O, Joes in it, Pip!'

I leaned over Joe, and, with the aid of my forefinger, read him the whole letter.

'Astonishing!' said Joe, when I had finished. 'You ARE a scholar.'"

Great Expectations, Chapter 7

The Final Years

Dickens' fame continued to increase. He undertook a second, highly successful tour of the United States and performed many public readings of his work. The excitement of these readings (women in the audience were known to faint when he performed the scene of Nancy's murder from Oliver Twist) made him ill, and he died of a stroke later that year, at the age of fifty-eight.

His work was remarkable for its blend of comedy and pathos and his burning sympathy for the poor and the oppressed. He had a fixed dislike of all institutions, including the Church, the law, the monarchy, and the government, and his work is free of the prejudices associated with class and the Empire. His contemporaries possessed ability but could not match Dickens either for perception or compassion and perhaps this accounts for the enduring popularity of his novels.

Jane Austen (1775 - 1817)

Jane Austen was the seventh of eight children. She had six brothers and one sister and grew up in the countryside between Winchester and Basingstoke. When she was eight, she and her sister were sent to Oxford to be taught by the widow of one of her father's friends. A few months later they moved to Southampton where Jane and Cassandra caught 'putrid fever' (probably typhoid) and had to be taken home to their frightened mother. Jane nearly died and received little further formal schooling: from then on her education took place at home.

Her father was rector of Steventon and he encouraged his children to read good books; when his daughters left school, he taught them himself. The family was very close and Jane seems to have had an idyllic childhood.

Although she travelled little, met few people outside her family and their limited circle of acquaintances, and spent her days in domestic pursuits, she acquired a subtle knowledge of human nature and a command of the language that has rarely been surpassed. Her insightful-ness, sense of humour, and an ability to make day-to-day events as interesting in print as they are in real life, make her one of the most accomplished writers in the English language.

There are few authenticated pictures of Jane Austen, but a silhouette found pasted inside a copy of Mansfield Park is believed to be of the authoress.

Sense and Sensibility

Jane Austen spent years revising and rewriting her stories; not a word is wasted and there are no tedious passages or unnecessary digressions. She often admitted that she knew nothing about war or politics and chose to show instead the human foibles and peculiarities which she understood so well. The absence of contemporary events give her books a timeless feel, and ensure that they are as fresh today as when they were first published.

Sense and Sensibility was her first published novel. It is the story of two sisters, Elinor and Marianne Dashwood, who are forced to leave the great house in which they grew up and move to a small cottage on a relative's estate. The way in which they adapt to their new life is a reflection of their respective characters. Elinor is reserved, sensible and clear-sighted; Marianne is romantic, hot-tempered, and self-willed. When Elinor discovers that the man she loves is already engaged, she bears it with heroic fortitude, but when Marianne is jilted by the handsome but faithless Willougby she falls ill and nearly dies. Jane Austen reveals her sympathy for the more rational sister, and, in the course of the novel, Marianne learns to appreciate Elinor's quiet good sense, and abandons the romantic ideas that have been the cause of her suffering.

Pride and Prejudice

When Pride and Prejudice appeared it rapidly established itself as the most popular novel of the 'season', and has been enjoyed by generations ever since.

It is the exuberant, witty tale of Elizabeth Bennet and her five sisters. Their father's estate is entailed and will pass, on his death, to a distant cousin; in consequence, all six girls must make good 'matches'. The following scene takes place early in the novel. Elizabeth and her sisters are attending a dance where they make the acquaintance of their new neighbours, the young, eligible Mr Bingley and his friend, Mr Darcy:

> "Elizabeth Bennet had been obliged, by the scarcity of gentlemen, to sit down for two dances; and during part of that time, Mr Darcy had been standing near enough for her to overhear a conversation between him and Mr Bingley, who came from the dance for a few minutes, to press his friend to join it.
>
> 'Come Darcy,' said he, 'I must have you dance. I hate to see you standing about by yourself in this stupid manner. You had much better dance.'
>
> 'I certainly shall not. You know I detest it, unless I am particularly acquainted with my partner. At such an assembly as this, it would be insupportable. Your sisters are engaged, and there is not another woman in the room, whom it would not be a punishment to me to stand up with.'
>
> 'I would not be so fastidious as you are,' cried Bingley, 'for a kingdom! Upon my honour, I never met with so many pleasant girls in my life, as I have this evening; and there are several of them you see uncommonly pretty.'
>
> '*You* are dancing with the only handsome girl in the room,' said Mr Darcy, looking at the eldest Miss Bennet.
>
> 'Oh! she is the most beautiful creature I ever beheld! But there is one of her sisters sitting down just behind you, who is very pretty, and I dare say, very agreeable. Do let me ask my partner to introduce you.'
>
> 'Which do you mean?' and turning round, he looked for a moment at Elizabeth, till catching her eye, he withdrew his own and coldly said, 'She is tolerable; but not handsome enough to tempt *me*; and I am in no humour at present to give consequence to young ladies who are slighted by other men. You had better return to your partner and enjoy her smiles, for you are wasting your time with me.'
>
> Mr Bingley followed his advice. Mr Darcy walked off; and Elizabeth remained with no very cordial feelings towards him."
>
> *Pride and Prejudice, Chapter 3*

Mansfield Park

Mansfield Park is a quiet, subtle novel, and Fanny Price is very different from Elizabeth Bennet. She is sent to live with her wealthy aunt and uncle when she is nine years old, and grows up in the great house at Mansfield Park, alongside her four cousins. Her own family is large and impoverished, and she is never allowed to forget that she is a dependant. Poor Fanny is shy and frightened of everyone, except her cousin Edmund. He befriends her and she bestows on him all the love and respect of a warm heart.

Emma

When Jane Austen was planning her fourth novel she wrote: 'I am going to take a heroine whom no one but myself will much like,' and it must be admitted that Emma Woodhouse is far from perfect. She is vain and self-satisfied and interferes in the affairs of everyone around her.

Fortunately, she is also warm-hearted and sincere and receives plenty of good advice from Mr Knightley, a friend of the family whose affection for Emma does not blind him to her faults.

Emma Woodhouse

"Emma Woodhouse, handsome, clever, and rich, with a comfortable home and happy disposition, seemed to unite some of the best blessings of existence; and had lived nearly twenty-one years in the world with very little to distress or vex her.

She was the youngest of the two daughters of a most affectionate, indulgent father; and had, in consequence of her sister's marriage, been mistress of his house from a very early period. Her mother had died too long ago for her to have more than an indistinct remembrance of her caresses; and her place had been supplied by an excellent woman as governess, who had fallen little short of a mother in affection.

The real evils, indeed, of Emma's situation were the power of having rather too much her own way, and a disposition to think a little too well of herself: these were the disadvantages which threatened alloy to her many enjoyments. The danger, however, was at present so unperceived, that they did not by any means rank as misfortunes with her."

Emma, Chapter 1

Persuasion

Jane Austen often seems to be laughing at her characters, and slyly poking fun at their preoccupation with wealth, social standing and success. In Persuasion her sarcasm is gentler, and her heroine is more thoroughly good than any of her predecessors. Anne Elliot is ignored by her vain father and patronised by her sisters; when she was nineteen she was persuaded to refuse the hand of the man she loved and, when she meets Wentworth again seven years later, he appears completely indifferent to her. Captain Wentworth does his best to fall in love with the high-spirited Louisa Musgrove but when she meets with a near-fatal accident in a famous scene set in Lyme Regis, it is Anne who inspires him with her courage.

> "There was too much wind to make the high part of the new Cobb pleasant for the ladies, and they agreed to get down the steps to the lower, and all were contented to pass quietly and carefully down the steep flight, excepting Louisa; she must be jumped down them by Captain Wentworth. In all their walks, he had had to jump her from the stiles; the sensation was delightful to her. The hardness of the pavement for her feet, made him less willing upon the present occasion; he did it, however; she was safely down, and instantly, to shew her enjoyment, ran up the steps to be jumped down again. He advised her against it, thought the jar too great; but no, he reasoned and talked in vain; she smiled and said 'I am determined I will:' he put out his hands; she was too precipitate by half a second, she fell on the pavement on the Lower Cobb, and was taken up lifeless!"
>
> *Persuasion, Volume 1, Chapter 12*

Northanger Abbey

Catherine Morland is an inexperienced, sweet-natured girl of seventeen whose opinion of the world has been formed by reading novels. When she goes to stay in Bath, she has every expectation that she will meet with high adventure and, of course, fall in love.

Jane Austen delights in making fun of her heroine's romantic ideas, and the series of mishaps which befall poor Catherine are some of the funniest, and most perceptive that she ever wrote.

Catherine's friend, the pretty but insincere Isabella.

William Shakespeare (1564 - 1616)

William Shakespeare was born in Stratford-upon-Avon and attended the local grammar school. He married a woman from a neighbouring village and had three children. After a lapse of seven years he re-emerged in London, a supremely gifted poet and playwright, with an unparalleled mastery of language and an understanding of the human soul which elevates his work to the divine.

Nobody knows how this transformation came about. The plays of Shakespeare have been studied by millions but the man who wrote them remains an enigma.

> "Sweet Swan of Avon! What a sight it were,
> To see thee in our waters yet appear."
>
> *Ben Johnson*

For many of his contemporaries William Shakespeare's genius must have been hard to understand. Here was a man who knew 'small Latin and less Greek', reared in a provincial backwater, yet so brimming over with inspiration that his dramas flowed from his pen with barely a pause for thought. London audiences were mesmerised and Queen Elizabeth and James I attended select performances of his work, yet Shakespeare was always a quiet man, wary of the court and disliking rowdy company.

At the height of his creative powers, he retired from the theatre and returned to Stratford. He died a few years later in 1616, aged fifty-two.

> "Read him therefore again and again and if then you do not like him, surely you are in some manifest danger not to understand him."
>
> *John Heminges, Henry Condell (friends of Shakespeare)*

William Shakespeare – from a drawing that appeared in the first edition of his plays.

Sonnets

"To the only begetter of these ensuing sonnets, Mr W. H." Shakespeare dedicated his one hundred and fifty four sonnets to an unknown person: the mysterious, unidentified 'Mr W. H.'.

The nature of this friendship has been the source of much discussion over the centuries but a study of the poems themselves would suggest that they exalt a higher form of love than that which is the object of most modern literature:

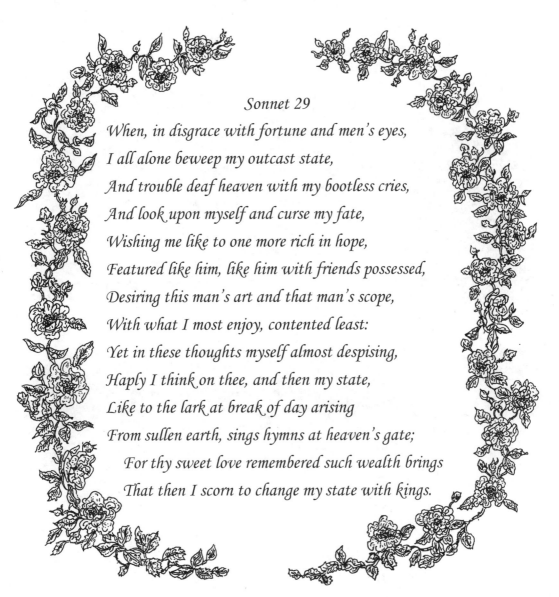

Sonnet 29

When, in disgrace with fortune and men's eyes,
I all alone beweep my outcast state,
And trouble deaf heaven with my bootless cries,
And look upon myself and curse my fate,
Wishing me like to one more rich in hope,
Featured like him, like him with friends possessed,
Desiring this man's art and that man's scope,
With what I most enjoy, contented least:
Yet in these thoughts myself almost despising,
Haply I think on thee, and then my state,
Like to the lark at break of day arising
From sullen earth, sings hymns at heaven's gate;
For thy sweet love remembered such wealth brings
That then I scorn to change my state with kings.

Hamlet, Prince of Denmark

When Hamlet, the young Prince of Denmark, is called home from university, he finds his father dead and his mother married to his uncle. He discovers that his father was murdered, and it is his duty to avenge the crime. Hamlet shrinks from this act of violence, and tragedy results from his inability to act decisively.

Here Hamlet talks to Rosencrantz and Guildenstern, two courtiers newly returned to Denmark:

"How weary, stale, flat, and unprofitable seem to me all the uses of this world."

HAMLET: What's the news?

ROSENCRANTZ: None, my lord, but that the world's grown honest.

HAMLET: Then is doomsday near: but your news is not true. Let me question more in particular: what have you, my good friends, deserved at the hands of Fortune that she sends you to prison hither?

GUILDENSTERN: Prison my lord?

HAMLET: Denmark's a prison.

ROSENCRANTZ: Then is the world one.

HAMLET: A goodly one, in which there are many confines, wards and dungeons, Denmark being one o'th' worst.

ROSENCRANTZ: We think not so my lord.

HAMLET: Why, then 'tis none to you, for there is nothing either good or bad but thinking makes it so. To me it is a prison.

ROSENCRANTZ: Why, then, your ambition makes it one; 'tis too narrow for your mind.

HAMLET: O God, I could be bounded in a nutshell, and count myself a king of infinite space, were it not that I have bad dreams.

Hamlet, Act 2, Scene 2

Romeo and Juliet

Romeo and Juliet is the story of two feuding families and the love that springs up between their children.

Romeo and Juliet marry without their parents' consent and a series of tragic misunderstandings leads to their deaths. They are two of Shakespeare's most endearing characters, and their deaths are, perhaps, the saddest, for they have done little to deserve them. The play is an eloquent warning to those who allow anger and jealousy to become the ruling passions of their lives.

> "Two households, both alike in dignity
> In fair Verona, where we lay our scene,
> From ancient grudge break to new mutiny
> Where civil blood makes civil hands unclean.
> From forth the fatal loins of these two foes
> A pair of star-crossed lovers take their life
> Whose misadventur'd, piteous overthrows
> Doth with their death bury their parents' strife"
>
> *Prologue*

JULIET: Wilt thou be gone? It is not yet near day.
It was the nightingale, and not the lark,
That pierced the fear-full hollow of thine ear.
Nightly she sings on yon pom'granate tree.
Believe me, love, it was the nightingale.

ROMEO: It was the lark, the herald of the morn,
No nightingale. Look, love, what envious streaks
Do lace the severing clouds in yonder east.
Night's candles are burnt out, and jocund day
Stands tiptoe on the misty mountain tops.
I must be gone and live, or stay and die.

JULIET: Yon light is not daylight; I know it, I.
It is some meteor that the sun exhaled
To be to thee this night a torchbearer
And light thee on thy way to Mantua.
Therefore stay yet. Thou need'st not to be gone.

ROMEO: Let me be ta'en, let me be put to death.
I am content, so thou wilt have it so.
I'll say yon grey is not the morning's eye,
'Tis but the pale reflex of Cynthia's brow;
Nor that is not the lark whose notes do beat
The vaulty heaven high above our heads.
I have more care to stay than will to go.
Come, death, and welcome; Juliet wills it so.
How is't, my soul? Let's talk. It is not day.

JULIET: It is, it is. Hie hence, be gone, away.

Romeo and Juliet, Act 3, Scene 5

"O Romeo, Romeo! wherefore art thou Romeo?"

Macbeth

Macbeth is probably the grimmest of Shakespeare's plays. It exposes, with unflinching clarity, the ability of ambition to warp men's minds and harden their hearts. Macbeth and his wife sacrifice everything in the pursuit of power and their plight, by the end of the play, is truly pitiable: after committing murders and atrocities, the light has been extinguished from their lives and they see no way of escaping the despair that has engulfed them.

MACBETH:
> What is that noise?

SEYTON:
> It is the cry of women, my good lord. *[Exit]*

MACBETH:
> I have almost forgot the taste of fears.
> The time has been my senses would have cooled
> To hear a night-shriek, and my fell of hair
> Would at a dismal treatise rouse and stir
> As life were in't. I have supp'd full with horrors;
> Direness, familiar to my slaughterous thoughts,
> Cannot once start me.
> *[Enter Seyton]*
>   Wherefore was that cry?

SEYTON:
> The Queen, my lord, is dead.

MACBETH:
> She should have died hereafter;
> There would have been a time for such a word.
> Tomorrow, and tomorrow, and tomorrow
> Creeps in this petty pace from day to day,
> To the last syllable of recorded time;
> And all our yesterdays have lighted fools
> The way to dusty death. Out, out, brief candle!
> Life's but a walking shadow; a poor player,
> That struts and frets his hour upon the stage,
> And then is heard no more: it is a tale
> Told by an idiot, full of sound and fury,
> Signifying nothing.

Macbeth, Act 5, Scene 5

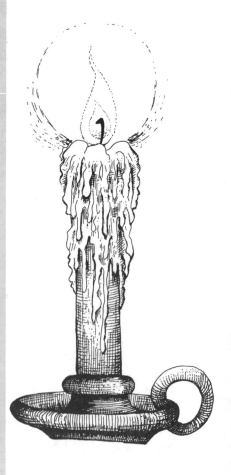

The Merchant of Venice

The Merchant of Venice is neither a tragedy nor a comedy, and its characters are neither wholly good nor wholly bad. The hero is Antonio, a Venetian merchant who borrows a large sum of money from a Jewish usurer called Shylock. Shylock has received many insults from the merchant, who despises him both for his religion and his profession, and seizes this chance to gain power over his enemy. He states that if misfortune overtakes Antonio's vessels, and he cannot repay the loan, he must forfeit a pound of his flesh. Rashly, Antonio agrees and Shylock leaves, delighted with the bargain. Here he explains to a friend the reasons he has to dislike the merchant:

Shylock

SALERIO:

Why, I am sure if he forfeit thou wilt not take his flesh. What's that good for?

SHYLOCK:

To bait fish withal. If it will feed nothing else it will feed my revenge. He hath disgraced me, and hindered me half a million; laughed at my losses, mocked at my gains, scorned my nation, thwarted my bargains, cooled my friends, heated mine enemies, and what's his reason? - I am a Jew. Hath not a Jew eyes? Hath not a Jew hands, organs, dimensions, senses, affections, passions; fed with the same food, hurt with the same weapons, subject to the same diseases, healed by the same means, warmed and cooled by the same winter and summer as a Christian is? If you prick us do we not bleed? If you tickle us do we not laugh? If you poison us do we not die? And if you wrong us shall we not revenge? If we are like you in the rest, we will resemble you in that. If a Jew wrong a Christian, what is his humility? Revenge. If a Christian wrong a Jew, what should his sufferance be by Christian example? Why, revenge. The villainy you teach me I will execute, and it shall go hard but I will better the instruction.

The Merchant of Venice, Act 3, Scene 1

A Midsummer Night's Dream

Midsummer night was traditionally a time of magic and enchantment, and in this, one of Shakespeare's most famous plays, the mortal and fairy worlds come very close together. The story is set in Ancient Greece. The Duke has agreed that Hermia should be forced to marry Demetrius but she loves Lysander. Before becoming infatuated with Hermia, Demetrius had loved Helena. In this scene Hermia and Lysander try to console Helena by explaining that they plan to run away together:

HERMIA: God speed fair Helena! Wither away?
HELENA: Call you me fair? That fair again unsay!
    Demetrius loves your fair. O happy fair!
    Your eyes are lode-stars, and your tongue's sweet air
    More tuneable than lark to shepherd's ear,
    When wheat is green, when hawthorn buds appear.
    Sickness is catching: O were favour so,
    Yours would I catch, fair Hermia, ere I go:
    My ear should catch your voice, my eye your eye,
    My tongue should catch your tongue's sweet melody.
    Were the world mine, Demetrius being bated[1]
    The rest I'd give to be to you translated.
    O, teach me how you look, and with what art
    You sway the motion of Demetrius' heart.
HERMIA: I frown upon him; yet he loves me still.
HELENA: O that your frowns would teach my smiles such skill.
HERMIA: I give him curses; yet he gives me love.
HELENA: O that my prayers could such affection move!
HERMIA: The more I hate, the more he follows me.
HELENA: The more I love, the more he hateth me.
HERMIA: His folly, Helena, is no fault of mine.
HELENA: None but your beauty: would that fault were mine!
LYSANDER: Helen, to you our minds we will unfold:
    Tomorrow night, when Phoebe[2] doth behold
    Her silver visage in the wat'ry glass,
    Decking with liquid pearl the bladed grass
    (A time that lovers' flights doth still conceal)
    Through Athen's gates have we devised to steal.
HERMIA: And in the wood, where often you and I
    Upon faint primrose beds were wont to lie,
    Emptying our bosoms of their counsel sweet,
    There my Lysander and myself shall meet;
    And thence from Athens turn away our eyes,
    To seek new friends, and stranger companies.
    Farewell, sweet playfellow; pray thou for us,
    And good luck grant thee thy Demetrius!

A Midsummer Night's Dream, Act 1, Scene 1

    [1] *bated:* excepted   [2] *Phoebe:* the moon

Julius Caesar

The story of Caesar's assassination has become inextricably linked with Shakespeare's play. So much so in fact, that it is hard to believe that Mark Antony did not say 'Friends, Romans, Countrymen, lend me your ears' or that Caesar did not mutter as he fell 'Et tu Brute?'

Shakespeare put some of his most inspired speeches into the mouths of these Roman heroes and evokes all the passion and drama of ancient Rome. In this extract Caesar's wife, Calpurnia, implores her husband not to leave the house. It is the fifteenth of March, the day on which it has been predicted Caesar will meet his death.

CALPURNIA: What mean you, Caesar, think you to walk forth?
You shall not stir out of your house today.

CAESAR: Caesar shall forth. The things that threatened me
Ne'er looked but on my back; when they shall see
The face of Caesar they are vanished.

CALPURNIA: Caesar, I never stood on ceremonies
Yet now they fright me. There is one within,
Besides the things that we have heard and seen,
Recounts most horrid sights seen by the watch.
A lioness hath whelped in the streets,
And graves have yawned and yielded up their dead;
Fierce fiery warriors fight upon the clouds
In ranks and squadrons and right form of war,
Which drizzled blood upon the Capitol;
The noise of battle hurtled in the air,
Horses did neigh and dying men did groan,
And ghosts did shriek and squeal about the streets.
O Caesar, these things are beyond all use,
And I do fear them.

CAESAR: What can be avoided
Whose end is purposed by the mighty gods?
Yet Caesar shall go forth, for these predictions
Are to the world in general as to Caesar.

CALPURNIA: When beggars die there are no comets seen,
The heavens themselves blaze forth the death of princes.

CAESAR: Cowards die many times before their deaths,
The valiant never taste of death but once.
Of all the wonders that I yet have heard
It seems to me most strange that men should fear,
Seeing that death, a necessary end,
Will come when it will come.

Julius Caesar, Act 2, Scene 2

Historical Plays

Shakespeare wrote ten plays chronicling the lives of seven English kings. They are, for the most part, historically accurate and present a vivid picture of the battles, uprisings and political scheming that took place in the reigns of King John, Richard II, Henry IV, Henry V, Henry VI, Richard III and Henry VIII.

These are more than historical accounts, however: Shakespeare brought his understanding of human nature to bear upon his portrayal of the kings, and shows them to be human beings, influenced by the same joys and sorrows as their subjects.

In this extract, Richard II has lost his crown and his kingdom, and is about to be taken prisoner by his cousin, the usurping Henry Bolingbroke:

> KING RICHARD:
>> For God's sake, let us sit upon the ground,
>> And tell sad stories of the death of kings:–
>> How some have been depos'd; some slain in war;
>> Some haunted by the ghosts they have depos'd;
>> Some poison'd by their wives; some sleeping kill'd;
>> All murder'd:– for within the hollow crown
>> That rounds the mortal temples of a king
>> Keeps Death his court; and there the antic[1] sits,
>> Scoffing his state, and grinning at his pomp;
>> Allowing him a breath, a little scene,
>> To monarchize, be fear'd, and kill with looks;
>> Infusing him with self and vain conceit, –
>> As if this flesh, which walls about our life,
>> Were brass impregnable; and humour'd thus,
>> Comes at the last, and with a little pin
>> Bores through his castle-wall, and – farewell, king!
>> Cover your heads, and mock not flesh and blood
>> With solemn reverence; throw away respect,
>> Tradition, form, and ceremonious duty;
>> For you have but mistook me all this while:
>> I live with bread like you, feel want, taste grief,
>> Need friends:– subjected thus,
>> How can you say to me, I am a king?
>
> *Richard II, Act 3, Scene 2*

[1] antic = madman

King Lear

King Lear is the story of a man who gives his kingdom to the two daughters who despise him, and banishes the daughter who loves him. Like the famous Greek tragedies it portrays a character whose own arrogance brings about his downfall, and who is taught wisdom through suffering – to read or watch it is an elevating experience, even though almost all the principal characters die.

In this scene King Lear has been turned out onto the heath by his two daughters. A storm is raging and the old king is filled with anger at his daughters' ingratitude.

LEAR:
Blow winds and crack your cheeks! Rage, blow!
You cataracts and hurricanes, spout
Till you have drenched our steeples, drowned the cocks!
You sulphurous and thought-executing fires,
Vaunt-couriers[1] of oak-cleaving thunderbolts,
Singe my white head! And thou, all-shaking thunder,
Strike flat the thick rotundity o' the world,
Crack nature's moulds, all germens[2] spill at once
That make ingrateful man!

FOOL:
O, nuncle, court holy water[3] in a dry house
is better than this rain water out o'door.
Good nuncle, in, and ask thy daughters
blessing. Here's a night pities neither wise
men nor fools.

LEAR:
Rumble thy bellyful! Spit fire, spout rain!
Nor rain, wind, thunder, fire are my daughters;
I tax not you, you elements, with unkindness.
I never gave you kingdom, called you children;
You owe me no subscription[4]. Why then,
let fall
Your horrible pleasure. Here I stand your
slave,
A poor, infirm, weak and despised old
man.
But yet I call you servile ministers
That will with two pernicious daughters
join
Your high-engendered battles 'gainst a
head
So old and white as this. Oho! tis foul.
                    King Lear, Act 3, Scene 3

King Lear, on the heath.

---

[1] *vaunt-couriers*: forerunners [2] *germens*: seeds [3] *court holy water*: flattery, fair words
[4] *subscription*: support

Homer

Homer's poetry occupied a unique position in the ancient world: it was regarded as a sacred text and it provided a definitive statement about the deeds and motives of the Gods and the purpose of human life. It is still regarded as the finest literature ever produced by Western civilisation.

The Iliad

The Iliad describes a few crucial days in the siege of Troy. Achilleus allows his friend, Patroklos, to borrow his armour and lead his troops into battle. Patroklos is killed and Achilleus is devastated when he receives the news of his death:

" 'Oh, son of warrior Peleus, there is terrible news for you to hear, which I wish had never happened. Patroklos lies dead, and they are fighting over his body. It is naked now – Hektor of the glinting helmet has his armour.'

So he spoke, and the black cloud of sorrow enveloped Achilleus. He took up the sooty dust in both his hands and poured it down over his head, soiling his handsome face: and the black ashes settled all over his sweet-smelling tunic.

And he lay there with his whole body sprawling in the dust, huge and hugely fallen, tearing at his hair and defiling it with his own hands. And the serving-women that Achilleus and Patroklos had won in war shrieked loud in their hearts' grief, and ran out to flock round the warrior Achilleus: all of them beat their breasts with their hands, and the strength collapsed from their bodies. And to one side Antilochos mourned with his tears falling, and he held the hands of Achilleus as his glorious heart groaned: he was afraid that Achilleus might take a knife and cut his own throat. Achilleus gave out a terrible cry, and his honoured mother heard him, where she sat by the side of her old father in the depths of the sea, and she wailed loud in her response."

Extract from The Iliad, translated by Martin Hammond

"And Achilleus came close on him like Enyalios, the god of war, shaking his terrible spear of Pelian ash over his right shoulder."

The Odyssey

The Odyssey describes the homecoming of Odysseus from the siege of Troy. His kingdom has been occupied by enemies during his twenty year absence and he re-enters his palace disguised as a beggar. He is still recognised, however, by his faithful old dog:

"...A dog that was lying there lifted his head and ears. This was Argos, whom long ago Odysseus himself had brought up at home but had little pleasure in, because all too soon he had departed to sacred Ilium. In days gone by, the younger men had taken him with them to hunt wild goats and deer and hares; but now, with his master gone, he lay unwanted on the deep pile of dung from the mules and cattle that was waiting there in front of the doors till the king's servants should carry it away to fatten the wide estates; on this the dog Argos lay, full of vermin. But now, as he saw Odysseus close by and knew him, he wagged his tail and dropped his ears, though he could not now move nearer to his master. Then Odysseus glanced aside, wiped away a tear unheeded by Eumaeus and hastened to put a question to him: 'Eumaeus, surely this is a strange thing, a dog like this lying on a dunghill. He is handsome to look at; I wonder if he had speed to match his looks. Or was he only one of those dogs whose masters pamper them at table and keep them for show alone?'

Eumaeus the swineherd answered him: 'The plain truth is that this dog's master was one who has died far from his home. If in looks and power Argos could be again such as Odysseus left him when he set out for Troy, then you would not be slow to wonder when you saw what strength and speed he had. There was no beast in any nook of the bushy woodland that could escape him when he pursued. How sure he was in tracking the prey! But now his plight is pitiable; his master has perished far from his own land, and the women care nothing and will not tend him. When masters are not there to command, serfs lack zeal to do as they should, for Zeus the Thunderer takes half the virtue away from a man when once the day of bondage has come on him.'

So saying, he went through the palace entrance and down the hall to the haughty suitors. As for Argos, the fate of dark death fell on him suddenly when in this twentieth year he had once again set eyes upon Odysseus."

The Odyssey, translated by Walter Shewring

See also History Section, Homer, pages 84 and 85.

The Ramayana

The Ramayana is the ancient story of Lord Ram, composed by the Sanskrit poet, Valmiki. In the late fifteen hundreds, Tulsidas rewrote the story: he named his poem the Ramacharitmanasa, or the 'Holy Lake of Ram's Deeds'. It is one of the great masterpieces of world literature, and is as beloved in India as the Bible or Shakespeare are in the West.

The Ramacharitmanasa tells the story of Ram, son of King Dasaratha. He is divinely wise and beautiful and all who meet him are filled with joy. The subjects of the kingdom long for Ram to become king and Dasaratha gladly agrees to relinquish the throne. Unfortunately, one of Dasaratha's wives becomes jealous of Ram and contrives to have him banished to the forest for fourteen years. The people are distraught but Ram comforts them with loving words and departs in the company of his young wife, Sitā, and his devoted brother, Lakshman.

Hanuman is Ram's most faithful adherent and has become a symbol of loyalty and devotion.

"Whenever Sitā, Lakshman and Raghurāī (Rām) came out near a village on the way, people, – young and old, man and woman – came directly they heard the news, forgetting their own private affairs, and as they gazed on their beauty, obtained the fruition of their eyes and were made happy for ever. At the sight of the two heroes their eyes filled with tears, they felt a thrill of joy, and became all-enraptured, their state of mind as indescribable as though a beggar had discovered a pile of heavenly jewels. Everyone was telling his neighbour: 'Now is the time to prove the value of sight.' One in his delight to see Rām would go with him, gazing as he went; another, drawing his beautiful image into his heart by way of his eyes, was utterly overpowered in body, soul and speech."

The Ramacharitmanasa, Chaupai 113, Tulsidas, translated by F. S. Growse

The Bible

Not only does the Bible have enormous historical and religious significance but it is also one of the major works of world literature. The fact that it is so little studied today is partly a reaction against established religions but, more significantly, highlights an eclipse of learning in general.

The translation completed in the reign of King James I of England is still widely held to be the best version in the English language.

Doth not wisdom cry? and understanding put forth her voice?

She standeth in the top of high places, by the way in the places of the paths.

She crieth at the gates, at the entry of the city, at the coming in at the doors.

Unto you, O men, I call; and my voice is to the sons of man.

O ye simple, understand wisdom: and, ye fools, be ye of an understanding heart.

Hear; for I will speak of excellent things; and the opening of my lips shall be right things.

For my mouth shall speak truth; and wickedness is an abomination to my lips.

All the words of my mouth are in righteousness; there is nothing froward or perverse in them.

They are all plain to him that understandeth, and right to them that find knowledge.

Receive my instruction, and not silver; and knowledge rather than choice gold.

For wisdom is better than rubies; and all the things that may be desired are not to be compared to it.

Counsel is mine, and sound wisdom: I am understanding; I have strength.

By me kings reign, and princes decree justice.

By me princes rule, and nobles, even all the judges of the earth.

I love them that love me; and those that seek me early shall find me.

Riches and honour are with me; yea, durable riches and righteousness.

My fruit is better than gold, yea, than fine gold; and my revenue than choice silver.

I lead in the way of righteousness, in the midst of the paths of judgment:

That I may cause those that love me to inherit substance; and I will fill their treasures.

Proverbs, Chapter 8, King James Version

Beowulf

Beowulf is the oldest work in Anglo-Saxon literature. It is an epic poem, written in Old English and is set in a semi-mythological Scandinavian past. It tells the story of Beowulf – 'the strongest of all men ever to have seen the light of life on earth' – and his slaying of the evil monster Grendel.

In this extract Beowulf introduces himself to King Hrothgar, and tells him that he has come to rid him of Grendel. The monster has been killing and consuming the Danes after they have been feasting, and they are now too afraid to make merry in Heorot, the grand banqueting hall.

Beowulf spoke – his corslet, cunningly linked
by the smith, was shining: 'Greetings, Hrothgar!
I am Hygelac's kinsman and retainer. In my youth
I achieved many daring exploits. Word of Grendel's deeds
has come to me in my own country;
seafarers say that this hall Heorot,
best of all buildings, stands empty and useless
as soon as the evening light is hidden under the sky.
So, Lord Hrothgar, men known to my people
to be noble and wise advised me to visit you
because they knew of my great strength:
they saw me themselves when, stained by my enemies' blood,
I returned from the fight when I destroyed five,
a family of giants, and by night slew monsters
on the waves; I suffered great hardship,
avenged the affliction of the Storm-Geats and crushed
their fierce foes – they were asking for trouble.
And now, I shall crush the giant Grendel
in single combat. Lord of the mighty Danes,
guardian of the Scyldings, I ask one favour:
protector of the warriors, lord beloved of your people,
now that I have sailed here from so far,
do not refuse my request – that I alone, with my band
of brave retainers, may cleanse Heorot.
I have also heard men say this monster
is so reckless he spurns the use of weapons.
Therefore (so great Hygelac, my lord,
may rest content over my conduct) I deny myself
the use of a sword and a broad yellow shield
in battle; but I shall grapple with this fiend
hand to hand; we shall fight for our lives,
foe against foe; and he whom death takes off
must resign himself to the judgement of God.

Beowulf, translation by Kevin Crossley-Holland, Oxford World's Classics

Recommended: **Beowulf: A Glossed Text** The original poem with word for word translation by Michael Alexander, Penguin Classics

Henry Fielding (1707 - 1754)

Inspired with a love of the classics, Henry Fielding set himself the task of writing novels as moving, humorous and insightful as the masterpieces of Greek and Roman literature.

Joseph Andrews: The first of Fielding's novels began as a parody of a bestseller of the time, but it soon blossomed into a classic in its own right. It recounts the adventures that befall Joseph Andrews, his sweetheart Fanny, and the loveable, scatterbrained Parson Adams, as they journey across an England peopled by robbers, rakish squires, innkeepers, eccentrics, and dissolute priests. The innocence of the three principal characters makes them a prey to every scoundrel that they meet, but their goodness of heart protects them, and they pass unscathed through a succession of mishaps and comical misadventures.

Tom Jones: Written at the peak of Fielding's career, Tom Jones is generally considered to be his masterpiece. The tale of the foundling boy, and his love for the virtuous Sophia is told in Fielding's inimitable style, and gives a clear picture of the high-spirited, exhilarating times in which he lived.

In this extract Sophia has just been thrown from her horse and would have fallen to the ground if Tom Jones had not leapt forward to catch her:

"She (Sophia) was so affected with the fright that she was not immediately able to satisfy Jones, who was very solicitous to know whether she had received any hurt. She soon after, however, recovered her spirits, assured him she was safe, and thanked him for the care he had taken of her. Jones answered: 'If I have preserved you, madam, I am sufficiently repaid; for I promise you, I would have secured you from the least harm at the expense of much greater misfortune to myself than I have suffered on this occasion.'

'What misfortune?' replied Sophia eagerly. 'I hope you have come to no mischief?'

'Be not concerned, madam,' answered Jones. 'Heaven be praised you have escaped so well, considering the danger you was in. If I have broke my arm, I consider it as a trifle, in comparison of what I feared on your account.'

Sophia then screamed out: 'Broke your arm! Heaven forbid!'

'I am afraid I have, madam,' says Jones, 'but I beg you will suffer me first to take care of you. I have a right hand yet at your service, to help you into the next field, whence we have but a very little walk to your father's house.'

Sophia, seeing his left arm dangling by his side, while he was using the other to lead her, no longer doubted of the truth. She now grew much paler than her fears for herself had made her before. All her limbs were seized with a trembling, insomuch that Jones could scarce support her; and as her thoughts were in no less agitation, she could not refrain from giving Jones a look so full of tenderness that it almost argued a stronger sensation in her mind than even gratitude and pity united can raise in the gentlest female bosom without the assistance of a third more powerful passion."

Tom Jones, Book 4, Chapter 13

Mrs Gaskell (1810 - 1865)

Victorian England was torn between pride in its new, industrial towns, and nostalgia for the countryside which so many people had left behind. The novels of Elizabeth Gaskell reflect this dilemma; **North and South** and **Mary Barton** are set in Northern, manufacturing towns, and the conflicts between the mill owners and the workers are recounted with compassion combined with a strong sense of the injustice of such a system.

Elizabeth Gaskell had, however, been brought up in the country, and one feels that it is in depicting rural scenes and people that she is happiest. **Wives and Daughters** is set in a small country town and is the most light-hearted of her novels. In this extract Mr Gibson tells his seventeen-year-old daughter, Molly, that he has decided to remarry.

"He went into the house by a private door, and made his way into the drawing-room, half expecting, however, that Molly would be in the garden. She had been there, but it was too hot and dazzling now for her to remain out of doors, and she had come in by the open window of the drawing-room. Oppressed with the heat, she had fallen asleep in an easy-chair, her bonnet and open book upon her knee, one arm hanging listlessly down. She looked very soft, and young, and childlike; and a gush of love sprang into her father's heart as he gazed at her.

'Molly!' said he, gently taking her little brown hand that was hanging down, and holding it in his own. 'Molly!'

She opened her eyes, that for one moment had no recognition in them. Then the light came brilliantly into them and she sprang up, and threw her arms round his neck, exclaiming, –

'Oh, papa, my dear, dear papa! What made you come while I was asleep? I lose the pleasure of watching for you.'

Mr Gibson turned a little paler than he had been before. He still held her hand, and drew her to a seat by him on a sofa, without speaking. There was no need; she was chattering away.

'I was up so early! It is so charming to be out here in the fresh morning air. I think that made me sleepy. But isn't it a gloriously hot day? I wonder if the Italian skies they talk about can be bluer than that – that little bit you see just between the oaks – there!'

She was rather struck by his unusual silence.

'Do you know, papa, I don't think you are looking well?'

'Don't I look well? That must be all your fancy, goosey. I feel uncommonly well; and I ought to look well, for – I have a piece of news for you, little woman.' (He felt that he was doing his business very awkwardly, but he was determined to plunge on.) 'Can you guess it?'

'You're going to be married again,' said she, helping him out, with a quiet dry voice, and gently drawing her hand out of his.

'Yes. To Mrs Kirkpatrick – you remember her? They call her Clare at the Towers. You recollect how kind she was to you that day you were left there?'

She did not answer. She could not tell what words to use. She was afraid of saying anything, lest the passion of anger, dislike, indignation – whatever it was that was boiling up in her breast – should find vent in cries and screams, or worse, in raging words that could never be forgotten. It was as if the piece of solid ground on which she stood had broken from the shore, and she was drifting out to the infinite sea alone."

Wives and Daughters, Chapter 10

Oliver Goldsmith (1730 - 1774)

Born in Ireland, Oliver Goldsmith trained as a doctor, but seems to have had little interest in the profession. He travelled round Europe begging and playing the flute, and then settled in London where he supported himself by writing poetry, articles, and plays.

His only novel, **The Vicar of Wakefield**, recounts the adventures of the unworldly Dr Primrose and his family. The freshness and innocence of the story, combined with a gentle humour, have made it one of the best-loved books in the English language.

In this extract Dr Primrose describes his ideas of hospitality, and a novel way of disposing of unwanted guests.

"As we lived near the road, we often had the traveller or stranger visit us to taste our gooseberry-wine, for which we had great reputation; and I profess, with the veracity of an historian, that I never knew one of them find fault with it. Our cousins, too, even to the fortieth remove, all remembered their affinity, without any help from the herald's office, and came very frequently to see us. Some of them did us no great honour by these claims of kindred, as we had the blind, the maimed, and the halt amongst the number. However, my wife always insisted that, as they were the same *flesh and blood*, they should sit with us at the same table.

However, when any one of our relations was found to be a person of very bad character, a troublesome guest, or one we desired to get rid of, upon leaving my house I ever took care to lend him a riding-coat or a pair of boots, or sometimes an horse of small value, and I always had the satisfaction of finding he never came back to return them. By this the house was cleared of such as we did not like; but never was the family of Wakefield known to turn the traveller or the poor dependant out of doors."

The Vicar of Wakefield, Chapter 1

Conclusion

The list of books recommended in this section does not pretend to be comprehensive: inevitably, many people's favourites will have been omitted and modern writers are not represented at all.

However, if you have read, and enjoyed, the books on this list you will have been introduced to the pillars upon which world literature stands and you will have a much better understanding of the subject than many people who have, perhaps, read far more books than you. Furthermore, by concentrating initially on books that are of an indisputable quality, you have a good chance of developing a love for literature which will remain with you for the rest of your life and which will, hopefully, lead you to continue reading and enjoying books for many years to come.

Crowns have their compass – length of days their date –
Triumphs their tomb – felicity, her fate –
Of nought but earth can earth make us partaker,
But knowledge makes a King most like his Maker.

Shakespeare

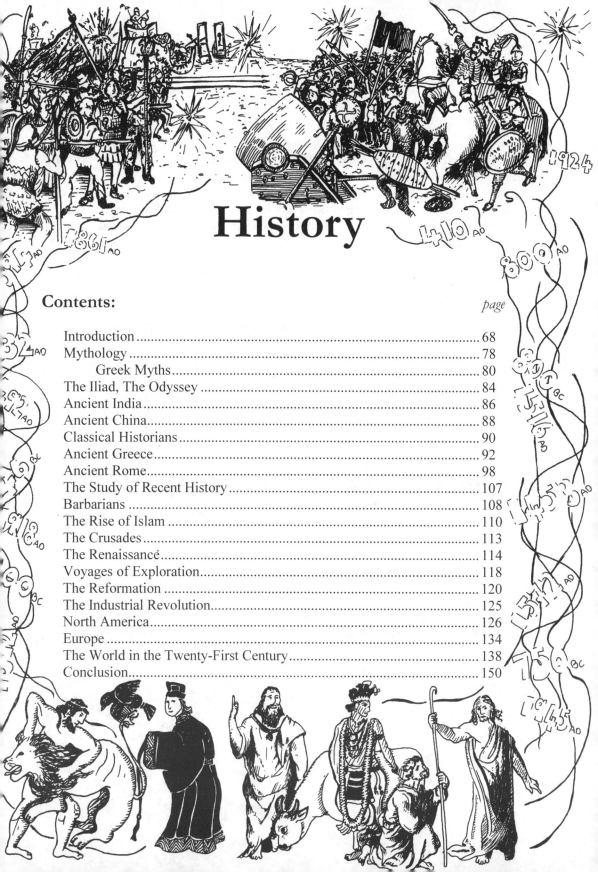

History

Contents:

History

Some time ago, I taught maths and science in a small school in the north of England. The pupils came from a range of backgrounds and varied widely in their abilities. The school had no set curriculum and did not enter pupils for any examinations. It was up to me to work out how to introduce my subjects in a way that would interest the students and would be of use to them.

After a little trial and error, I discovered that the answer lay in introducing everything in terms of its historical perspective: we studied astronomy in terms of the lives of Copernicus, Kepler and Newton; in mechanics we looked at the work of Galileo; to understand electricity we studied the work of Benjamin Franklin and Michael Faraday; in Geometry we studied Euclid; and for trigonometry we tried to understand the work of the ancient Babylonians.

I found that this approach had something to offer everyone. The more technically-minded students followed the mathematics and logic involved in each area, step-by-step, while the other pupils appreciated the drama and the struggle that lay behind each new discovery.

At the same time, something else happened: I found that by focussing on the origin and history of mathematical and scientific ideas, I came to understand the subjects much better myself – it put everything into the correct perspective.

> "I am not one who has innate knowledge, but one who, loving antiquity, is diligent in seeking it therein."
>
> *Confucius, The Analects*

If this applies to maths and science, then it must apply to every area of human endeavour. Whether it be health, transport, literature, farming, government, education, industry, technology, exploration, or the factors that govern the politics of the modern world, the current state of affairs can only be properly understood through a clear understanding of its history.

Hannibal's march across the Alps

In 218 BC Hannibal, commander of the Carthaginian forces in Spain, and the greatest general of his time, led 100,000 men and 47 elephants against Rome, Carthage's bitterest enemy. But between him and Italy lay an insurmountable barrier...

My men, you have accomplished much; you have subjugated Spain, you have crossed the Pyrenees, you have tricked the Romans and you have forded many rivers. But we are not yet at the walls of Rome; there is one last effort to be made— the crossing of the Alps.

Assumptions that Arise from Bad History Teaching

Unfortunately, history can be used to distort the truth just as it can be used to illuminate it. We tend to think that these distortions are only perpetrated by evil dictators and their propaganda machines, but in fact everyone has a tendency to colour their view of history according to their own beliefs and prejudices.

Commonly-held beliefs that are often woven into the teaching of history include some of the following:

- Human history is a story of steady progress from ancient barbarism to modern civilisation.

- Man's understanding of the world has steadily increased over time.

- People's lives today are better than they have ever been before.

- Levels of health are better now than ever before.

- People live longer now than they did in the past.

- History is full of wars and destruction.

- Europe is the cradle of civilisation and the rest of the world should be grateful when Western ideas are imposed upon them.

None of these assumptions can be supported by an objective analysis of the available facts. A dispassionate examination of the subject favours the notion that history repeats itself over and over again; it is more like a circle in which civilisations rise and fall than a straight line along which mankind is progressing towards some imminent conclusion.

When this is understood, history starts to take on a new meaning and the past ceases to be an alien place inhabited by barbarians, living in squalor and bent on destruction. It becomes familiar territory belonging to people very like ourselves and from whom we can learn about the joys and the pitfalls of human existence.

"There is really no limit to historians' lies."

Titus Livy

It is a strange world up here in the mountains, Hannibal. The natives and beasts look half dead with cold.

Yes, and look, a number of them are holding the pass up there.

Hmmm, it will be impossible for us to pass that way whilst the barbarians are there—unless we want to lose our army. Something will have to be done...

69

Problems that Arise from a Misunderstanding of History

If the assumptions that we make about history are false, then the consequences are profound: the lifestyle of the developed world is based on the notion that our civilisation is vastly superior to anything that has gone before and this assumption is used to justify almost any degree of intrusion into the lives of people living in other parts of the world. This philosophy of superiority was used to justify the colonial policies of previous centuries and it is still being used to justify the exploitation of mineral and agricultural resources in poor countries around the world. What if this were a mistaken philosophy and we were simply repeating old behaviour patterns? In that case surely a proper understanding of history would help us to find appropriate solutions.

The fact is that historical assumptions have a profound effect upon daily life as well as upon politics and global economics:

- People take drugs and medicines because they believe that healthcare arrangements in previous centuries were ineffective.
- Parents vaccinate their children because they believe that in the past it was common for children to die from childhood ailments.
- People tolerate the indignities of having to go out to work because they believe that working practices were harsher and less humane in the past than they are now.
- People are prepared to pay high rents and mortgages in order to have a roof over their heads because they believe that the system is fairer now than it used to be.
- People send their children to school because they believe it represents an improvement on previous educational arrangements.

Perhaps these assumptions are true, perhaps they are not: the problem is that people believe them to be true without ever having taken the trouble to really investigate.

After having looked at history from many different angles, I believe it to be the area in which the maxim 'a little knowledge is a dangerous thing' is the most apt: it would be better to have no knowledge of history than to allow one's actions to be guided by misconceptions of what took place in the past. The more effort one makes to be open-minded and impartial in one's study of history, the more evident it

becomes that it is practically impossible to establish exactly what happened at any time in the past. This is itself a valuable lesson, because it teaches us to be less absolute in our judgements and to realise that no matter what facts are being presented to us about the current world situation, there are probably other ways of looking at it that are equally valid.

The Difference Between History and Propaganda

If a real study of history represents an effort to understand the past, then much of what passes for history is in fact propaganda.

Propaganda is used as a means to make people identify with a particular cause, country or religion. This is very obvious in history books that have survived from the beginning of the twentieth century. European children were taught that the world was inhabited by savages who ought to be thankful to the European powers for occupying their territory and imposing European customs upon them.

This way of looking at life was responsible for the First World War, in which the European powers fought each other in order to resolve which of them was to control the rest of the world, and it contributed to the Second World War which was characterised by such brutal racism that even now people cannot understand how it can have taken place.

Since those times, history teaching may have improved a little but it still tends to try to impose a particular idea of history upon the student, rather than allowing them to form their own ideas, based upon their own experiences and observations.

Objectivity in History

The lack of objectivity in history teaching can best be appreciated when one takes a step back from discussing the details of the recent past to look at the overall picture. People have been living on this planet for a very long time; there have been times of peace and times of war and there have been times of plenty and times of hunger. Any clear-sighted view of history tells us that the times of peace and plenty are the good times and that the times of war and hunger are the bad times.

All of us would prefer to live our lives in peace and prosperity and we would all dearly love to believe that our children and grandchildren will be able to do the same.

When we consider history, therefore, we should be looking for times and places in which people have managed to live in harmony with each other, and with Nature – not just for ten or twenty years, but for a few centuries. These are the people who we should respect and from whom we should seek to learn.

When we make an assessment of the achievements of our own civilisation, it should be on the basis of whether or not it has managed to improve the level of human happiness; whether it has led to a reduction in war, an increase in security, a reduction of poverty and an improvement in health – not just for a favoured minority, but for everyone whose life it affects.

Prejudice has no Place in History

Instead of using history as a means to identify people and civilisations from which we can learn, there is a tendency to use it as a way of passing on national, religious or ethnic prejudices to another generation: children are taught that everything done by their own country, religion or race has always been good, and that everything that has been done by their neighbours is bad.

These one-sided, myopic views of history have always been divisive and dangerous, but they seem to be particularly out of place in the modern world. It makes some people identify with minority groups and feel the weight of historical injustice weighing down upon them, and it makes other people – those with access to wealth and power – feel self-righteous as they convince themselves that people of other classes, races and religions have always been untrustworthy, undeserving, ungrateful or simply in the wrong.

Human Values in History

When teaching history, or when reading about historical events, it is best to focus upon ordinary people instead of upon the fates of countries, races, or religious groupings: everyone in history has behaved in a way that is easy to understand in the context of the situations in which they found themselves.

History becomes interesting when it is seen as the stories of countless people, each of whom is essentially the same as oneself. Some of them have had to endure things that you hope you will never have to endure, some have done things that you

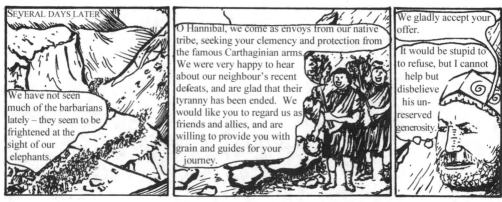

hope you will never do, and a few have led their lives in such a way as to be a source of inspiration and hope for everyone.

School as Medium for History Teaching

If people have any positive memories about the academic work that they did at school, it is quite likely to be related to history – but this says more about the universal appeal of history than about school's ability to teach it.

Project and course work represent the best side of school history teaching because they give pupils a chance to work at their own pace on a topic that interests them. Project work involves cooperation between the school and the home, with teachers giving ideas and support while the children have to find material in the library, on the internet and from books and magazines that they have at home.

Schools are not so good when they teach a specific curriculum and make people sit history tests. Everything in history is open to various interpretations and setting an exam in the subject forces students to adopt the views favoured by the examiners. The more impersonal the examination, the more this applies: it may be possible for post-graduate university students to put forward an unconventional argument – and for it to be accepted – but if a sixteen-year-old school pupil does something similar, they simply fail the exam.

The Home as a Good Place to Study History

Different people are interested in different aspects of history; studying at home allows them to pursue this interest without being put under pressure to conform to anyone else's idea of what a proper study of history should entail.

The ready availability of history books and the huge number of historical documents published on the internet means that people's homes are now able to offer better resources for study than schools, and they certainly provide a more conducive atmosphere in which to read, consider and discuss historical questions.

When is the Best Time to Start Learning History?

Schools tend to start teaching history at too young an age. History is not a collection of facts and dates, it is about real people, and what they did and why they did it. This is not a subject that holds much interest for young children – they are not really interested in what adults are doing today, let alone in what they were doing hundreds of years ago.

In practice, people need not ever be made to study history; it is a subject of such fundamental significance, and so inherently interesting, that, providing they are given the freedom to make their own decisions, everyone sooner or later becomes a student of history.

The history section of this book reflects the traditional way of studying the subject:

- First become acquainted with the myths and legends that were important to the people who founded the earliest-known civilisations.

- Next, study everything about these early civilisations in as much detail as surviving records allow.

- Finally, try to understand the series of events that led from the decline of these civilisations to the world in which we ourselves are living today.

What is the Best Way to Study History?

The best way to study history is from good history books. There are a few classic history texts that have a long established reputation (sometimes going back for thousands of years), upon which all our understanding of the subject is based. Despite their pretensions to the contrary, most modern history books are simply reworked versions of these classics, inferior to the original in almost every respect. The worst offenders are school textbooks which patronise the reader and assume that they are too young and stupid to understand the original material and therefore present them with a simplified, incomplete version that is lacking both in interest and intellectual integrity.

A serious student should initially concentrate upon those books that are recognised as being classics in their field. Some of these books are themselves very

old and have the added advantage of providing a perspective on history from a time other than our own.

Any written material dating back even a few decades provides an insight into the life and views of people living at the time that they were written, thus novels, comics, diaries, newspapers, etc. are all worth reading to give a broader understanding of the context within which historical events were enacted.

Reading allows the student to gradually build up an overall picture of history into which they are then able to fit new information as it is presented to them, whether it be from television, magazines, encyclopaedias, films, historical dramas, literature, or discussions with other people.

There never comes a time when you can say that you have learnt all there is to know about history: it is an inexhaustible subject and the more you learn, the more you realise how much more there is to know. This is a good thing because it means that once you have discovered a love for history, you have found something that will stay with you for the rest of your life.

Historical Themes

When studying history, you do not have to start at the beginning and slowly work up to the present day. Instead, concentrate on different periods of history and different regions of the world, moving from one to another as you see fit. Some common themes start to emerge that remain of interest no matter which period of history you are studying:

- **The Art of Good Government** – The successes and failures experienced by human societies in their efforts to maintain good government is one of the main themes of history.

- **Kings, Queens, Emperors and Dictators** – The lives and deaths of absolute rulers hold a fascination that provides one of the most compulsive aspects of historical studies.

- **War** – Is war an inevitable part of the human condition? Have people ever lived without war?

- **Ancient Civilisations** – Are people today more, or less, civilised than they were thousands of years ago?

- **Migration** – The migration of peoples from one country to another is responsible for radical changes in the course of world history.

- **The Industrial Revolution** – How has industry and technology changed people's lives? Is life better now than it used to be?

- **Children** – What was life like for children at different times and in different parts of the world?

- **Health** – How healthy or unhealthy were people in previous times? How long did they live? What did they eat?

- **United States** – In little over two hundred years a group of former British colonies has transformed itself into the world superpower. How did it happen?

Dates in History

Historians have developed the habit of placing a huge amount of importance on knowing exactly when historical events took place. This often leads them to lose sight of the true significance of the events themselves and to concentrate instead upon relatively unimportant details relating to times and dates.

Most people cannot remember the 'significant' dates in their own lives. When pressed they may be able to remember the date that they were married, but they will probably not know the date they started their first job, the date they started school, the date they first met a particular friend, or the date they lost someone who was dear to them. It is not the dates that are important but the fact that the events took place. The same principle applies to history; the important thing is to know that something happened, to understand why it happened and to learn from the fact that it did happen.

Becoming obsessed with historical dates allows people to give the impression that they are studying history whilst in reality they are avoiding the real issues involved. A proper study of history makes the student look a little deeper into themselves and into the nature of human beings. It shows how certain ways of behaving always yield the same kinds of results: intolerance breeds hatred and civil unrest; nationalism leads to war; materialism leads to injustice and disillusionment; religious bigotry leads to stagnation; bad rulers create havoc in their countries; good rulers can provide peace

and stability; society works best when individuals take responsibilities upon themselves; ideologies never work etc.

History can be about learning from these lessons and ensuring that mistakes made in the past are not repeated today. Dates and times have no real relevance to this process.

Archaeology

The admissibility of historical evidence is a contentious subject. Recent centuries have seen a rejection of traditional stories which were once seen as the most reliable source of historical information, in favour of archaeological evidence. This has led to all sorts of confusion and embarrassment for historians. Time and again new archaeological evidence has been found that contradicts old archaeological evidence, forcing historians to readjust their theories so that they become closer to the traditional beliefs that are supposed to have been supplanted. Inexplicably, this has not caused historians to change their approach.

Logically, archaeological remains should be considered as the least interesting and least instructive of all historical data. In order to demonstrate this point to yourself, try to imagine how an historian of the future would try to reconstruct your life on the basis of archaeological evidence that *you* leave behind. It is just as foolish for us to imagine that a few fragments of pottery, or an animal's jaw bone will tell us all that there is to be known about someone who lived thousands of years ago.

The History of Language

One thing that has survived from ancient times, and which has been passed on to us in a living form, is language. But a careful study of language raises more questions than it answers: many modern languages share a common origin (for example the majority of the languages spoken in Europe and Asia seem to be derived from a common source), but instead of becoming more refined with the passage of time, languages appear to deteriorate. Ancient languages are marked by the precision of their grammar, the diversity of their vocabulary and the facility with which they lend themselves to verse and poetry. This is wholly at odds with the idea that human history marks a path of steady progress.

Continued on page 159 77

Mythology

Why study mythology?

The problem for the modern historian is that historical records do not go back further than about two and a half thousand years. Even when taking archaeological remains into account, the timescale being studied by historians is very small when set against the millions of years that human beings are thought to have been on the planet.

Mankind appears to have emerged from the prolonged period of 'pre-history' having already made the discoveries that distinguish human beings from animals: agriculture, the plough, the cultivation of all the significant food crops, the use of fire, building, architecture, art, sculpture, mathematics, and, most significantly, language.

To imagine that, prior to this time, people were living a 'caveman' existence and then suddenly transformed themselves into the sophisticated civilisations of the ancient world is untenable, but modern academics can throw no light on what actually took place. It therefore makes sense to study the myths and legends which have survived from those times.

These stories reflect what ancient peoples believed to be the origins of their knowledge and wisdom. They are stories that had been handed down from generation to generation and they deserve to be taken seriously.

Mythology and History

Mythology has the advantage of being both interesting and enjoyable: if mythological stories had been boring, they would not have survived to the present time. They do not simply describe events that took place in the past, but also contain a message about morals and about how life should be led. Sometimes, this message is appreciated from a different perspective each time the story is read.

Myths and legends are largely ignored by modern schools and make a good starting point for people who are withdrawn from school and have negative associations with things that they did when they were there. Traditionally, the stories were told orally and it is therefore particularly appropriate to study them without much written work – the stories can be read aloud, you can draw or paint scenes from them, and you can write poems, retell the stories yourself, etc.

Fantasy and Science Fiction

Superficially, fantasy and science fiction appear to be similar to the ancient myths and legends, but closer reading shows that they are not.

The thing that makes the ancient stories interesting is that they *have* been passed down from one generation to the next for thousands of years. Modern stories almost certainly will not be.

Norse Myths

The mythology of the Norsemen who invaded Northern Europe from Scandinavia harked back to the ancient beliefs that had been common to barbarian tribes across Europe and Asia long before the advent of Greek civilisation.

They describe a heaven, Asgard, inhabited by gods and goddesses who rule over a world of giants, dwarfs, and men:

"Down in the shady gloom at the foot of the World Tree the Gods held their council, to decide how they might bring help to mankind, and what must be done in the long war against the Giants. Down there under the Ash, beside the Well, stood a fair hall where dwelt the Norns, the three weird sisters Urd, Verlandi, and Skuld, who knew more even than Odin himself. For Urd could see all that had chanced in the past, while Verlandi had the power of knowing what was being done in all the worlds at the present; but Skuld was the wisest of all, for she could see into the future – and that not even Odin himself could do.

Often in time to come the Norns appeared at the birth of a hero to spin his web of fate and give him gifts of good and evil that should determine his future life.

They could tell Odin of the course of the world, and from them he knew, as well as from his own wisdom, of Ragnarok, the Last Great Battle, which must come at the end of the world when the Gods and their Giant foes would fight out to the bitter end the great contest between Good and Evil."

Myths of the Norsemen, Roger Lancelyn Green, Puffin Books

Celtic Myths

Britain, Ireland and much of France were home to the Celtic peoples for many years before the coming of the Romans. Traces of their civilisation still exist in the form of stone circles, standing stones, ley lines, sacred groves and hill forts. Celtic languages and culture have managed to survive in spite of the wars and invasions that have ravaged Europe over the past two thousand years.

Celtic myths and legends have a quality of their own. They weave magical events into the lives of ordinary men and women, and are marked by their strong affinity with the world of Nature. Nevertheless, the hierarchy of gods and goddesses that occurs in many other mythologies is also present in Celtic tales.

Amongst the most enduring of Celtic legends are those that relate to the wise warrior-king, King Arthur, and his advisor, the wizard Merlin. In these stories, King Arthur is neither the strongest knight nor even the wisest counsellor, but he possesses a quality of kindness that makes him universally loved and respected and which enables him to bring peace to his feuding subjects.

Recommended Book:
The Mabinogion, translated by Gwyn Jones and Thomas Jones, Everyman

Greek Myths

Ancient Greece was the birthplace of Western civilisation: agriculture, city life, writing, philosophy, mathematics, and art, all trace their origins to Greek settlements around the Mediterranean. The Roman empire spread this culture throughout Europe, and with it a belief in the Greek gods.

It was a renewed interest in everything to do with ancient Greece that was one of the driving forces behind the European Renaissance in the late middle ages; and this in turn was the cause of events that have led to the Industrial Revolution, the colonisation of North America, the development of science and the current world situation.

For this reason Greek myths and legends have an enormous cultural significance: they provide the foundations upon which Western civilisation is built.

The Greek Gods

The Greek gods are not the all-powerful, omniscient 'God' of many religions, they were supernatural beings, each of whom had a distinct personality, and acted as intermediaries between mankind and the formless, incomprehensible energy which was believed to have created the universe. They are remarkably similar both to the Norse gods and to the gods of Hindu mythology.

Principal Greek gods (Roman equivalents in brackets):

- **Zeus** *(Jupiter)* Ruler of the gods
- **Poseidon** *(Neptune)* Brother of Zeus. Ruler of the oceans
- **Hades** *(Pluto)* Brother of Zeus and Poseidon. Ruler of the underworld
- **Hera** *(Juno)* Wife of Zeus
- **Apollo** The patron of music and poetry
- **Dionysus** *(Bacchus)* God of Nature and wine
- **Hermes** *(Mercury)* Messenger of the gods
- **Aphrodite** *(Venus)* Goddess of love
- **Demeter** *(Ceres)* Goddess of Nature
- **Artemis** *(Diana)* Goddess of the chase
- **Athena** *(Minerva)* Goddess of war and wisdom
- **Hephaestus** *(Vulcan)* Blacksmith to the gods
- **Eros** *(Cupid)* Son of Aphrodite and god of love
- **Aries** *(Mars)* God of war

Psyche, wife of Eros, the god of love.

Recommended Books:
(Try to find older translations of the Greek myths, they are usually superior to modern versions.)
The Metamorphoses, Ovid
Tales of the Greek Heroes, Roger Lancelyn Green, Puffin Books

The Origin of the World

Greek mythology provides well-reasoned explanations for every aspect of life, including the origin of the world:

"At first, the sea, the earth, and the heaven, which covers all things, were the only face of nature throughout the whole universe, which men have named Chaos; a rude and undigested mass, and nothing more than an inert weight, and the discordant atoms of things not harmonizing, heaped together in the same spot. No Sun as yet gave light to the world; nor did the Moon, by increasing, recover her horns anew. The Earth did not as yet hang in the surrounding air, balanced by its own weight, nor had Ocean stretched out her arms along the lengthened margin of the coasts. Wherever, too, was the land, there also was the sea and the air; and thus was the earth without firmness, the sea unnavigable, the air void of light; in no one of them did its present form exist. And one was ever obstructing the other; because in the same body the cold was striving with the hot, the moist with the dry, the soft with the hard, things having weight with those devoid of weight.

To this discord God and bounteous Nature put an end; for he separated the earth from the heavens, and the waters from the earth, and distinguished the clear heavens from the gross atmosphere. And after he had unravelled these elements, and released them from that confused heap, he combined them, thus disjoined, in harmonious unison, each in its proper place. The element of the vaulted heaven, fiery and without weight, shone forth, and selected a place for itself in the highest region; next after it, both in lightness and in place, was the air; the Earth was more weighty than these, and drew with it the more ponderous atoms, and was pressed together by its own gravity. The encircling waters sank to the lowermost place, and surrounded the solid globe."

The Metamorphoses of Ovid, Book 1

The Origin of Man

The new world was ruled over by a race of giants called the Titans, who were themselves ruled by Cronos (Time). Cronos believed that he would be overthrown by one of his own children, and, to prevent this from happening, he ate his babies at birth until one of them, Zeus, was spirited away by his wife. Zeus did indeed overthrow his father and released his brothers and sisters from their captivity within Cronos' body. They became the Immortals and ruled over earth from Mount Olympus.

One Titan, Prometheus, assisted the gods against Cronos and was entrusted by Zeus to create and educate human beings. Prometheus created people from clay and taught them the arts of agriculture, speech, building and weaving but also, against the instructions of Zeus, he taught them how to use fire so that they could work with metal. Zeus foresaw the havoc and destruction that people would wreak with this gift but Prometheus was unrepentant: he said that the time would come when the gods themselves would need the assistance of men.

The gods chained Prometheus to a rock where he remained until he was freed by Heracles. According to Greek mythology, people wear a ring on their finger in fulfilment of a pledge to Prometheus that the suffering he endured on their behalf would never be forgotten by a grateful human race.

Heracles

Heracles was the greatest of the Greek heroes; in the course of his life he performed twelve seemingly-impossible tasks and is credited with founding many of the oldest states and institutions of the ancient world. Before any of this came about, however, he had to choose the path he wished to follow:

"As Heracles sat alone on the hillside one day, wondering if he was fated to be a cow-herd all his life, or whether it would not be better to become a wild robber of the mountains, he saw two lovely maidens coming towards him. One of them was dressed in simple white, and had modest, down-cast eyes and a calm, gentle face from which seemed to shine both goodness and wisdom; but the other wore bright colours, and came striding along glancing boldly about her – now admiring herself, and now looking to others for admiration. She was decked with rich jewels, and her face was artfully touched with paint and with powder.

As they drew near to Heracles, the second, as if anxious to forestall her companion, pushed eagerly ahead and spoke to him:

'Dear Heracles,' she said, 'I see that you have reached the age when you must choose what kind of life yours is to be. So I have come to urge you to take me as your friend and let me guide you on your way. I promise that if you do I will lead you by the easiest and most delightful paths. You shall taste every pleasure, and no troubles or toils shall come near you. Your life shall be passed in the pursuit and enjoyment of pleasant things, with no labour of body or mind, except to please yourself without any thought for the cares of others.'

She paused, and Heracles asked: 'Lady, tell me your name.'

Then she answered softly: 'Heracles, those who love me call me Happiness, but my enemies, it is true, have another name which I do not care to mention.'

Meanwhile the modest maiden had come up, and now she spoke: 'I too, noble Heracles, am come to offer you a way of life. Follow me, and you will do great deeds and leave a name which will never be forgotten. But you cannot win what is glorious and excellent in the world without care and labour: the gods give no real good, no true happiness to men on earth on any other terms. As for my companion, who is called Vice and Folly and other such names, do not be misled by her: there is no pleasure and no happiness like those which you earn by strife and labour and with the sweat of your brow.'

'Do not believe this foolish girl, who is called Virtue!' interrupted Vice hastily. 'My way to happiness is short and pleasant; hers is hard, and long, and the end is doubtful.'

'Come, Heracles,' said Virtue quietly, 'choose which of us you will follow. Her path leads through easy, worthless pleasures that grow stale and horrible and yet are craved after more and more. But follow me through toil and suffering to the great heritage which Zeus has planned for you.'

'Lady!' cried Heracles, 'I choose your path!' "

Tales of the Greek Heroes, Roger Lancelyn Green, Puffin Classics

Theseus of Athens

Theseus

The ancient Athenians regarded Theseus as the founder of their state. He was believed to be Heracles' cousin and the son of Ægeus, a local king. At that time, the people of Athens were obliged to pay a tribute of seven young men and seven young women to Minos, the powerful king of Minoa, and to his father's grief Theseus volunteered to take the place of one of the hostages. His ship set out for the Minoan kingdom of Crete, with black sails to mark the tragic nature of its voyage, and on his arrival in Minoa, Theseus discovered that he was to be released into a labyrinth and devoured by the Minotaur – a monstrous creature, half man, half bull.

Fortunately, he won the love of Ariadne, the King's daughter, who told him how to overcome the Minotaur, and gave him a silken skein to unwind as he wandered through the labyrinth, so that he could find his way out. Their plan was successful, and they escaped to the Athenian boats with Theseus' fellow hostages.

In the elation of the homecoming, the ship's captain forgot to change the sails to white and Ægeus, who saw the black sails on the horizon, presumed that the hostages had been killed and hurled himself off the cliff top into the sea below, which has ever after been called the Ægean, in his memory.

Theseus became king and united the various communities of the region into the state of Athens. He then voluntarily relinquished power in favour of democratic institutions. This established Athens as a model for innovative and idealistic forms of government, a reputation that it has retained to this day.

"In the days of old the gods had the whole earth distributed among them. There was no quarrelling; for you cannot rightly suppose that the gods did not know what was proper for each of them to have, or, knowing this, that they would seek to procure for themselves by contention that which more properly belonged to others. They all of them obtained what they wanted, and peopled their own districts; and when they had peopled them they tended us, their nurselings and possessions, as shepherds tend their flocks, excepting only that they did not use blows or bodily force, as shepherds do, but governed us like pilots from the stern of the vessel, holding our souls by the rudder of persuasion according to their own pleasure; - thus did they guide all mortal creatures. Now Hephaestus and Athene, who were brother and sister, having a common nature, and united also in the love of philosophy and art, both obtained as their common portion this land, which was naturally adapted for wisdom and virtue; and there they implanted brave children of the soil, and put into their minds the order of government…"

Critias, Plato: describing Athens in the time before the great flood that destroyed Atlantis

The Iliad

The Iliad describes the siege of ancient Troy and the death of Hector. For the Greeks and Romans it marked the dividing line between mythology and their actual history.

It begins with Achilleus refusing to play his part in the war because of the injustice he has suffered at the hands of Agamemnon, the Greek leader. Without their principal hero, the Greeks are hard-pressed and forced back into their own camp. In this extremity, Achilleus allows his charioteer, Patroklos, to lead out his troops to repulse the Trojans. Patroklos, carried away by the exhilaration of success, advances right up to the walls of Troy, where he suffers a reversal of fortune and is killed. In his grief and remorse Achilleus fights and kills Hector, the Trojan hero.

Woven into this tragic theme are events that shaped the future history of Europe:

- Paris, a Phœnician prince from Troy, becomes embroiled in an argument between Aphrodite and Hera as to which of them is more beautiful. He takes the side of Aphrodite who then assists him in his pursuit of Helen, the young wife of the aged King Menelaus.

- Paris carries Helen off to Troy.

- King Menelaus persuades the disparate Greek cities to unite their forces and to launch a campaign against Troy.

- Troy is destroyed, thereby beginning the ascendancy of Greek culture in the Mediterranean.

- One of the Trojan heroes, Aeneas, escapes and settles in central Italy. His descendants found the city of Rome, which in its own turn overthrows Greek power, thus completing a cycle in history.

Hector bids farewell to his wife, Andromache.

Homer: Legend identifies Homer as a blind poet who lived about nine hundred years before the birth of Christ. His epic poems, The Iliad and The Odyssey, are regarded as the most well-crafted and beautiful works of literature ever produced by a Western culture. Many people find it hard to accept that works of such perfection could have been created by a single person living so long ago. Anyone who comes to love these works, however, cannot help but be filled by admiration and respect for their author - no matter how remote a historical figure he has now become.

The Odyssey

The Odyssey describes the homecoming of Odysseus from the war against Troy.

> "Goddess of song,
> teach me the story of a hero."
> *First line of The Odyssey*

Odysseus is the cleverest of the Greek kings, and it is he who devises the plan to build a wooden horse in which he and the other Greek heroes hide after the deaths of Hector and Achilleus. The Trojans are deceived into believing that the Greek fleet is sailing for home and they drag the wooden horse into their city. The Greek fleet returns in the dead of night, Odysseus leaves his hiding place, opens the gates of the city and Troy is sacked.

However, he has the misfortune to anger Poseidon, god of the sea, and as a result is beset by constant storms as he tries to make his way home.

Odysseus has many adventures, in the course of which he loses all his men, all his ships and all his plunder. He frequently forgets why he is travelling and where he is going but, ten years after setting out from Troy, he arrives back in his kingdom of Ithaca.

With the help of the goddess Athena he is reunited with his faithful wife, Penelope, and destroys the suitors who have been demanding that she choose a new husband from amongst them.

Heinrich Schliemann (1822 – 1890)

Heinrich Schliemann was born in Germany and developed a passion for Homer's poetry in his boyhood. Contrary to the established belief, maintained by scholars for a thousand years, that the Iliad and the Odyssey were works of fiction, he was convinced that they described actual historical events.

He left school at the age of 14 and started work apprenticed to a grocer, but he soon started to travel and conduct business in his own right. He was working in California when it joined the Union in 1850 and Heinrich became an American citizen. By the age of forty-one he had amassed a sufficient fortune to allow him to retire and fulfil his youthful ambition.

He organised an archaeological expedition to Turkey and excavated the hill of Hissarlik which his study of Homer's texts told him to be the most likely site of ancient Troy. To the consternation of classical scholars and university professors everywhere, he did indeed discover the remains of an ancient city – now accepted to be ancient Troy. He then went on to locate Odysseus' kingdom of Ithaca and excavated buildings old enough to have been his palace. The world was forced to admit that, in all probability, the events described in Homer's epic poems actually did take place.

Recommended Books:
The Iliad, Homer
The Odyssey, Homer

Ancient India

Even though India has been plagued by countless wars and foreign invasions, it has never been subject to a total collapse of civilisation. Consequently, it has preserved a cultural tradition that stretches back for thousands and thousands of years. Even today there is no clear distinction made between history and religion, and the greatest heroes and heroines of Indian history are closely related to the gods and goddesses of the most ancient scriptures.

The Ramayana

Ram, prince of the ancient city of Ayodaya, is banished to the jungle for ten years due to the intrigues of his stepmother. While in the jungle his beautiful wife, Sita, is kidnapped by the tyrannical king of Lanka, Ravan.

Ram gathers together an army of monkeys and bears who invade Lanka in an effort to release Sita from captivity, but they prove ineffectual against the might of the demon king. Ram then takes pity upon his followers, destroys the king of Lanka, frees Sita from captivity, and ushers in a golden age of peace and happiness.

Ram and Sita

In order to win Sita's hand in marriage, Ram must bend Shiva's enormous bow:

"He took up the bow with most superlative ease; as he grasped it in his hand, it gleamed like a flash of lightning; and again as he bent it, it seemed like the vault of heaven. Though all stood watching, before any one could see him grasp it, he had lifted it from the ground and raised it aloft and drawn it tight, and in a moment broken it in halves; the awful crash resounded through the worlds.

So awful a crash re-echoed through the worlds that the horses of the Sun left their course and strayed, the elephants of the four quarters groaned, earth shook, the great serpent, the boar, and the tortoise tottered. Gods and sages put their hands to their ears and began anxiously to consider the cause; but when they learnt that Ram had broken the bow, they uttered shouts of victory."

The Ramayana

The Mahabharata

The Mahabharata is an epic tale describing wars and intrigues that took place at an undetermined period in history. It incorporates innumerable tales harking back to even earlier times, but a web is slowly woven which draws all the characters into a civil war that pits friends and brothers in a mortal struggle against each other.

Throughout the story, one person stands out from all the rest: Krishna, a prince who is reputed to be an incarnation of the God Vishnu. Krishna refuses to take part in the battle himself but agrees to drive the chariot of his beloved friend, Prince Arjuna.

Arjuna is a renowned warrior but when he sees the two opposing armies drawn up against each other, both containing people whom he loves and admires, he loses the will to fight. The resulting discourse between Arjuna and Krishna comprises the Bhagavad Gita.

" 'O day of darkness! What evil spirit moved our minds when for the sake of an earthly kingdom we came to this field of battle ready to kill our own people?
Better for me indeed if the sons of Dhrita-rashtra, with arms in hand, found me unarmed, unresisting, and killed me in the struggle of war.'

Thus spoke Arjuna in the field of battle, and letting fall his bow and arrows he sank down in his chariot, his soul overcome by despair and grief.
Then arose the Spirit of Krishna and spoke to Arjuna, his friend, who with eyes filled with tears, thus had sunk into despair and grief.

'Thy tears are for those beyond tears; and are thy words words of wisdom? The wise grieve not for those who live; and they grieve not for those who die - for life and death shall pass away.
Because we all have been for all time: I, and thou, and those kings of men. And we all shall be for all time, we all for ever and ever.
From the world of the senses, Arjuna, comes heat and comes cold, and pleasure and pain. They come and they go: they are transient. Arise above them, strong soul.
The unreal never is: the Real never is not. This truth indeed has been seen by those who can see the true.
Weapons cannot hurt the Spirit and fire can never burn him. Untouched is he by drenching waters, untouched is he by parching winds.
Beyond the power of sword and fire, beyond the power of waters and winds, the Spirit is everlasting, omnipresent, never-changing, never-moving, ever One.' "

The Bhagavad Gita (from chapters 1 and 2)

Recommended Books:
The Bhagavad Gita, translated by Juan Mascaró, Penguin Classics
The Mahabharata, translated by Kisari Mohan Ganguli, Munshiram Manoharlal Publishers Ltd

Ancient China

China had a civilisation that succeeded in providing hundreds of millions of people with a stable government for thousands of years. This civilisation was already in decline when Europeans first visited China, and it is difficult for us today to get a clear understanding of what life was like when Chinese civilisation was at its peak, thousands of years ago.

Pan Ku

According to Chinese mythology, the world was created by Pan Ku when he separated heaven and earth by hatching from the egg within which he was contained. After 18,000 years he died and the various parts of his body became the sun, the moon, the stars, the wind, the mountains, the seas and all the living creatures. One version of the origin of human beings is that they were formed from the parasites that lived on the body of Pan.

Pan was followed by three Supreme Sovereigns; the first was responsible for the art of divination, the second invented agriculture and the third saved the world from destruction.

The Model Rulers

The Supreme Sovereigns were succeeded by five Model Rulers or sages: Huangdi, Zhuan Xiu, Ku, Yao and Shun. The first of these, Huangdi, is known as the Yellow Emperor and he is credited with inventing the bow and arrow, boats, carts, ceramics, house building, medicine, the calendar and writing. His wife started the cultivation and weaving of silk.

The Yellow Emperor is also believed to have been the first Daoist master.

> "When a sage king rules, his influence is felt everywhere, but he does not seem to be doing anything."
> *Chuang Tsu*

Huangdi - the Yellow Emperor

The Early Emperors

Yu - 'founder' of the Xia dynasty

The last of the model rulers, Shun, was concerned about the hardships caused to the people by flooding. He appointed an official called Yu, to tackle the problem.

Yu travelled tirelessly, dredging the channels that became the rivers of north China. He succeeded Shun as the ruler of the empire but when he died the people rejected his choice of successor and installed his son on the throne – thereby starting the first Chinese dynasty, the Xia.

The Xia dynasty was followed by the Shang and then the Zhou. The Zhou dynasty was overthrown by Qin Shihuangdi in 221 BC.

Qin Shihuangdi burned almost every book and text that had survived from previous times, with the result that his reign now marks the beginning of recorded Chinese history.

> "How sublime the way Shun and Yu undertook the empire, and yet as if it were nothing to them!"
>
> *Confucius, The Analects*

Confucius

Confucius lived around 500 BC. He followed in the Daoist tradition that was already fundamental to Chinese life, and which advocated reverence of the family, proper management of agricultural resources, and respect for justice, and considered the pursuit of self-knowledge to be the chief purpose of human life.

Confucius drew upon this source of wisdom to codify a way of life that was to make China the envy of the world for thousands of years to come: the country has never been free from difficulties, but few places on earth have enjoyed comparable wealth, stability, and general well-being as that experienced by China for the two thousand years after the death of Confucius.

Recommended Books:
The Analects, Confucius, Dover Thrift Editions, translated William Edward Soothill
Chuang Tsu

Classical Historians

Ancient history provides the logical starting point for historical studies, not only because many aspects of the modern world owe their origins to events that took place between two thousand and two and a half thousand years ago, but also because it is easier for us to take an objective view of ancient history than it is of modern history – the issues involved are less likely to touch upon those religious, national or ethnic sensitivities which have a tendency to cloud our judgement.

The classical world of ancient Rome and ancient Greece is distinguished by having produced historians whose thoughtful and perceptive accounts of people and events provide an ideal framework upon which to build an understanding of history.

Herodotus

The theme of Herodotus' Histories is the war that took place between the Greeks and the Persians during the fifth century B.C. He not only describes the war itself but also manages to include an account of his travels around the ancient world and a description of its peoples.

Herodotus was nicknamed the 'father of history' by the Roman writer and statesman, Cicero, but his style is very different from that of modern historians. His Histories do not suffer from being dry, analytical, or pretentious: instead they continue the age-old tradition of storytelling, and use an historical account to entertain, inform and inspire the reader.

> "These are the researches of Herodotus of Halicarnassus, which he publishes, in the hope of thereby preserving from decay the remembrance of what men have done, and of preventing the great and wonderful actions of the Greeks and the Barbarians from losing their due meed of glory; and withal to put on record what were their grounds of feud."
>
> *Opening paragraph of The First Book, entitled Clio, Herodotus*

Arrian

Arrian was one of the most interesting people of his time: as well as being the first non-Italian to govern a Roman province, he was a successful general, a respected administrator, and author of "The Campaigns of Alexander the Great".

In addition to all this he was a student of the renowned philosopher, Epictetus and the notes that he made of Epictetus' sayings form the celebrated and immensely influential "Discourses".

> "I did not write these discourses of Epictetus as a literary composition...nor did I myself release them to the public, for, as I say, it was not my intention to write a book. Rather, I tried to note down whatever I heard him say, so far as possible in his own words, to preserve reminders for myself in future days of his cast of mind, and frankness of speech."
>
> *Arrian's Preface to the Discourses*

Titus Livy

Titus Livy is the most famous of the Roman historians. He lived at the time of the early Emperors, but his histories cover the time from the founding of Rome onwards.

He was regarded as being incorruptible and resisted the temptation to curry political favour by distorting history.

Much of his later work has been lost, but his accounts of the founding of Rome, the early Roman Republic and the war against Carthage have shaped people's views of these events for the past two millennia.

"Next day...the two most famous generals and the two mightiest armies of the two wealthiest nations in the world advanced to battle, doomed either to crown or to destroy the many triumphs each had won in the past. In all hearts were mixed feelings, confidence alternating with fear. As men surveyed their own and their enemy's ranks, weighing the strength of each merely by what their eyes could tell them, thoughts of joy and of foreboding jostled for preeminence in their minds."

Livy's account of the Battle of Zama, in which Hannibal and Scipio faced each other at the end of the second war with Carthage.

Plutarch

Plutarch

Plutarch lived during the first century AD but, unlike his contemporary, Arrian, he never became involved in the grand affairs of state. He preferred instead to pass most of his life in his home town in central Greece.

His fame rests on the biographical accounts that he wrote of the principal characters in Greek and Roman history, and the comparisons that he then drew between them.

These biographies are collectively known as 'Plutarch's Lives' and include such diverse figures as Julius Caesar, Romulus, and Alexander the Great. Until recently they formed an indispensable part of every educational programme.

Recommended Books:
The Histories, Herodotus, translated by George Rawlinson, Everyman's Library
The Campaigns of Alexander, Arrian, translated by Aubrey de Sélincourt, Penguin Classics
The Early History of Rome, Livy, translated by Aubrey de Sélincourt, Penguin Classics
Rome and the Mediterranean, Livy, translated by Henry Bettleston, Penguin Classics
Rome and Italy, Livy, translated by Betty Radice, Penguin Classics
The War with Hannibal, Livy, translated by Aubrey de Sélincourt, Penguin Classics
Plutarch's Lives, Volume 1 & 2, translated by John Dryden, The Modern Library Classics
The Discourses of Epictetus, Arrian, translation revised by Robin Hard, Everyman

Ancient Greece

Greek civilisation is considered to have been at its peak from 800–300 BC. It was based upon the cultivation of wheat, grapes and olives, the use of domesticated animals, the development of cities, the use of bronze, and ship building.

Compared with their neighbours in Persia, Egypt, and Mesopotamia, the ancient Greeks were a new and emerging civilisation. It is not their antiquity that makes them interesting to the modern historian but the fact that it is *their* culture which gave birth to the Western civilisation that dominates the world today.

The Greeks rarely united to form one organised government but their ideas and culture dominated the whole Mediterranean world of their time, including that of ancient Rome: even though the Romans eventually conquered every corner of the Greek world, Rome was dependent upon Greek scholars for the organisation of its empire and the education of its citizens.

In their respective fields, the leading figures of ancient Greece gained reputations that have rarely been equalled by subsequent generations of scholars, philosophers, artists, playwrights, mathematicians, scientists, and military leaders.

Thus as Roman influence grew, it was Greek culture that was spread far and wide: from Britain in the West to the shores of the Black Sea in the East and from Germany in the North to Africa in the South.

As Roman military power eventually waned, the cultural heritage from ancient Greece survived. It provided the inspiration for the European Renaissance and it provides the basis for mathematical thought, for Western philosophy, for Western drama, for Western art, and for Western science.

Ancient Greece saw the emergence of Western Europe as a new and distinct civilisation, quite different from anything that had existed in the East for thousands of years. Why and how this happened is a subject of inexhaustible fascination.

> "Lead me, Zeus, and thou, O Destiny,
> To wheresoever your decrees have
> ordained."
>
> *Cleanthes' Hymn to Zeus*

Hades, god of the Underworld.

Pythagoras

Pythagoras is believed to have lived around 800 BC, although this date was disputed even by ancient historians and should not be taken too seriously.

He is believed to have travelled widely in his youth, with his journeys taking him to Egypt and Mesopotamia. In Mesopotamia he was suspected of trying to steal ancient mystical secrets and was imprisoned.

Eventually, however, the priests recognised him to be an exceptionally able student and instead of withholding information from him, undertook to train and educate him – even though in their eyes he was from an inferior, barbarian tribe, more suited for slavery than learning.

After many years, Pythagoras returned to the Mediterranean and settled in Sicily. Legend has it that he was desperate to pass on what he had learnt to his fellow countrymen but could find no one who was willing to learn. Eventually a poor goat-herd became his student – on condition that Pythagoras would pay him the same wages as he would have earned if he had been working.

From this unpromising beginning, Pythagoras's reputation slowly grew until he could number his students in hundreds or perhaps thousands. His work attracted criticism from an early stage: he admitted women to his meetings, he was vegetarian, he was accused of being secretive and his followers seemed to enjoy a disproportionate degree of success and wealth.

Pythagoras was believed to have been killed when an angry mob of citizens attacked the home of one of his most powerful followers, but some people claimed that he escaped from the resulting fire and lived on for many more years – continuing to teach but hidden from the glare of unwelcome publicity by the discretion of his students.

Today the name of Pythagoras is most closely associated with mathematics – 'Pythagoras's Theorem' describes the relationship between the sides of a right-angled triangle *(pages 322 and 326)* – but in classical times he was widely regarded as one of the founding geniuses of Greek civilisation.

"There was a man, a Samian by birth; but he had fled from both Samos and its rulers, and, through hatred of tyranny, he was a voluntary exile. He too, mentally, held converse with the Gods, although far distant in the region of the heavens; and what nature refused to human vision, he viewed with the eyes of his mind. And when he had examined all things with his mind, and with watchful study, he gave them to be learned by the public; and he sought the crowds of people as they sat in silence, and wondered at the revealed origin of the vast universe, and the cause of things, and what nature meant, and what was God; whence came the snow, what was the cause of lightning; whether it was Jupiter, or whether the winds that thundered when the cloud was rent asunder; what it was that shook the earth; by what laws the stars took their course; and whatever besides lay concealed from mortals."

Ovid's recounting of the story of Pythagoras, The Metamorphoses, Book XV

The Greek Cities

Ancient Greece was made up of independent city states, each of which had its own institutions and mode of government. The most powerful of these two states were Sparta and Athens. Athens' military strength lay in its navy and Sparta's in its army. This balance of power helped to maintain an uneasy peace throughout the Greek world up until the time of the Persian invasion.

Sparta

The term 'Spartan' has come to suggest an unnecessarily harsh regime but the city of Sparta was respected throughout the ancient world for the stability of its administration and for the system of government created by its semi-mythological statesman, Lycurgus.

Lycurgus is reputed to have been the first major figure to popularise the works of Homer. After visiting Crete, Egypt, and the mainland of Asia, where he was able to see the best and worst of human societies, he set about reforming his home state.

He established a balance of power between two kings and a senate of twenty-eight leading citizens, with every important decision having to be ratified by a gathering of the people; he redistributed the land so that everyone had an equal amount, withdrew gold and redistributed wealth; his final reform was to make everyone eat in communal surroundings so that it was not possible for some people to eat better than others.

This last ordinance in particular exasperated the wealthier men. They collected in a body against Lycurgus, and from ill words came to throwing stones, so that at length he was forced to run out of the market-place, and make to sanctuary to save his life; by good-hap he outran all, excepting one Alcander, a young man otherwise not ill accomplished, but hasty and violent, who came up so close to him, that when he turned to see who was so near him, he struck him upon the face with his stick, and put out one of his eyes. Lycurgus, so far from being daunted and discouraged by this accident, stopped short and showed his disfigured face and eye beat out to his countrymen; they, dismayed and ashamed at the sight, delivered Alcander into his hands to be punished, and escorted him home, with expressions of great concern for his ill-usage. Lycurgus, having thanked them for their care of his person, dismissed them all, excepting only Alcander; and, taking him with him into his house, neither did nor said anything severely to him, but, dismissing those whose place it was, bade Alcander to wait upon him at table. The young man, who was of an ingenuous temper, without murmuring did as he was commanded; and being thus admitted to live with Lycurgus, he had an opportunity to observe in him, besides his gentleness and calmness of temper, an extraordinary sobriety and an indefatigable industry, and so, from an enemy, became one of his most zealous admirers, and told his friends and relations that Lycurgus was not that morose and ill-natured man they had formerly taken him for, but the one mild and gentle character of the world. And thus did Lycurgus, for chastisement of his fault, make of a wild and passionate young man one of the discreetest citizens of Sparta.
Plutarch's Lives Vol 1: Lycurgus, translated by John Dryden, The Modern Library Classics

Conflict Between Greece and Persia

In 500 BC Persia had an empire of enormous wealth and power. At that time, the emerging Greek cities were regarded as troublesome tributary states at the edge of the empire, more closely related to the barbarian world than to the civilised nations.

There was, however, something distinctly different about the Greeks: they had a greater love for personal liberty and individual freedom than was evident anywhere else in the ancient world at that time. (This was not an idealistic pursuit of freedom for mankind in general – they were happy to have slaves and to subjugate foreign nations – but individual Greek citizens were not in the habit of serving kings and rulers and were prepared to defend their liberty with their lives.)

This brought the Greek states into conflict with the Persian king, Darius I, who expected total obedience from everyone under his sway.

Darius I

The resulting wars are generally regarded as a turning point in world history. Persian kings sent armies of ever-increasing size to annihilate the Greek cities but these armies were routed by much smaller Greek forces who were fighting to preserve their homes and their freedom. As a result of these wars, Persia, and correspondingly Eastern culture in general, lost its influence over the Mediterranean; Greek culture reached its zenith over the ensuing century.

The city of Athens claimed credit for the victory and, after the defeat of Persia, succeeded in establishing an empire which allowed it to dominate the rest of the Greek world. This aroused jealousy amongst other prominent Greek cities; Sparta led an alliance that defeated Athens after a prolonged war and it was not long after this that the whole of Greece fell under the control of Philip of Macedon, father of Alexander the Great.

Recommended Books:
The Histories, Herodotus
Plutarch's Lives: Themistocles, Lysander, Pericles, Alcibiades, Aristides, Nicias,
   Timoleon, Pelopidas, Cimon, Agesilaus, Plutarch
Fifteen Decisive Battles of the World: Chapter 1 The Battle of Marathon,
   Chapter 2 Defeat of the Athenians at Syracuse, Sir Edward Creasy
History of the Peloponnesian War, Thucydides

Socrates

The years following the defeat of Persia are regarded as the golden age of Greek culture and Socrates is the most renowned of all the people who lived at that time. This is remarkable in itself because he was not a great general, neither was he a leading politician, artist, or writer. He described himself as being an old soldier and he spent his time in discussing questions of philosophy in the Athenian market place.

The leading people of the time became jealous of the influence that he held over their sons and hatched a plot to have him removed from the city. They brought Socrates to trial under the accusation that he was corrupting the young by not preaching a proper reverence for the ancient gods.

In his defence, Socrates launched a blistering attack on the hypocrisy of his accusers, who, in their confusion, sentenced him to death by poison.

Socrates' prison cell was poorly guarded and the people of Athens probably expected him to preserve his life by fleeing the city – thereby saving them from the disgrace of killing so famous a citizen, or the embarrassment of having him living amongst them after he had exposed their faults.

"Many are the marvels which I might narrate in praise of Socrates; most of his ways might perhaps be paralleled in another man, but his absolute unlikeness to any human being that is or ever has been is perfectly astonishing."
The Symposium, Plato

His pupil, Plato, describes how the old philosopher chooses an honourable death in favour of a dishonourable life and voluntarily drinks the poison:

"Whatever the popular view is, and whether the alternative is pleasanter than the present one or even harder to bear, the fact remains that to do wrong is in every sense bad and dishonourable for the person who does it."
Socrates (Crito 49, Plato)

Plato: We owe most of our knowledge of Socrates to Plato. In later life Plato himself became a leading figure in Athenian life (amongst other things, he founded the famous Academy in Athens) but most of his literary work was dedicated to preserving the memory of Socrates. Amongst his best-known works are **Euthyphro, The Apology, Crito,** and **Phaedo,** which describe the circumstances surrounding Socrates' trial and death, and **The Republic** which outlines some of Socrates' ideas on education and government.

Alexander the Great

Alexander is one of those rare characters in history – an exceptional child of an exceptional parent. His father, Philip of Macedon, had subjugated the disparate Greek states and united them under his personal rule, but was assassinated when Alexander was only twenty years old.

The young Alexander was able to marshal the resources of his father's kingdom to launch the most audacious campaign of conquest that the world has seen. Two years after the death of his father he led a small Macedonian force against the Greeks' traditional enemy, the Persians, and, in the course of three years and three decisive battles, annihilated the military might of the vast Persian empire, and brought about the death of their ruler, King Darius III. Three further years saw Alexander established as the supreme ruler of lands that included Egypt, the Middle East, Persia, and Central Asia, in addition to his native Greece.

Western India had once been part of the Persian empire, and under the pretext of wanting to preserve the integrity of his conquests, Alexander invaded the Punjab. It is unclear how far he intended to extend his conquests because, after another victorious campaign, his soldiers mutinied and demanded to be taken home. The army returned to the Middle East via the Persian Gulf.

Alexander contracted a fever and died a year later in the city of Babylon at the age of thirty-three. In just under ten years his armies had conquered almost the whole of the known world.

Alexander's tomb is believed to have been inscribed with this famous epitaph:
"A tomb now suffices for him for whom the whole world was not enough."

Alexander the Great

Recommended Books:
The Campaigns of Alexander, Arrian, translated by Aubrey de Sélincourt, Penguin Classics
Plutarch's Lives: Alexander, Plutarch

Ancient Rome

Historians in ancient Rome traced their origins back to Aeneas, the son of Aphrodite who survived the destruction of his native Troy. After years of travelling, he settled amongst the tribes of central Italy, where destiny decreed that his descendants were to found a city that would avenge the wrongs that his people had suffered at the hands of the Greeks.

The city itself was said to have been founded by Romulus at the spot where he and his twin brother, Remus, were discovered being suckled by a she-wolf. Romulus and Remus were the illegitimate sons of the King's niece. The King had ordered them to be killed because he feared that, if they lived, they might seek to depose him from his throne, but instead of killing the baby boys, the King's servant set them adrift on the River Tiber. They were washed ashore and were discovered by a shepherd who took them home and brought them up as his own sons.

"In their very infancy, the size and beauty of their bodies intimated their natural superiority; and when they grew up, they both proved brave and manly, attempting all enterprises that seemed hazardous, and showing in them a courage altogether undaunted. But Romulus seemed rather to act by counsel, and to show the sagacity of a statesman, and in all his dealings with their neighbours, whether relating to feeding the flocks or to hunting, gave the idea of being born rather to rule than to obey. To their comrades and inferiors they were therefore dear; but the king's servants, his bailiffs and overseers, as being in nothing better than themselves, they despised and slighted, nor were the least concerned at their commands and menaces. They used honest pastimes and liberal studies, not esteeming sloth and idleness honest and liberal, but rather such exercises as hunting and running, repelling robbers, taking of thieves, and delivering the wronged and oppressed from injury. For doing such things they became famous."

Plutarch: Life of Romulus – describing the early life of Romulus and Remus,
before they suspected their royal parentage

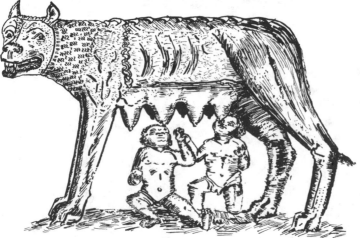

Romulus and Remus were inseparable as children, but they quarrelled over who should rule the new city that they planned to found after deposing their uncle, the King. Fighting broke out, Remus was killed in the confusion and the soothsayers of the time claimed that these events presaged a glorious but bloody future for the new settlement.

King Numa

King Numa

Romulus' reign lasted for thirty-seven years, and was marked by constant strife and warfare. The city that he founded was bitterly divided and these divisions were exacerbated by the mysterious nature of his death. He is said to have disappeared when a cloud enveloped his throne while he was reviewing his troops. One group of senators claimed that Romulus had been carried directly to heaven, by his father, the god Mars, but many ordinary people believed that he had been brutally murdered by jealous rivals to the throne.

Whatever the truth, it was clear that Romulus had died without naming a successor, and the people of Rome eventually decided to ask Numa Pompilius, a learned man from a neighbouring town, to become their next king.

Numa was as different from Romulus as one man could be from another. Romulus had populated his city by opening its doors to every vagabond, criminal, exile and fortune-seeker in the area, and he had found wives for his men by kidnapping the daughters of his neighbours. Numa, on the other hand, was committed to peace and the pursuit of truth. He taught the Romans to lead simple lives, to be true to their word, to value honesty and integrity, and to revere the gods.

He ruled Rome for forty-three years of uninterrupted peace. After his death, the city returned to its previous habit of warfare and conquest, but the values of honour and simplicity, that he had instilled in his subjects, remained the defining characteristics of ancient Rome for centuries to come, and were universally acknowledged to be the qualities that underpinned her greatness, and allowed her to build an empire that established Europe as a centre of world civilisation.

"Men of all classes took Numa as their unique example and modelled themselves upon him, until the effect of this change of heart was felt even beyond the borders of Roman territory. Once Rome's neighbours had considered her not so much as a city as an armed camp in their midst threatening the general peace; now they came to revere her so profoundly as a community dedicated wholly to worship, that the mere thought of offering her violence seemed to them like sacrilege."

Livy 1.21

Recommended Books:
Plutarch's Lives: Romulus, Numa Pompilius, Plutarch

The Roman Republic

Rome had seven kings, starting with Romulus and finishing with Tarquin II, a ruthless tyrant who fell from power after his son raped Lucretia, the beautiful young wife of one of his trusted aides. The people and senate of Rome revolted against the King, exiled him from the city, and inaugurated a Republic which lasted almost five hundred years. Over that time Rome grew from being a relatively insignificant settlement at the edge of the civilised world into the capital of a vast empire.

Each year, two consuls were elected by the senate. While in office the consuls enjoyed almost absolute power – but voluntarily relinquished that power at the end of the year. Neighbouring kings saw this as a threat to themselves and were eager to extinguish this experiment in Republican government. The Romans became involved in a war that was to last for several hundred years, and would only end when the whole of Italy had fallen under their control. Roman armies, comprised of free citizens led by generals selected on the basis of their proven abilities, were nearly always victorious against armies composed of subject peoples and mercenaries; Rome steadily grew in power and strength, and warfare became an accepted way of life for its citizens.

Rome's success was not, however, due simply to its military prowess. The Roman senate established an unparalleled reputation for dealing fairly with both friends and enemies, and won the respect even of those people who found themselves under Roman control.

Cato the Younger, renowned for his fearless defence of the Republic

"I hope my passion for Rome's past has not impaired my judgement; for I honestly believe that no country has ever been greater or purer than ours or richer in good citizens and noble deeds; none has been free for so many generations from the vices of avarice and luxury; nowhere have thrift and plain living been for so long held in such esteem."

Livy 1.1

Recommended Books:
Plutarch's Lives: Marcus Cato, Caius Marius, Sulla, Pompey, Crassus, Caesar, Cato the Younger, Cicero, Marcus Brutus, Antony, Plutarch
Books I-X and XXI-XLV of The History of Rome from its Foundation, Livy,
Julius Caesar, Shakespeare

War With Carthage

The growth of Roman power in Italy coincided with the rise to prominence of a city on the North coast of Africa. The name of this city was Carthage, and it became established as the centre of trade in the Western Mediterranean. It was inevitable that, as the two cities sought to extend their region of influence into Sicily, Spain and Southern France, they would come into conflict with each other. Initially, it was Carthage that had the upper hand: it had a long-standing network of alliances with cities in Africa, Europe and the Middle East, a much more powerful navy than Rome, and access to almost unlimited amounts of money with which to hire mercenary troops that could confront the Roman legions on land.

Despite occasional setbacks, however – most noticeably against the Carthaginian general, Hannibal – Roman forces always proved superior to the Carthaginian mercenaries. Over the course of a hundred years and three wars, Carthage was first defeated and then utterly crushed; the city was reduced to rubble and its citizens sold into slavery.

The End of the Republic

Once Carthage had been destroyed, Rome became the undisputed superpower of its time, exercising control over the whole Mediterranean region and most of Europe. No individual state or city was strong enough to oppose Rome on its own, and people were fearful of creating alliances that might incur Roman displeasure.

The Republican institutions that had helped Rome to attain this supremacy could not survive the changes brought about by the wealth, power, and military glory that were now available to the city. The Senate gradually lost control of public affairs and the real power was found to be in the hands of generals who commanded armies that could destroy cities, and devastate countries, at will. These generals fell prey to the lust for glory, and the fear of rivals that has often characterised military rulers, and the newly-established Roman empire was ravaged by Roman armies, under the command of feuding Roman generals, fighting bitter civil wars.

Julius Caesar emerged as the supreme leader of these armies and public opinion supposed that he would make himself king. For this reason he was assassinated by a group of high-born conspirators, but far from restoring the Republic, his death marked the end of the old form of government and the beginning of rule by Emperors.

The Roman legions represented absolute military power.

The Roman Emperors

The story of the Roman emperors is one that both fascinates and appals. Whilst he was emperor, a man enjoyed supreme power, having absolute control over Rome's vast armies, and unrestricted access to its enormous wealth, but Roman society had not retained the tradition of honour that had been the hallmark of the Republic since the time of Numa, with the result that the emperor was liable to be murdered at any time by corrupt officials, avaricious members of his own family or mutinous soldiers – the average reign of the Roman emperors lasted for less than eight years, and fewer than one in four of them died a natural death.

When viewed solely in terms of the lives and deaths of the emperors it is surprising that the Roman Empire should have lasted for as long as it did. In fact, it was the people of the Empire who ensured its survival: being part of the Roman Empire meant that there were good roads, that travel was possible, that there was an efficient system of law and, above all, that there was a measure of security provided by the Roman legions. Roman rule was benign when compared to other empires of the time: peoples from all corners of the Empire were able to become Roman citizens and were free to follow the religion of their choosing. This meant that even when the Empire was riven by civil war and was being devastated by the ravages of opposing armies, ordinary people did what they could to support the restoration of centralised government. The Empire had been forged by the campaigns of Roman legions, but it was maintained by a collective desire of its various peoples to live in a civilised society.

Antoninus Pius and Marcus Aurelius: The history of remorseless brutality that characterises the reigns of the Roman emperors is broken by Antoninus Pius and his adopted son Marcus Aurelius. They were both students of the philosopher Epictetus, and were so successful in putting his teachings into practice that the Roman world was able to enjoy a brief period of peace during the time that they ruled.

Antoninus Pius

"Titus Antoninus Pius has been justly denominated a second Numa. The same love of religion, justice, and peace, was the distinguishing characteristic of both princes. But the situation of the latter opened a much larger field for the exercise of those virtues. Numa could only prevent a few neighbouring villages from plundering each other's harvests. Antoninus diffused order and tranquillity over the greatest part of the Earth. His reign is marked by the rare advantage of furnishing very few materials for history; which is, indeed, little more than the crimes, follies, and misfortunes of mankind."

The History of the Decline and Fall of the Roman Empire, Edward Gibbon

Jesus of Nazareth

"And seek not ye what ye shall eat, or what ye shall drink, neither be ye of doubtful mind. For all these things do the nations of the world seek after: and your Father knoweth that ye have need of these things. But rather seek ye the kingdom of God; and all these things shall be added unto you."

Luke 12, 29-31

Jesus of Nazareth

The Roman Empire provided the backdrop to many remarkable lives, but the person who has had the greatest effect upon the future history of the world was not an emperor or a politician, but someone who travelled around the Middle East preaching a doctrine of love to ordinary people.

Jesus of Nazareth emerged from obscurity at the age of thirty-two to preach with such power and authority that he was mobbed by crowds of thousands of people wherever he travelled.

The religious leaders of the province felt threatened by his activities: they conspired against him, brought him to trial and condemned him to death for threatening their authority.

There was, however, something of such universal appeal in Jesus' message that it was not extinguished by his removal. His fame spread slowly to all the corners of the empire.

"Come unto me, all ye that labour and are heavy laden, and I will give you rest. Take my yoke upon you, and learn of me; for I am meek and lowly in heart: and ye shall find rest unto your souls."

Matthew 11, 28-29

Recommended Books:
New Testament, King James Version
The Gospels of Matthew, Mark, Luke, and John give four individual accounts of the life of Jesus

Christianity and the Roman Empire

One of the factors that contributed to the growth of the Roman Empire was its religious tolerance: whenever a new province was added to the Empire, a temple was built in Rome to honour the gods of that province; no attempt was made to impose Roman religion upon the local people, and local priests were allowed to retain their status in society unless they actually took up arms against their Roman rulers.

However, this policy had never worked in Judea, where the local leaders were implacably opposed to any accommodation with the 'pagans' from Rome and where the religion was based on the idea that the Jewish people were the chosen ones, loved by God more than any other people on Earth.

This idea appears to have influenced the early Christians and their belief that *they* were the only

Emperor Constantine

true believers in God proved a very divisive element in an already tottering empire.

Initially, Christianity spread amongst the slaves and the poorer classes of society, and this made Christians easy targets for blame and persecution when things were not going well. However, this only served to strengthen Christianity's position as the principal opponent of a regime that was perceived to be corrupt and unable to deal with the problems of over-taxation, barbarian invasion and moral decay. It continued to gain converts in all parts of the Empire and eventually started to assume an important role in Roman politics.

Constantine came to power with the aid of the Christian Church and, as one of his reforms, he made Christianity the official religion of the whole Roman Empire: he had probably underestimated the attachment that people felt for their traditional religions, and the forced conversion to Christianity did not prove to be the unifying factor that he had hoped for. The Church was unable to arrest the decay of Roman civilisation in Western Europe and, within a century, the Empire had collapsed in chaos.

The Collapse of the Empire

Constantine moved the capital of the Empire from Rome to a new city that he built at the gateway to Asia: Constantinople. This placed the administration in the heart of the most prosperous and secure region of the Empire but it made it more difficult to keep control of the vast western half, which was under constant pressure from 'barbarian' tribes living to the north and east.

Sometimes, these tribes came simply to rob and plunder, but, more often than not, they came to settle and seek sanctuary from enemies who were driving them from their homelands. For a while these barbarian settlers provided much of the manpower for the legions who guarded the borders of the Empire.

Inevitably, the Empire eventually split in two; the Eastern half was wealthy and stable but in culture and custom became more like an Asian civilisation than a European one, while the Western half fell more and more under the control of the barbarian invaders who lacked the training to run the complex administration required to maintain it as a single state.

They were plagued by the problem that Roman civilisation had been unable to resolve since the fall of the Republic: there was no recognised system for the transfer of power from one ruler to the next. This led to an endless succession of civil wars which devastated the farmland, decimated the population, drained the Empire of its resources and which frequently left its borders undefended. The barbarian kings gave up trying to work with the Roman system of government and took control of areas of land which they governed with the aid of tribal laws that were completely alien to the Roman tradition. The symbolic end of the Roman Empire came when Alaric, king of the Goths, sacked the city of Rome itself in 410 AD.

The Dark Ages

The demise of the Western Roman Empire was a disaster for its citizens. All the benefits of a civilised society – roads, cities, farms, sewers, fresh water, law courts, theatre, literature, trade, secure borders, communication and a stable currency were lost in the space of a single generation. Roads fell into disrepair, trade ceased, people were forced to survive on what they could produce for themselves, there was no recourse to law when goods were stolen, warlords established control over small areas, disease became rife, life expectancy fell and Roman times were remembered as a golden age almost indistinguishable from myths and legend.

It was nearly a thousand years before Europe was to again enjoy the benefits of civilised life.

Recommended Books:
The Decline and Fall of the Roman Empire, Edward Gibbon
Fifteen Decisive Battles of the World: Battle of Chalons, Sir Edward Creasy

Slavery and Freedom

One of the principal themes that runs through the history of the ancient world is the quest for personal freedom.

All ancient civilisations depended upon the existence of an underclass of people who had few rights and who did all the menial work that was essential to the smooth running of a complex society. Eastern civilisations such as those of Persia, Mesopotamia, Egypt, India and, to a large extent, China, relied upon a caste system that destined the majority of the population, and their offspring, to a state of perpetual servitude. People had no opportunity to rise through the social strata, and their lives were forfeit to the whim of an absolute ruler.

Ancient Greece and Rome

The Greek states provided a radical departure from this model – every citizen had the right and the duty to take part in the government of their city, and individuals could augment their standing in the community through their own personal merits. This freedom, however, only extended to certain sections of the population and all the routine tasks were still done by slaves who were regarded as the property of their free owners.

Rome was able to bring this form of government – free citizens ruling with the aid of slave labour – to a vast empire, but the end of the Roman Republic, and the assumption of supreme power by the emperors, effectively deprived even Roman citizens of true political freedom. This undermined the very thing that had allowed Rome to prosper and the demise of the Empire became inevitable.

Slavery and Work

When Roman power collapsed, Europe fell under barbarian control: personal freedoms increased but the trappings of civilisation were lost. Since then, Europeans have succeeded in gradually rebuilding their civilisation and in exporting it to almost every corner of the world, so that it now occupies a supreme position in world affairs (in this context the modern USA owes its origins to European expansion). One of the criteria by which this achievement should be judged is the degree to which personal freedoms have been maintained over the course of this expansion.

In modern societies, many people work very long hours simply so that they can pay off a mortgage that allows them to have a roof over their heads. Parents are not free to bring up their own children. Working conditions are so onerous that they enforce the separation of parents and children for the greater part of each day. It is not uncommon for mothers to have to go out to work, simply in order to survive. People have no land of their own, and many people do not even have time to cook for themselves.

In the ancient world this would have been considered a particularly harsh form of slavery and it suggests that civilisation has not progressed significantly since the days of ancient Rome.

The Study of Recent History

One of the advantages of studying ancient history is the fact that the passage of time has made the issues that were so significant to ancient historians appear almost irrelevant to the modern reader. This allows us to read their books without being influenced by the political or religious prejudices that they have inadvertently allowed to slip into their work.

The same cannot be said for recent history: when studying recent events everyone tends to identify with people of their own nationality, race, religion, or ideology, and, even if it were possible to find an account of recent events that was completely impartial and objective, it would be difficult to prevent one's own preconceptions from distorting the truth.

For this reason, as wide a variety of resources as possible should be used when studying modern history. This allows you to build up an understanding of historical events without being unduly influenced by any single point of view.

- **Books:** History books can still be your principal resource, providing they are balanced by other things.

- **Picture Books:** Books containing photographs of people, portraits, buildings, landscapes, etc., can give a better feel for historical events than long, written descriptions.

- **Works of Art:** Works of art give a direct insight into other cultures. A good way to understand them is to try to copy them.

- **Magazine Articles:** Magazines are sometimes able to print pictures and articles that would never find their way into a book.

- **Autobiographies:** The lives of prominent people are interesting in their own right and details about where they lived, how they lived, their family life, etc. give an insight into ordinary life that is often lacking in history books.

- **Television Programmes:** Television is probably not the best medium for presenting history but it can provide prominent historians with an opportunity to explain their ideas to a wider audience.

- **Contemporary Novels:** Novels inadvertently give a clear description of the conditions that exist at the time that they are written, and are therefore useful historical documents as well as being enjoyable to read.

- **Second-Hand Magazines and Comics:** Magazines and comics that are up to a hundred years old are readily available from second-hand book shops. They probably give a clearer picture than anything else of the mood in the country at the time at which they were written.

- **Documents from the Internet:** There are a huge number of historical letters, official reports, newspaper articles, etc. freely available on the internet. These provide a student working at home with unparalleled access to resources – better, in fact, than that enjoyed by a researcher working in a university library before the advent of the internet.

Barbarians

The central European peoples (Goths, Vandals, Franks and Huns) who invaded, occupied and ruled over the remains of the Western Roman Empire are collectively known as the barbarians. This is something of a pejorative term used by people to describe anyone who threatens their civilisation – to the Chinese, the Indians were barbarians, and to the Indians, the Greeks were barbarians – but the fact that the barbarian tribes were able to flourish in the harsh conditions of their homelands, while the lush Roman provinces became depopulated and weak, suggests that it is wrong to characterise them as inferior to their civilised neighbours.

Barbarian Attributes

The Roman Empire had offered people security, but at a price. Taxes were high and were largely used to maintain huge standing armies which were often at war with each other. In the early days of Rome, the rulers had been austere, honourable and just: the people gave them power but they prided themselves on using it wisely. As the centuries passed, the ruling class became indolent, corrupt, lazy and cruel, with the result that the people only supported their government out of fear of the alternative.

The alternative eventually proved to be barbarian rule. Barbarian society was organised on a tribal basis with disputes settled by local chieftains; men and women enjoyed approximately equal rights, and slaves were assimilated into the rest of society over a period of time. People survived through their own hard work, they did not pay taxes, there was no centralised government, there was no upper class, there were no cities, people could not read or write, craftsmen were treated with respect, and everyone had to be self-sufficient in terms of what they produced and also in their ability to defend themselves.

Surprisingly perhaps, this created a very fertile society, for the barbarians were able to repopulate Roman provinces that had fallen into decay during the final years of the Empire.

Barbarians and the Church

As the barbarian kings sought to re-establish order across Western Europe, they were forced to turn to the remnants of the Christian Church for help. Gradually, probably for political reasons rather than out of conviction, the barbarian leaders converted to Christianity, and Europe was reunited in a loose coalition of states under the auspices of the Church.

The Church had no military power, but it had a monopoly on learning which was sufficient, over a period of time, to make it the most powerful institution in Europe. It is interesting to note that, at this time, the Church was able to extend its influence beyond the Rhine and into Germany, something that Rome itself had not been able to do, even at the height of its power.

Recommended Books:
Fifteen Decisive Battles of the World: Chapter VII The Battle of Tours, Sir Edward Creasy

European Countries

Rome had divided Western Europe into provinces on the basis of geography and economic activity. The barbarian invaders maintained these boundaries and divided out the Empire according to the existing pattern of government. Hence Gaul fell into the hands of the Franks and the Burgundians, and eventually became France; the Visigoths occupied Spain, Italy and the Balkans; and the Angles and Saxons occupied Britain.

Kings now ruled these countries as independent states and although people still paid lip-service to the idea of creating a single Christian state to match the glory of the departed Roman Empire, the realities of the times made this impossible.

Charlemagne and the Holy Roman Empire

Charlemagne, king of the Franks, subjugated several neighbouring states and became the most powerful European ruler since the fall of Rome. In 800 AD the Pope crowned him Emperor of the 'Holy Roman Empire'. It is not clear whether Charlemagne sought this honour or whether it was cleverly bestowed by a Pope who thereby established a tradition in which successive popes conferred the title on their favoured European monarch.

The Holy Roman Empire in the time of Charlemagne

Charlemagne's empire 814 AD | Slavic peoples tributary to Charlemagne

The Rise of Islam

The barbarian invasion and the collapse of the Western Roman Empire eventually gave rise to the feudal system in Europe. The majority of people became little better than slaves and were the property of the local landowner. The landowners themselves owed allegiance to the king and no one enjoyed any degree of freedom. Towns were small, trade almost non-existent, and the economy completely agricultural.

The Church had developed a form of Christianity that owed as much, or more, to the superstitions that survived from previous religions as it did to the teachings of Jesus. By maintaining a monopoly of learning and by playing on people's fears, it acquired almost complete control over the daily lives of ordinary people.

Meanwhile another part of the old Roman Empire underwent a resurgence of culture and vigour. Based on the teachings of the Prophet Muhammad, a new religion, Islam, became established across the Middle East and Northern Africa.

Islamic Culture

The world of Islam had everything that Western Europe lacked: it had a legal system, it had art, it had culture, it was well organised and it was united.

Islamic scholars were noted for their knowledge of mathematics, and Islamic doctors renowned for their healing abilities. Islamic architecture matched and surpassed that of ancient Greece, and Islamic government provided security.

The Spread of Islam

It is not surprising that this dynamic new civilisation was able to spread its influence to the four corners of the known world. Muhammad founded a small state, Medina, in Arabia, and within twenty years of his death in 632 his Arab followers had gained control of Egypt, Syria, Iraq and Western Persia. Over the next one hundred and fifty years Muslim rule spread to Spain, Morocco, Afghanistan and Central Asia.

After this, Islamic politics became complicated and rival factions frequently fought each other, but Islam remained the dominant world force for at least another five hundred years, mounting successive invasions of India and a gradual expansion into Europe.

"Thy Lord hath not forsaken thee, neither hath he been displeased.
And surely the Future shall be better for thee than the Past,
And in the end shall thy Lord be bounteous to thee and thou be satisfied.
Did he not find thee an orphan and gave thee a home?
And found thee erring and guided thee,
And found thee needy and enriched thee."

The Koran XCIII

The Arabian Nights

The wealth and breadth of Islamic culture is reflected in 'The Arabian Nights', a collection of stories drawn from China, Egypt, Persia, Syria, Iraq, Arabia and North Africa.

In addition to familiar stories such as Aladdin, and Ali Baba and the Forty Thieves, which recount tales of princes, princesses, genii, and magicians, there are others that refer back to legends that were prevalent before the dawn of modern history.

One of the most famous of these is the story of the city of Many-Columned Iram: a goatherd, while wandering through the desert in search of his lost flock, finds himself in the midst of a vast city of indescribable splendour. He recounts his experience to the Sultan, and the Sultan's vizier explains that he must have stumbled upon the mystical city of Many-Columned Iram.

*"Her forehead was flower-white,
her cheeks like the anemone ruddy bright."*

The City of Many-Columned Iram

Ad the Greater had two sons, Shadid and Shaddad who, when their father died, ruled conjointly in his stead, and there was no King of the Kings of the earth but was subject to them. After awhile Shadid died and his brother Shaddad reigned over the earth alone. Now he was fond of reading in antique books; and, happening upon the description of the world to come and of Paradise, with its pavilions and galleries and trees and fruits and so forth, his soul moved him to build the like thereof in this world, after the fashion aforesaid. Now under his hand were an hundred thousand Kings, each ruling over an hundred thousand chiefs, commanding each an hundred thousand warriors; so he called these all before him and said to them, "I find in ancient books and annals a description of Paradise, as it is to be in the next world, and I desire to build me its like in this world. Go ye forth therefore to the goodliest tract on earth and the most

continued overleaf...

spacious and build me there a city of gold and silver, whose gravel shall be chrysolite and rubies and pearls; and for support of its vaults make pillars of jasper. Fill it with palaces, whereon ye shall set galleries and balconies and plant its lanes and thoroughfares with all manner trees bearing yellow-ripe fruits and make rivers to run through it in channels of gold and silver."

Shaddad presently assembled from all lands and countries architects and engineers and men of art and labourers and handicraftsmen, who dispersed over the world and explored all the wastes and wolds and tracts and holds. At last they came to an uninhabited spot, a vast and fair open plain clear of sand-hills and mountains, with founts flushing and rivers rushing, and they said, "This is the manner of place the King commanded us to seek and ordered us to find." So they busied themselves in building the city even as bade them Shaddad, King of the whole earth in its length and breadth; leading the fountains in channels and laying the foundations after the prescribed fashion. Moreover, all the Kings of earth's several reigns sent thither jewels and precious stones and pearls large and small and carnelian and refined gold and virgin silver upon camels by land, and in great ships over the waters, and there came to the builders' hands of all these materials so great a quantity as may neither be told nor counted nor conceived. So they laboured at the work three hundred years; and, when they had brought it to end, they went to King Shaddad and acquainted him therewith. Then said he, "Depart and make thereon an impregnable castle, rising and towering high in air, and build around it a thousand pavilions, each upon a thousand columns of chrysolite and ruby and vaulted with gold, that in each pavilion a Vizier may dwell."

So they returned forthwith and did this in other twenty years; after which they again presented themselves before King Shaddad and informed him of the accomplishment of his will. Then he commanded his Viziers and his Chief Officers and such of his troops and others as he put trust in, to prepare for departure and removal to Many-Columned Iram, in the suite and at the stirrup of Shaddad, son of Ad, King of the world; and he bade also such as he would of his women and his Harim and of his handmaids and eunuchs make them ready for the journey. They spent twenty years in preparing for departure, at the end of which time Shaddad set out with his host, rejoicing in the attainment of his desire till there remained but one day's journey between him and Iram of the Pillars. Then Allah sent down on him a mighty rushing sound from the Heavens of His power, which destroyed them all with its vehement clamour, and neither Shaddad nor any of his company set eyes on the city. Moreover, Allah blotted out the road which led to the city, and it stands in its stead unchanged until the Ressurection Day and the Hour of Judgement.

Taken from The Arabian Nights, translated by Sir Richard Burton,
The Modern Library Classics

The Crusades

The remorseless rise of Islamic power became a source of anxiety to Pope Urban II in Rome: perhaps he had a genuine religious objection to Christian 'holy places' being in the hands of 'the infidel' or perhaps he was simply motivated by political considerations – in any case he managed to temporarily bury the long-standing animosity that existed between the Western Church of Rome and the Eastern Church which was based in Byzantium (Constantinople). He called upon all the peoples of Europe to unite and launch a crusade against Islam.

The European armies that sailed to the Middle East captured Jerusalem and set up a Christian kingdom in Palestine. The success of this expedition was probably

King Richard I of England – one of several European monarchs who dedicated himself to the crusades.

due in part to divisions between competing Muslim rulers who, up until that time, would not have taken the threat of attack by Christian Europe very seriously.

Once alerted to the danger, the world of Islam marshalled its forces and launched a counter-offensive against Christendom. It proved to be a long war, interspersed with more Christian crusades, but the Islamic forces usually had the upper hand and it was they who slowly but surely extended the area under their control to include the Balkans, the Greek islands, and Sicily.

Byzantium fell in 1453 and, judging from historical precedents, one would have expected Western Europe to follow suit in the not-too-distant future.

However, this did not happen. Instead of falling prey to foreign invasion, Europe underwent a change from within and a Renaissance of new ideas, new forms of government, new science and new art gave it the strength to resist attack and marked its emergence as a significant power in world affairs.

The Renaissance

What Was the Renaissance?

By the thirteen hundreds, Italy had become divided up into various power blocs: the King of Naples controlled the South; the Pope controlled the centre; the Venetian Republic controlled the North-East; Milan controlled the Northern plain and the Florentine Republic controlled the West.

Each of these mini-states developed its own independent cultural life. Art, science, mathematics, sculpture, engineering, building and military science, all started to flourish at the same time. Each state was wealthy enough to be able to sponsor and encourage its most able citizens: schools of painting developed, and universities were founded, innovative building projects were undertaken and traditional dogmas were challenged.

This spirit of experimentation spread spontaneously throughout Europe and gave rise to the voyages of exploration and to new theories on astronomy. The size of cities increased, trade revived and the feudal system started to crumble. Every aspect of European life was affected by this process which is now referred to as 'The Renaissance'.

What Caused the Renaissance?

No one has ever adequately explained why the Renaissance took place – it is an event that has no obvious parallel elsewhere in history. One factor that provided it with momentum was the rediscovery of lost manuscripts from ancient Greece. These possibly arrived in Italy from Byzantium, brought by scholars fleeing the threat of Muslim invasion.

Artists and sculptors in the Renaissance sought to recapture the beauty of Greek art, and Renaissance thinkers rejected the superstition of the medieval Church in favour of the clarity and logic of the Greek philosophers.

Botticelli's Venus: Greek gods and goddesses provided the theme for much of Renaissance art as Renaissance artists struggled to recapture the genius of Greek painting.

114

Leonardo da Vinci (1452 - 1519)

Leonardo was born in the town of Vinci, in Tuscany. At the age of fourteen he was apprenticed to the leading Florentine artist of the time, Andrea del Verrocchio.

When he was twenty-six he set up his own workshop, by which time his teacher had vowed never to paint again, so inferior did he feel to his pupil's genius.

Leonardo left Florence four years later to work for Ludovico Sforza, as the chief engineer and architect in the city of Milan.

He never allowed his interest to be confined to a single discipline but studied mathematics, anatomy, optics, engineering, architecture, painting, drawing and sculpture. What he learnt in one field, he applied to others.

He is renowned for the innovation and experimentation that he brought to all areas of his work, most noticeably in painting. It led to some of his pictures never being completed and to others being lost due to the deterioration of the materials, but it also led to the creation of masterpieces such as the Mona Lisa (La Gioconda) which was perhaps his favourite work. He took it with him wherever he travelled and is believed to have worked on it over many years.

Later in his life Leonardo returned to Florence and also worked in Rome taking commissions from Cesare Borgia and the Pope; in 1516 he was invited to join the French court and travelled to France, where he passed the last three years of his life.

> "I love those who can smile in trouble,
> who can gather strength from distress,
> and grow brave by reflection.
> 'Tis the business of little minds to shrink,
> But they whose heart is firm,
> and whose conscience approves their conduct
> will pursue their principles to death."
>
> *Leonardo da Vinci*

Recommended Books:
The Notebooks of Leonardo da Vinci, Leonardo da Vinci
Life of the Artists, Vasari

115

Niccolò Machiavelli (1469 - 1527)

Niccolò Machiavelli is one of the most enigmatic of the principal Renaissance figures. He first came to public prominence at the age of twenty-nine when he was appointed secretary to the council responsible for administrative affairs in the newly-created Florentine Republic. In this capacity he undertook diplomatic missions to the French king, the Pope, to the German emperor and to Cesare Borgia. He was also responsible for organising the military defences of the Republic – a job that brought him into contact with Leonardo da Vinci.

He fell from office when the Republic was dissolved in 1512 and played no further role in public life. His fame rests mainly upon two works that were published after his death, The Discourses and The Prince. These books are remarkable for the cold, clinical logic with which they analyse the relationship between citizen and State and between the State and its rulers.

They remain the most compelling treatises yet written on European political life and have influenced courts and governments over many centuries. Even so, it is not clear why they were written or whether Machiavelli was seriously offering advice for others to follow or satirising the corrupt morals of the Renaissance rulers of his time. In this extract from The Prince he gives advice on 'How human affairs are governed by fortune, and how fortune can be opposed':

"I compare fortune to one of those violent rivers which, when they are enraged, flood the plains, tear down trees, wash soil from one place to deposit it in another. Everyone flees before them, everybody yields to their impetus, there is no possibility of resistance. Yet although such is their nature, it does not follow that when they are flowing quietly one cannot take precautions, constructing dykes and embankments so that when the river is in flood they would keep to one channel or their impetus be less wild and dangerous. So it is with fortune. She shows her potency where there is no well regulated power to resist her, and her impetus is felt where she knows there are no embankments and dykes built to restrain her."

The Prince, Chapter XXV

Recommended Books:
The Prince, Niccolò Machiavelli, translated by George Bull, Penguin Classics
The Discourses, Niccolò Machiavelli, translated by Lesley J. Walker, Penguin Classics

Galileo Galilei (1564 - 1642)

Galileo lived at a time when the established authorities of Church and State had seen that their power was being threatened by new ideas, and were moving towards a brutal phase of repression.

He was born in Pisa and started to attend the University of Pisa at the age of sixteen or seventeen, as a medical student. He could not accept the dogma that was being taught by the science professors and spent his time studying mathematics. After five years he left the university without a degree, but four years later was appointed mathematics professor at the same university.

It was at this stage of his career that he conducted his famous experiment of dropping two metal balls, one large and one small, off the

top of the leaning tower of Pisa: they hit the ground at the same time, thereby disproving the theories of the professors who were assembled to watch. For this, and other such actions, his contract was not renewed and after four years he moved to become professor of mathematics in Padua, in the Republic of Venice. It was here that he learnt about the invention of the telescope, and he built a device which enabled him to make a series of observations supporting the theory that the Earth goes round the Sun, rather than the reverse.

His gift of a telescope to the Doge of Venice won him renown in the city, which was the capital of a seafaring empire, but he made the politically-unwise choice of leaving its security to take up the prestigious post of court mathematician in Florence.

His logical, mathematical approach to working out why things float, determining the path followed by a cannon ball, and studying the movement of a pendulum won him acclaim from many quarters but it also aroused the resentment of professors who had been schooled in traditional theories and who were being made to look foolish by Galileo. These professors eventually conspired with the Catholic Church to bring him to trial on the basis that he was openly supporting the heretical idea that the Earth moves round the Sun.

Galileo was condemned and forced to renounce this view, and he was kept under house arrest for the rest of his life. Three hundred and fifty nine years later, in 1992, the Church acknowledged that it had been wrong to treat the greatest scientist of his time in this way.

Voyages of Exploration

From the collapse of the Roman Empire to the beginning of the Renaissance, Europe had little contact with the outside world. In that time the Church had become immersed in superstition and ignorance, and did all that it could to reinforce the idea that the lands beyond Europe were not safe to visit. It preached that the world was flat, that the periphery was inhabited by sea monsters, that madness awaited anyone who sailed to the edge of the Earth and that it was God's will that everyone should stay where they were. Many of these ideas had no connection with the original doctrine of the Christian Church, but were superstitions absorbed from the barbarian tribes that had, supposedly, been converted to the Christian faith.

The Renaissance saw all these ideas being challenged by European intellectuals; and classical texts, that provided a more conventional view of the Earth's geography, once again found their way into circulation. These texts affirmed that the world was a globe and gave a description of the climatic zones – cold regions at the poles and a tropical zone round the equator. They also gave a reasonably clear picture of the geography of Europe, Africa and Asia.

Henry the Navigator (1394 - 1460)

Henry was prince of Portugal at a time when the Moors were finally being expelled from the Iberian peninsular. His study of ancient texts convinced him that it ought to be possible to find a sea route round Africa to India, which would enable Europe to trade directly with the East. He foresaw that if this route were found, it would bring an end to Europe's dependence upon Islamic traders who had been able to control overland trade between Europe and Asia for well over five hundred years.

With this in mind, he established Europe's first school for navigators and equipped expeditions for the exploration of the African coast and the search for a sea route to the Far East.

This work did not culminate until nearly forty years after his death, when Vasco da Gama sailed round the south of Africa, across the Indian Ocean and into the Indian harbour at Calicut where he negotiated exclusive trading rights for Portugal with the local ruler.

Discovery of America

Christopher Columbus became convinced at a young age that it should be possible to find a route to the East by sailing West. He initially put his plan to the king of Portugal, who refused to help him, probably because Portugal was close to completing its long-term aim of finding a route round Africa, but also because the king's advisors were convinced that Christopher Columbus had underestimated the circumference of the Earth.

The king and queen of Spain, perhaps worried by the prospect of a Portuguese monopoly on Eastern trade, did, however, agree to sponsor his expedition and it set out with three ships in 1492.

It is a testament to the indomitable personality of Christopher Columbus that he managed to persuade his crews to keep sailing away from the known world for thirty-three consecutive days until land was sighted on the 12th October.

Columbus *had* seriously underestimated the circumference of the Earth: rather than arriving on the eastern shores of China (which he steadfastly maintained that he had done), he did, in fact, make landfall in the Bahamas and discovered a new continent, the existence of which does not appear to have been known either to Europeans or the civilisations of the East.

Unfortunately, Christopher Columbus's arrival spelt disaster for the inhabitants of this New World. Spain claimed the continent as its own property, and established colonial governments that treated the existing inhabitants as slaves. Civilisations, such as the Aztec, Incan and Mayan were discovered and destroyed. European diseases brought despair and death to millions of people.

This catalogue of events represents one of the grimmest chapters in recorded history and does not reflect well upon European 'civilisation'. Perhaps it was inevitable that the native peoples of America would find themselves at a disadvantage both technologically and militarily when they were reunited with the rest of mankind, but this cannot excuse the inhumanity with which they were treated by a society that laid such emphasis on its own moral superiority.

Christopher Columbus' ship, the 'Santa Maria'

The Reformation

The Renaissance awoke people's desire for change and this was bound to cause problems for the Church, which had been controlling the way people thought for over a thousand years. The shift towards people once again thinking for themselves was a slow and painful process which was bitterly resisted by some sections of society and especially by the Church hierarchy. Religion became the principal point of dispute between reformers and those who wished to maintain the status quo.

King Henry VIII

There were many long-held grievances against the Church: the opulence of its buildings; the luxurious lifestyle of its priests; its bureaucracy; its lack of sympathy with the plight of ordinary people and the way in which it supported the ruling classes, but all this had been endured while people believed that the Church was the divine representative of God on Earth. Everything changed when leading figures of the Renaissance suggested that it was in fact simply a human institution, open to corruption and abuse just like any other, and, as a result, new movements arose that resisted the authority of the bishops and cardinals and demanded a simpler form of Christianity, more akin to that practised by the first Christians.

This process became known as the Reformation. Not surprisingly, it started in those areas that had not been part of the Roman Empire, and in which there still lingered a deep-seated distrust of centralised control by a rich elite based in Rome. Scandinavia and many German states led the way, creating new Christian sects based on the ideas of Martin Luther and they were followed by parts of Switzerland, the Netherlands and Scotland where the new sects were modelled on the ideas of John Calvin.

England was added to the list of 'Protestant' countries when King Henry VIII argued with the Pope over his divorce from his first wife, Catherine of Aragon. Initially, Henry's Church was not Protestant – he retained all the rites and rituals of the Roman Church – but politics forced him to become more closely aligned with Protestant countries and economics made the enormous wealth of the Church too tempting a target to be ignored. He dissolved the monasteries and effectively privatised their enormous holdings of land by selling them off to the highest bidder – thereby creating a new class of landowners.

Leaders of the Reformation

The key figures of the Reformation are distinctly different from the artists, sculptors, mathematicians and scientists who are associated with the Renaissance. They are troubled figures, struggling to reconcile common sense with religious dogma and perplexed by the difference between their own lives and that of the disciples in the Bible:

Martin Luther (1483 - 1546)

Martin Luther received what we would now consider to be a conventional education – primary school, secondary school, university – but at the age of twenty-three he abandoned his law studies and entered a monastery.

His exceptional abilities as a scholar led to his appointment at the age of twenty-nine to the post of professor of Biblical Philosophy at the new University of Wittenberg. Five years later he published (possibly by nailing them to the cathedral door) Ninety Five Theses in which he attacked the practice of selling indulgences (exemption from the penalties of sin in exchange for money) to raise funds for the new cathedral in Rome.

His aim was undoubtedly to stimulate reform of the Church rather than to cause a schism, but he became caught up in events beyond his control. He was excommunicated from the Catholic Church but received the support of Frederick the Wise, prince of Saxony. His reforms were instituted in Saxony, thereby creating the first Protestant state and the first Protestant Church.

His ideas were taken up enthusiastically by several German statesmen, but when they were espoused by peasants who demanded greater freedom and justice for themselves, Martin Luther failed to lend them his full support. The uprising was crushed with brutality and, consequently, he lost much of his popularity with ordinary people. The last years of his life appear to have been marked by increasing bitterness and his later writing includes attacks on Jewish people, the Pope and those Protestants who were demanding more radical reforms than he himself had initiated.

John Calvin (1509 - 1564)

Calvin was born in France and studied law and theology at French universities. His association with supporters of Martin Luther forced him to leave Paris when he was twenty-six years old and go into hiding. He published work that made him a leading figure in the Protestant world and his travels took him to Geneva, where he eventually settled.

Under his guidance, the city developed an austere form of life, partly inspired by his Protestant philosophy and partly out of necessity due to continuous threat of attack by Catholic armies. He instituted social measures such as schools and hospitals, which established the tradition of Protestant administrations being more concerned with the welfare of ordinary people than the Catholic regimes that they replaced.

Like Luther, Calvin saw nothing wrong in the execution of Christians who campaigned for more extreme reforms than he believed to be appropriate.

The Bitterness Aroused by Religious Disputes

The resurgence of art, science and philosophy in Italy and the change of mood that swept across Europe did not leave the Roman Church untouched. It retained its hierarchical structure with bishops and cardinals, the use of Latin in its services, and its ornate buildings, but it still underwent enormous changes – it ceased to be a medieval institution ruled by superstition and dogma and embraced many of the discoveries and much of the culture of the Renaissance.

In one respect, however, there was to be no compromise – the leaders of the Roman Church were implacably opposed to the creation of independent Protestant Churches and did everything that they could to eradicate them.

At first this was attempted by the traditional method of the excommunication of troublesome priests and princes but, as the extent of the dissatisfaction with the established Church became apparent, it became more ruthless.

Europe became divided into two halves: the north was Protestant and the south Catholic and to be caught in the wrong half could lead to torture and death at any time. Each side accused the other of being in league with the devil and the citizens of Europe no longer saw each other as fellow human beings or even as fellow Christians, but judged people solely on the type of Christianity they practised.

> "Use every man after his desert, and who should scape whipping? Use them after your own honour and dignity: the less they deserve, the more merit is in your bounty."
>
> *Shakespeare*

Saint Bartholomew's Eve

This divide was most graphically demonstrated in France where large numbers of French people became Protestants during the early years of the Reformation. Although they were all technically subjects of the French king, the majority of them lived in areas that paid nominal allegiance to the central government in Paris but which in practice enjoyed a large degree of autonomy. The Reformation coincided with the French monarchy acquiring the power to weld France into a single country. Opposition to this centralisation of power centred around the issue of religious freedom but in reality Protestants were struggling to protect their political, economic, and cultural independence from the encroachment of a despotic government.

Events culminated on Saint Bartholomew's Eve in 1572: a plan to assassinate certain Protestant leaders went out of control and led to a wholesale massacre in the streets of Paris.

Despite the best efforts of leading figures on both sides of the divide, a rapprochement between French Catholics and Protestants was never achieved and over the next hundred years virtually all the Protestants fled the country.

They settled in Britain, the Netherlands and Germany, where they did much to enrich the cultural and economic life of their adopted countries, being pivotal in the development of the wool trade and the creation of a prosperous middle class. France was correspondingly impoverished.

Freedom and the Reformation

The Reformation had modest beginnings and never took hold in the traditional centres of European wealth and power. Consequently, the leaders of Italy, Spain and France had no doubt that they would be able to crush the emerging Protestant communities and bring them back into the orbit of Roman influence. They failed to recognise that the process of 'Reformation', even though it had been started by princes, was now being driven by ordinary people. The Bible was being translated into local languages, people were learning to read and write and were running their own churches, they were enjoying paying less tax and felt that they were starting to take control of their own destiny.

Even though the Protestant countries were smaller and less wealthy than their Catholic neighbours, their citizens were determined not to lose their new rights and freedoms. The opposition of the Catholic Church actually accelerated this process: the rulers of Protestant countries were dependent on the goodwill of the people for their ability to withstand invasion and were therefore unable to oppose the increases in individual freedom that came with the new religion.

The Spanish Armada

The watershed of this process proved to be the attempted invasion of Britain by Spain. Backed by the Pope, King Philip of Spain prepared an armada with which to invade and subjugate the British Isles.

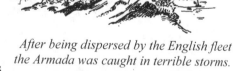

The building of the fleet was financed by gold and silver plundered from the Spanish conquests in the New World, and it was manned by nobility from all over Europe who planned to redistribute the estates of England and Wales

After being dispersed by the English fleet the Armada was caught in terrible storms.

amongst themselves in much the same way as the Normans had done five hundred years previously, after the battle of Hastings. The principal powers of Europe confidently expected to be able to stamp out Protestantism once the English ruler, Queen Elizabeth I, had been removed from power and her country defeated.

It did not work out in the way that they expected – the Armada was completely destroyed and failed to land a single soldier on British soil. Spain lost its aura of invincibility and went into decline as a major world power.

It became apparent that a divide had opened up in the Western Christian Church that would never be healed. The Pope had lost his authority over millions of Christians, who from that time forward intended to be guided by their consciences rather than by their priests.

Recommended Books: **Fifteen Decisive Battles of the World: Chapter X, The Defeat of the Spanish Armada**, Edward Creasy

British Civil War (1642 - 48)

The defeat of the Armada was not brought about by a well-organised British government, but by the people of Britain who saw that they had much to lose by being drawn back into the orbit of the Roman Church.

It marked a stage in the transfer of power from a small group of aristocrats to a broader-based group of landowners and merchants. For this to happen smoothly, the monarch had to agree to a gradual reduction in regal power. Queen Elizabeth acquiesced in this process but it is not surprising that her successors – James I and his son, Charles I – did not, and this led to a bitter civil war in which the 'Parliamentarians' eventually overwhelmingly defeated the 'Royalists'.

The historical significance of these events is that they gave rise to a society that was responsible both for the Industrial Revolution and the founding of the United States of America – both of which have a defining influence on the lives of people all over the world today.

Oliver Cromwell (1599 - 1658)

Oliver Cromwell was in the mould of the self-tortured leaders of the Reformation. He attended grammar school and the university of Cambridge and became a member of the English parliament at a time when conflict was mounting between Parliament and the King. He was instrumental in recruiting and training the 'New Model Army' which turned the war in favour of Parliament. When the army mutinied due to lack of pay, he brought it back under control and led it on murderous campaigns in Ireland and Scotland. He was the leading figure behind the execution of the defeated King and when Parliament was unable to form an administration of which he approved, he seized power and had himself declared 'Lord Protector', in which capacity he ruled Britain until his death, five years later. His government was particularly hated for its

'Puritan' measures that included closure of the theatres and the prohibition of any show of frivolity in public.

Oliver Cromwell is renowned for the struggles that he underwent with his conscience: he convinced himself that he was a special instrument of God's will and that God was pleased with the atrocities committed by his soldiers against Catholic people, particularly in Ireland. Viewed with the benefit of hindsight, his life appears to offer a classic example of a ruthless man using religion to justify indefensible actions.

The Industrial Revolution

The unique conditions existing in Britain after the Civil War gave rise to a fundamental change in the way that people lived and worked. The traditional relationship between landowner and farm worker was broken, and new landowners felt little compunction about introducing agricultural methods that yielded higher profits than traditional peasant farming. Common land was enclosed and people were driven from their homes.

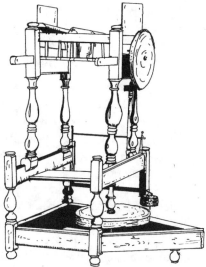

At the same time innovative craftsmen were developing machines that made age-old production techniques redundant; mechanised looms and spinning machines could produce cloth much more cheaply than the traditional cottage industries, and they deprived country people of another vital source of income.

Factories were built to house the new machinery and people who could no longer live on the land moved to work in them. This created a new underclass – the factory workers, who were totally dependent on money that they received from an employer; and a new upper class – the factory owners, who could generate tremendous wealth by the vigorous exploitation of the new technology and a compliant workforce.

Arkwright's Spinning Jenny, an invention that made the spinning wheel redundant.

Industrial Power

Industrial Revolution is a good term to describe the events that took place in Britain in the eighteenth century, because the process was not controlled by any central government. Events of previous centuries – the break with Rome, the defeat of the Armada, the Civil War, the rise of Parliament – had given rise to a population that contained a large number of well-educated, free-thinking people who had become used to following an independent course of action. These people invented things and exploited other people's inventions in a manner that could not be controlled by any government or institution.

Britain saw the construction of woollen mills and cotton mills, canal building, coal mining, and iron smelting; it saw the development of the steam engine and the building of railways; cities grew up out of nowhere and were linked by roads, railways and bridges, and fortunes were made and lost. Commerce, instead of agricultural production, started to drive the economy.

For the first time businessmen, instead of landowners or clerics, were able to dictate policy to a Western government, and they used their new-found power to build an empire based on commercial interests and profit.

The United States of America

Even though the Industrial Revolution began in Great Britain, and enabled Britain to briefly establish an Empire that encompassed the globe, it is in the United States of America that it has reached its fruition. The growth of America is, without doubt, the most significant story in the history of the world over the past three hundred years.

North America

The sparse population, the lack of gold and the absence of suitable conditions for sugar plantations meant that North America largely escaped the ravages of Spanish occupation. It did, however, become prey to colonisation by other European powers, most notably Britain, as soon as Spain was no longer able to exclude them from the continent.

British Colonies

Jamestown, the first British colony in North America, was established in 1607. It was owned and financed by wealthy backers who were eventually only able to get a return on their investment by importing people from Africa to work as slaves on tobacco plantations.

The colony of New Plymouth, founded thirteen years later, was very different. It was populated by a group of families who had embraced a Puritan doctrine that they were not allowed to practise freely in Britain.

Although nominally British, the colony was strongly independent, and unlike most European colonists around the world, its inhabitants were not looking for gold or power but simply for a place in which to settle.

Native Americans

One obstacle that stood between the settlers and the creation of a new world was the fact that the land of North America was already occupied by the native American Indians. It was only by depriving the existing inhabitants of their hunting grounds and their livelihoods that the new colonies could survive and grow.

Mitari warrior dressed for a ceremonial dance.

Growth of British America and Independence

British America grew on two fronts: self-sufficient settlements in the North and slave-owning plantation settlements in the South. Thirteen separate British colonies were established, each one virtually independent from the others.

Initially, all the colonists were grateful for the protection that the British administration afforded them against the threat posed by neighbouring French and Spanish colonies but, as Britain gradually assumed greater and greater power on the continent, the foreign threat diminished and the British army came to be seen not as a source of security but as an army of occupation.

Resentment grew as the British administration tried to enforce taxes and retain control over life in the colonies. Eventually the seemingly impossible happened and the thirteen colonies united to declare independence.

The bonds between Britain and America were naturally strong, but the savagery with which the British army attempted to suppress the 'rebellion' caused a rift to develop between the two countries that was to last for many years.

The American Constitution

After independence, the world expected the colonies to either splinter into warring states or else to fall under the control of a dictator: instead they agreed to abide by a common constitution that put the rights of the individual above the needs of the state, proving that the idealism that had led to the founding of the Northern colonies still lived on.

The issue that the Founding Fathers could not resolve when they drew up the constitution was that of slavery. Slavery was considered to be essential to the profits of the plantation owners of the South, but it made a mockery of a constitution that placed so much emphasis on the freedom of the individual and the right of *all* the people of America to be happy.

"We hold these truths to be self-evident, that all men are created equal, that they are endowed by their Creator with certain unalienable Rights, that among these are Life, Liberty and the pursuit of Happiness. – That to secure these rights, governments are instituted among Men, deriving their just powers from the consent of the governed, – That whenever any Form of Government becomes destructive of these ends, it is the Right of the people to alter or to abolish it, and to institute new Government, laying its foundation on such principles and organizing its powers in such form, as to them shall seem most likely to effect their Safety and Happiness."

From the Declaration of Independence July 4th 1776

Recommended Books:
A History of American Democracy (Translated from De la Démocratie en Amérique), Alexis de Toqueville
Fifteen Decisive Battles of the World: Chapter XIII, Victory of the Americans over Burgoyne at Saratoga, Sir Edward Creasy

Benjamin Franklin (1706 – 1790)

Benjamin Franklin plays a rather enigmatic role in the early history of America. He is the only person whose signature appears on the Declaration of Independence, The American Constitution, the Treaty of Alliance with France and the Treaty of Peace with England – which would suggest that his was the moving spirit behind the progress of Americans to becoming a free and independent people, but if this was the case, he achieved it whilst attracting the minimum attention to himself and allowing most of the credit to fall to others.

Such a course of action would have been consistent with the general tenor of his life. He left home at the age of seventeen and by the age of twenty-three had set up his own printing firm in his adopted home town of Philadelphia.

He succeeded in amassing a large fortune whilst retaining his reputation for honesty and integrity and was able to retire at the age of forty-two. He then dedicated himself to study and recreation. Within a few years he had established himself as one of the foremost scholars of his day. His scientific experiments, which demonstrated that lightning was a form of electricity, made him a celebrity on both sides of the Atlantic.

At the same time he was able to institute a series of social reforms that helped to make Philadelphia a centre of culture and model government. He was instrumental in starting the first public library, the first fire service, street cleaning and the founding of a college of further education.

As tension between the local governments and the British government mounted, he was persuaded to act as American ambassador in London. Once independence had been declared he became the American ambassador in Paris, where he succeeded in gaining support from the French government for the American cause.

Towards the end of his life he foresaw the danger that slavery posed to his country and he founded America's first anti-slavery society.

It is hard to imagine that anyone other than Benjamin Franklin could have been responsible for the idealism and optimism of America's declaration of independence from European colonial rule.

> "Good sense is a thing all need, few have, and none think they lack."
> *Benjamin Franklin*

Recommended Books:
The Autobiography of Benjamin Franklin,
Benjamin Franklin

Benjamin and his son performing their famous experiment with a kite during a thunder storm.

Frederick Douglass (1817 – 1895)

Frederick Douglass' life exposes a darker side of the birth of America. He was the first black American to rise to public notice, but remains largely unforgiven and unacknowledged by large sections of both the black and white communities.

He was born into slavery on a plantation in Maryland, and was separated from his mother, more or less at birth. His relatively pale skin makes it probable that the plantation owner was his father.

His early life was marked by the attempts of his 'owners' to break his spirit and to keep him in a state of ignorance, but he succeeded in teaching himself to read and write and came to his own understanding of the injustice to which he was being subjected. He was particularly appalled by the hypocrisy of the Christian churches that twisted the words of the Bible to justify

Frederick Douglass: "I had reached the point at which I was not afraid to die. This spirit made me a freeman in fact, though I still remained a slave in form."

the institution of slavery, when it was clear to him that Jesus preached a doctrine of freedom. He escaped to the Northern states (where slavery was not legal), and after a short time became an active campaigner for the abolition of slavery. Racism was deeply ingrained throughout America, even amongst the Northern population, and it was not long before he was forced to leave America and travel to Europe, where, he discovered, black people were neither despised nor segregated from white people in public places. He carried the unwelcome message back to America that people had more freedom in the country of their old oppressors than they did in the 'land of the free'.

Given the passion and the lack of compromise with which he attacked hypocrisy in the American churches, the American government, and in the people that he met, it is surprising that he lived to see his dreams come true: he advised Abraham Lincoln during the Civil War, and for many years was the American Marshal in Washington. He died peacefully in his late seventies, satisfied that he had lived a happy and fulfilled life in spite of the early obstacles that he had had to overcome.

Recommended Books:
The Life and Times of Frederick Douglass, Frederick Douglass

In this extract from Frederick Douglass' autobiography he explains how he learned to read. He was the first slave his mistress had ever 'owned':

"...the fatal poison of irresponsible power, and the natural influence of slave customs, were not very long in making their impression on the gentle and loving disposition of my excellent mistress. She regarded me first as a child, like any other. This was the natural and spontaneous thought; afterwards, when she came to consider me as property, our relations to each other were changed, but a nature so noble as hers could not instantly become perverted, and it took several years before the sweetness of her temper was wholly lost.

The frequent hearing of my mistress reading the Bible aloud when her husband was absent, awakened my curiosity in respect to this mystery of reading, and roused in me the desire to learn.

Up to this time I had known nothing whatever of this wonderful art, and my ignorance and inexperience of what it could do for me as well as my confidence in my mistress, emboldened me to ask her to teach me to read.

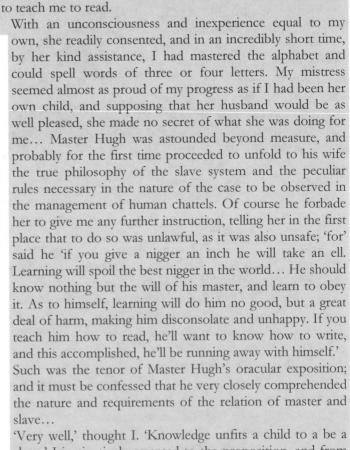

With an unconsciousness and inexperience equal to my own, she readily consented, and in an incredibly short time, by her kind assistance, I had mastered the alphabet and could spell words of three or four letters. My mistress seemed almost as proud of my progress as if I had been her own child, and supposing that her husband would be as well pleased, she made no secret of what she was doing for me... Master Hugh was astounded beyond measure, and probably for the first time proceeded to unfold to his wife the true philosophy of the slave system and the peculiar rules necessary in the nature of the case to be observed in the management of human chattels. Of course he forbade her to give me any further instruction, telling her in the first place that to do so was unlawful, as it was also unsafe; 'for' said he 'if you give a nigger an inch he will take an ell. Learning will spoil the best nigger in the world... He should know nothing but the will of his master, and learn to obey it. As to himself, learning will do him no good, but a great deal of harm, making him disconsolate and unhappy. If you teach him how to read, he'll want to know how to write, and this accomplished, he'll be running away with himself.'

Such was the tenor of Master Hugh's oracular exposition; and it must be confessed that he very closely comprehended the nature and requirements of the relation of master and slave...

'Very well,' thought I. 'Knowledge unfits a child to a be a slave.' I instinctively assented to the proposition, and from that moment I understood the direct pathway from slavery to freedom."

The Southern economy was dependent upon slave labour in the cotton plantations.

Civil War 1861 - 1865

By the middle of the nineteenth century it was clear that the two halves of the United States were going in different directions: the North was embracing the process of industrialisation and expansion; the South had a society based upon a rigid class structure and was resistant to change of any kind.

For many years the Southern States were allowed to monopolise the institutions of government but in 1861 Abraham Lincoln, who came from the Northern State of Illinois, was elected president, and the Southern States decided to break away from the Union and form an independent country.

This move led to a civil war which saw the first full-scale conflict between armies fully equipped with modern weapons. In the end the North gained the victory with the result that the Union was preserved and slavery was abolished – but the issue of slavery had never been acknowledged as the cause of the war and, when the fighting stopped, little was done to improve the lot of the freed slaves. The main effect of the conflict was to commit the United States to a process of industrialisation and westward expansion that had begun in the North before the war started.

Abraham Lincoln was re-elected to the presidency as the war was drawing to its close. This extract from his second inaugural address provides a moving testimony to his personal commitment to finding a just peace. Tragically, he was assassinated a few weeks after the speech was delivered.

"Fondly do we hope – fervently do we pray – that this mighty scourge of war may speedily pass away. Yet, if God wills that it continue, until all the wealth piled up by the bond-man's two hundred and fifty years of unrequited toil shall be sunk, and until every drop of blood drawn with the lash, shall be paid by another drawn with the sword, so still it must be said the judgements of the Lord are true and righteous altogether.

With malice toward none; with charity to all; with firmness in the right, as God gives us to see the right, let us strive on to finish the work we are in; to bind up the nation's wounds; to care for him who shall have borne the battle, and for his widow, and his orphan – to do all which may achieve and cherish a just and lasting peace, among ourselves, and with all nations."

Industrialisation, War, and America as a World Power

A United States soldier of the nineteenth century.

The factors that caused the Industrial Revolution to begin in Northern Europe were present in a magnified form in the Northern United States. The population was composed of well-educated, free-thinking people who were eager to better themselves; there was an absence of authoritarian and bureaucratic government; there was a rich supply of raw materials and there was the constant spectre of want and hardship to drive people forward.

Industrial growth was further stimulated by the policy of welcoming unlimited numbers of European immigrants to American shores. Plentiful supplies of new immigrants kept labour costs in the Eastern cities to the absolute minimum, and also guaranteed a steady stream of people who were prepared to take their chance as pioneers attempting to settle the vast tracts of lands between the Eastern and Western coasts of the continent. These pioneers provided a booming market for every industrial product ranging from picks and shovels to railroad tracks and steam engines.

By the beginning of the twentieth century the United States was overtaking Europe in industrial production and was emerging as the world's greatest economic power; perhaps inevitably, this rise to ascendancy has been accompanied by almost unremitting warfare. After the War of Independence, there was war with the native American Indians, the Civil war, wars against Britain, Mexico and Spain, and, in the first half of the twentieth century, involvement in both the first and second World Wars. These were followed by a 'Cold War' against the USSR, wars in Korea and Vietnam, and wars in the Middle East.

The country has risen to the pre-eminent position in world affairs without ever having experienced a prolonged period of peace.

"Give me your tired, your poor,
Your huddled masses yearning to breathe free
The wretched refuse of your teeming shore
Send these, the homeless tempest-tossed to me,
I lift my lamp beside the golden door.
The inscription carved on the base of the Statue of Liberty

The American Dream

America remains the only country in the world to have the pursuit of happiness enshrined as an unalienable right in its constitution.

Few people would claim that Americans have been completely successful in their pursuit of happiness, but the fact that it has been a legitimate goal for every successive generation has undoubtedly contributed to the rise in American power and influence around the world.

History and the Art of Government

The constitution of the United States was framed by well-educated and thoughtful people who drew much of their inspiration from the republics of the ancient world in their search for a perfect form of government. In particular many of America's political institutions are modelled upon those of ancient Rome.

The American democracy is not, however, built upon the same foundations of integrity and honour as those which marked the early days of the Roman Republic. Corruption and greed have plagued America's politics from its earliest days with the result that people have become increasingly cynical both about politicians and the process of government. The success of the United States in economic and military terms means that many of its political ideas have been adopted by other countries – and that other countries are now beset by a similar disillusionment with the political process.

To some extent this disillusionment is caused by the way in which people are taught to regard their history – they are told that modern systems of government are superior to anything that has gone before, but they are appalled by the behaviour displayed by their politicians.

A more perceptive study of history teaches us that many different forms of government have been tried by many different societies over many millennia. The aim of every system is to ensure that the best people are placed in the positions in which they can do the most good. No system appears to be able to do this indefinitely and that is why political processes are constantly subject to change and renewal – a change and renewal that can only come about through the efforts of ordinary people working to safeguard basic values such as justice and freedom.

Europe

During the years that America was transforming itself from a collection of agricultural settlements into the world's foremost economic power, European countries continued to struggle against each other for power and influence.

British Empire

Britain in particular found itself in an unusually powerful position. Its geographical isolation protected it from the wars that devastated other European countries, its adoption of the Protestant religion made it independent of the Pope, and therefore free to pursue whatever policies it wished, and it led the world in industrial innovation.

The ruling classes were quick to exploit this combination of factors to vastly increase their personal fortunes. By the judicious use of overwhelmingly superior military resources, Britain was able to set up a system of trade that encircled the globe and caused unprecedented wealth to flow back to the British Isles.

It was not difficult for the people involved in this trade to convince themselves that because it was successful it must be right, and thereby to justify to themselves all the suffering they knew their actions to be causing.

History and Religion

Over the past five hundred years religion has suffered much the same fate as government. It has lost the influence that it once held over everyday life, and many people now see it rather as a source of conflict than an instrument of peace. To make matters worse, religious leaders have condoned and profited from many of the worst events of modern history and do not stand out as particularly virtuous or particularly wise.

A study of history shows that this has not always been the case. There *have* been people in the past whose teachings have had a profound effect upon the people who heard them speak. These teachers stand out as having had an enormous impact upon human affairs, and it is clear that we owe many of our most significant laws, customs, and beliefs to their inspiration. Far more unites these teachers than divides them but somehow their teachings have been used, in the name of religion, to sow hatred and mistrust between different peoples.

Seeing this may not enable us to understand religion but it does show us that it is an area far too important to be ignored. Simply because modern religions fall short of the ideal, it does not follow that the subject matter of the world's great scriptures has lost its validity or that it is less relevant now than it was in the past.

Britain and China

Europe wanted porcelain, silks, and tea from China but had nothing that China wanted in exchange.

The British solution was to grow opium in India, and to sell it in China. The Chinese government tried to solve the problem of opium addiction by closing the ports to British vessels and Britain responded by sending gunboats which reopened the ports and allowed the drug trade to continue. These 'Opium Wars' provide a stark example of the types of activities in which the

Lin Zexu burns opium seized from British merchants

European powers were prepared to engage as they built up their power and influence around the world.

History and Technology

When studying the history of nations and empires, technology appears to play a decisive role in the rise and fall of civilisations – the technology of steam engines and guns enabled Britain to establish an empire that spanned the globe during the nineteenth century, and the world has now fallen under the sway of modern information technology largely controlled by the United States.

A more detailed examination reveals that it is not technology but the way in which it is used that has the most effect upon people's lives. For many years the Chinese possessed technology far more advanced than the rest of the world – they understood the properties of gunpowder, they had printing presses, they had refined techniques of pottery production, etc. – but they did not use it to launch a campaign of conquest. Instead they studied the art of living in harmony with their environment, and they only used their technology when it did not infringe this fundamental goal. The same appears to be true of other ancient civilisations, which managed to prosper for many hundreds of years without harming the land upon which they lived.

The past few decades have seen an acceleration in the development and deployment of new technologies which appear to do little to improve the quality of human life but which definitely pose a threat to the well-being of the environment. An historical perspective suggests that this is not a wise course to follow, and highlights the need for a radically different approach to the way in which new ideas are exploited and developed.

135

Europe in The Twentieth Century

By the start of the twentieth century, British supremacy in European and world affairs was being challenged by Germany.

Instead of learning from the American Civil War, and realising that modern weapons had introduced a new scale of horror into warfare, both countries rushed into a military conflict (First World War 1914-18)

Powered flight developed rapidly during the 1914-18 war as the opposing powers raced against each other to develop the world's first effective air force.

which was enormously costly in human life and which effectively ended European pretensions to Empire building and world dominion.

The war was eventually brought to an end by the intervention of the United States on the side of Britain and France. This marked the emergence of the United States as the world's most powerful country.

Britain and France were not able to give up power gracefully and in the wake of the war imposed humiliating peace terms on the defeated Germany. This created the

---

History and War

It is understandable that historians focus so much of their attention upon wars because war represents the ultimate catastrophe in human affairs. It is an entirely man-made disaster and, in addition to the devastation caused by the conflict itself, it has been responsible for the overwhelming majority of the famines and epidemics that have afflicted people over the years.

Wars occur when people can no longer see each other as fellow human beings, and when they allow themselves to be overwhelmed by feelings of fear, anger and greed.

It is obviously the job of every sane person to do whatever they can to avoid warfare – and this applies particularly to political and religious leaders. One of the biggest assets in this effort is a study of history. History books contain a detailed analysis of the causes of countless wars in the past, and should therefore provide a wise statesman with information that helps him to avoid war in the present – otherwise he is simply repeating mistakes that have already been made before.

A study of history is also useful to ordinary people in that it helps them to put the propaganda and panic that occurs at times of crisis into some sort of historical perspective. This can be surprisingly reassuring.

conditions that allowed Adolf Hitler and the Nazi party to take control of the country; their policies of expansion and racial hatred inevitably led to another war (Second World War 1939-45).

Although this war was principally fought on the Eastern Front – between Germany and Russia – it was once again brought to a conclusion by the intervention of the United States.

After the War

As a result of this war, American policy changed, and it became more involved in world politics. Rightly or wrongly, it identified Soviet Russia as the biggest threat to world peace and stationed forces throughout Europe to

After the 1939-45 war Germany was divided in two, the East was occupied by Russian forces and the West by American. Since reunification in 1990 the Brandenburg Gate in East Berlin has become a symbol of reconciliation.

maintain the peace and to protect it from Russian invasion. Since then, Europe has played something of the same role in relation to the United States as that played by the Greek states within the Roman Empire: it is still culturally significant but it is dependent on the United States for its military security and economic stability.

History and Health

One of the questions that must be of most interest to everyone who studies history is whether people lived longer in the past than they do now and whether or not people used to be more healthy than now.

We are generally led to believe that we are lucky because, thanks to modern civilisation, we now enjoy lower levels of child mortality, less disease, and a greater life expectancy than people who lived in the past – but at the same time we are assailed by information that tells us that many aspects of modern life are bad for the health and that people are not living as long as they used to.

History helps us to clear up these contradictions. Factors that promote long-term good health include a regular supply of clean water, good drains, the ready availability of fresh food, and, above all, the absence of war. There appear to have been civilisations in the course of world history which have supplied these needs and in which the average life expectancy has been at least as high as that enjoyed by people today: for example in the Old Testament three score years and ten (seventy years) is stated as the allotted span of human life.

This is significant because it means that we cannot expect to live long, disease-free lives simply by relying on medical science. Doctors are the first to acknowledge that their ability to prolong human life is relatively insignificant when compared to what people can do for themselves.

The World in the Twenty-First Century

The world in which we are now living has been strongly influenced by the events that have taken place in Europe and North America over the past five hundred years. Much of the world was colonised by competing Europen powers, and when these empires collapsed the vacuum was filled by the commercial power of the United States.

This means that cultural traditions that go back for thousands of years have been swept away, or at least seriously disturbed, over the course of a few generations. For better or for worse, there is now hardly anywhere in the world where people are living in a way that would be recognisable to their grandparents or to their grandparents' grandparents. An historical perspective helps us to understand why change has affected different people in different ways.

China

Prior to European intervention, the Chinese empire had lasted for at least four thousand years. Throughout that time it maintained a more civilised way of life for the Chinese people than the relatively short-lived Roman empire ever did for the people of the West.

Based upon the teachings of Confucius and other ancient sages, Chinese life revolved around the family and the ideal that people in public office should act with integrity and honour. China was self-sufficient, wanting nothing from the outside world but prepared to trade its manufactured goods for precious metals, especially silver.

Throughout this time the Chinese were confident that they were superior to all other peoples on Earth. This belief was not even shaken when they were militarily defeated by invaders from Mongolia and Manchuria, because their conquerors were forced to adopt Chinese customs in order to rule China successfully.

The arrogance and complacency fostered by so many millennia of civilisation and success was shattered by Europeans who had the military power to take what they wanted from China but who had no desire to settle and rule. They made it clear that, from their perspective, China was not the centre of world affairs, but simply a heathen outpost to be exploited for profit. China was not only defeated by Europe but humiliated, and this made Chinese people doubt, for the first time, the inherent superiority of their culture.

> "I am happy because I am a human and not an animal,
> a male and not a female,
> a Chinese and not a barbarian
> and because I live in Luoyang,
> the most wonderful city in the world."
> *Shao Yong, a mathematician living in the 1200s*

Communist Revolution

The last Chinese emperor abdicated early in the twentieth century, and China entered a miserable period of civil wars, Japanese invasion, and foreign exploitation.

Many political factions arose, but it was the Communist party of Mao Zedong that emerged triumphant, and succeeded in reuniting the country in the 1940s. Mao took the least attractive Western philosophy – Marxism/Stalinism – and imposed his own version of it on the Chinese people through a ruthless process of brainwashing, executions and terror campaigns. His policies led to famine and deprivation.

Since his death a measure of pragmatism has returned to Chinese government, and, although the system is nominally still Communist, to an outside observer it now appears to be taking on many of the characteristics of a traditional Chinese dynasty.

Mao Zedong

It is difficult for a student of history to understand how China, with such a long history of civilisation, could have fallen prey so easily to the relatively unsophisticated European powers.

In many areas of life, such as healthcare, medicine, politics and agriculture, Western scientists and researchers are only now beginning to appreciate the value of traditional Chinese techniques and their superiority over modern methods. It may still be that one of the most significant long-term effects of Western intervention will be to bring Chinese culture to the rest of the world, rather than the reverse.

"A tree so big it can fill the span of a man's arms grows from a tiny sprout,
A terrace nine stories high rises from a shovelful of earth,
A journey of a thousand miles starts with one step.
Thus, one of absolute virtue never sets about to do grandiose things and therefore is able to achieve great things."

Tao Teh Ching, Lao Tzu

Russia

Russia is the world's largest country, encompassing some of its most hostile territory, and in times of antiquity it was home to tribes feared by civilised peoples across Europe and Asia. More recently, in the Middle Ages, it formed the core of a feudal empire which slowly expanded until it controlled territory stretching from the Baltic Sea in the West to the Pacific Ocean in the East and from the Arctic Ocean in the North to the Black Sea in the South. For a time it even claimed ownership of part of North America – the area now known as Alaska.

The Bolshevik Revolution 1917

At the beginning of the twentieth century, Russia was still ruled by an autocratic elite who kept the majority of the population in ignorance and servitude. The most vocal and well-organised opposition came from Communist groups, including the Bolshevik party, who used the ideas of Karl Marx to justify their plans for a violent revolution.

Russian involvement in the war of 1914-18 exposed the weaknesses of the government: Russian soldiers found themselves fighting on the front line with no boots, no food and, sometimes, without any weapons. The army suffered defeat after defeat and people lost faith in the traditional belief that the Tsar was God's representative on Earth.

The Tsar was forced to abdicate and, after a period of confusion and anarchy, the Bolshevik party was able to seize power. Its leader, Lenin, believed that he had the right to impose his ideas upon the Russian people – but before he could do so he had to defeat the many elements of Russian society which were opposed to his arbitrary seizure of power. Lenin concluded a humiliating peace treaty with Germany, and fought a bitter civil war against the supporters of the deposed Tsar, the Socialists, and various nationalist movements which sought independence for their own provinces. Once he had gained victory, he instigated a series of purges against those in his own party who criticised the way in which he was using power.

Lenin died in 1924 and power fell into the hands of Joseph Stalin. Stalin paid lip-service to the principles of justice and freedom, which were supposed to be part of the Communist ideal, but in practice he ruthlessly persecuted anyone, or any section of society, that posed a possible threat to himself.

In many ways, the success of the Communist party's bid for power was a tragic accident: the Tsarist government was an anachronism which was bound to fall sooner or later, but it is hard to imagine that any of the rivals for power could have been as disastrous for the Russian people as Lenin's Bolshevik regime. In terms of human misery inflicted by government action, Stalin was the worst ruler that Russia has ever had.

Recommended Books:
War and Peace, Leo Tolstoy: *Tolstoy's novels and writings provide an insight into Russian life prior to the Bolshevik revolution and give a hint of what might have been possible if Russia had not become engulfed in a terrible cycle of war and revolution.*

1939 - 1945 War

In the war of 1939-45 Hitler invaded Russia. At first his armies were welcomed as liberators, but when it became clear that the Nazi party's ideology viewed Russians as potential slaves, people realized that they had no choice but to resist. The resulting war fought on the 'Eastern Front' is the most costly in human life in recorded history.

Although nominally victorious, Russia was left devastated. Stalin was able to ensure his own continuation in power by playing on the people's fear of further invasions and by constantly reiterating his aim of transforming Russia into a world superpower capable of standing up to the United States; the nation's wealth was poured into the maintenance of an enormous army at the expense of everyday essentials such as food and housing.

This led to a 'cold war' with the United States, which involved the two powers vying with each other to gain allies around the world and threatening each other with ever more destructive weapons. Stalin's death in 1953 did not bring the looked-for change, and the 'cold war' was maintained by his successors for another thirty years.

Reform

Mikhail Gorbachev came to power in 1985 and instituted a policy of reform and openness. The main effect of this was to make apparent the inherent weakness of the system of government being maintained by the Communist party: corruption was found to be rife, factories antiquated and inefficient, the nuclear industry in chaos and the armed forces overstaffed and under-supplied.

Independence movements sprang up in Poland, Hungary and Czechoslovakia, Lithuania, Latvia, Estonia, the Ukraine, Belarus, and in the central Asian states with the result that the U.S.S.R. (the Union of Soviet Socialist Republics, formed by Lenin) broke up into its constituent parts.

Russia effectively lost its trial of strength with the United States and has had to settle back into its role of being only one of several significant European powers.

This does, however, open up the possibility that the Russian people will be able to make use of the vast natural wealth of their country and put behind them their recent history of suffering and deprivation.

St Basil's cathedral, Moscow

Middle East

The Middle East is the home of some of the world's oldest civilisations, including the cities of Mesopotamia (now in modern Iraq), ancient Egypt, and the Persian Empire. In more recent times, both Christianity and Islam originated in this part of the world.

From around 800 AD Islam has provided the dominant cultural force in the region and for many years succeeded in making the Middle East one of the wealthiest and most powerful regions of the world.

Events in Europe – the discovery of a sea route to India, the discovery of the New World, the Industrial Revolution – caused the status and power of the Muslim world to go into decline and, by the beginning of the twentieth century, much of the Middle East had become an annex of the Ottoman Empire (Turkey), which was itself struggling to modernise and maintain its standing in European politics.

Wheat is believed to have been first grown in the area now known as Iraq and was the staple crop upon which the Egyptian civilisation was based.

The Ottoman Turks allied themselves with Germany in the 1914-18 war, and after their defeat, their Middle Eastern possessions were divided out between Britain and France – in contravention of promises made to Arab leaders during the course of the war.

Israel

In the arrangement made after the 1914-18 war, the British assumed responsibility for Palestine, but they soon found themselves involved in a situation that they could not control. Large numbers of Jewish refugees arrived from Europe and, after the 1939-45 war, these newcomers became determined to re-establish their biblical homeland. This inevitably brought them into violent conflict with the resident Palestinian population.

The British withdrew in chaos and the Jewish settlers seized control of a large part of the country. Neighbouring Arab states, recently independent, and impoverished by years of colonial rule, were unable to intervene effectively and the modern state of Israel was created. The country now provides a graphic example of how historical grievances can be used to foster alienation and distrust between neighbouring communities, and it would appear that something extraordinary is now required to enable the inhabitants of Israel and Palestine to live at peace with each another.

Oil

Middle Eastern politics are complicated by the fact that the Western, industrialised way of life is now dependent upon oil – oil is needed to run cars and lorries, to fly planes, to fuel tractors, to generate the enormous amounts of electricity that are consumed every day, and to provide the raw material for the chemical industry – and the Middle East is by far the world's largest producer of oil.

People living in developed countries are unable to contemplate any interruption to this flow of oil and, in order to ensure that it continues, pay for it with huge sums of money. This money has a destabilising effect and frequently allows corrupt regimes to hold power in oil-producing countries, against the wishes of the people.

Even though Western countries no longer officially rule over colonies and empires, they still seem able to exercise control over world affairs through the power of economics. This enables them to procure for themselves, more or less on their own terms, those things that they deem to be necessary for their wealth and comfort. Oil appears to be the ultimate example of this phenomenon, and it is hard to see how any form of moderation can be introduced into the present almost frenzied consumption of this finite resource.

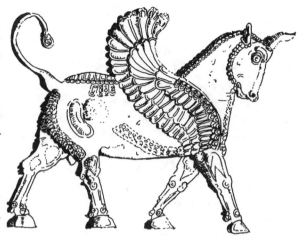

Detail of a winged bull, from a Persian frieze

The different communities of the Middle East share a common cultural heritage, as is demonstrated by this extract from an ancient Babylonian legend in which Uta-napishti (Noah) tells Gilgamesh of his experience in the flood.

Said Uta-napishti to him, to Gilgamesh:
'Let me disclose, O Gilgamesh, a matter most secret,
to you I will tell a mystery of gods.

'The town of Shuruppak, a city well known to you,
which stands on the banks of the river Euphrates:
this city was old – the gods once were in it –
when the great gods decided to send down the Deluge.

' "O man of Shuruppak, son of Ubar-Tutu,
demolish the house, and build a boat!
Abandon wealth, and seek survival!
Spurn property, save life!
Take on board the boat all living things' seed!

' "The boat you will build,
her dimensions all shall be equal:
her length and breadth shall be the same,
cover her with a roof, like the ocean below."

'I understood, and spoke to Ea, my master:
"I obey, O master, what thus you told me.
I understood, and I shall do it."

The Epic of Gilgamesh, Tablet XI

India

Like China, India does not have a tradition of centralised government: for most of recorded history it has been composed of a myriad of independent states, sharing a common religion but with different languages and customs.

Recent Indian history is marked by a series of Muslim invasions which began in the eleventh century and which, for a time, united the whole of India into the Mughal empire. Far from bringing stability, this proved to be a source of disharmony, the effects of which have survived to the present day. Over a period of time, the traditional principalities reasserted themselves, often with a Muslim upper class ruling over a subjugated Hindu population. The situation was complicated by the conversion to Islam of those people who felt most aggrieved by the Hindu caste system, and this created a society deeply divided on religious issues.

The British exploited these divisions by lending military support to one side or the other and thereby secured for themselves the favourable trading rights which allowed them to expand their commercial empire in the Far East. By the middle of the nineteenth century, Britain had gained control over the whole Indian subcontinent.

European interference in local affairs does not appear to have had as demoralising an effect in India as it had in China. When British power started to wane, in the wake of the 1914-18 and 1939-45 wars, Mahatma Gandhi was able to organise non-violent

demonstrations in which people simply refused to co-operate with the British forces. Gandhi's peaceful demonstrations proved to the British that Indian people were neither stupid nor uncivilised and once they lost belief in their own moral superiority their rule collapsed with surprising rapidity. They made a precipitate withdrawal and the country was divided into India, which was predominantly Hindu, and Pakistan, which was Muslim. Despite the best efforts of the new governments, the partition was accompanied by rioting, mass migration, and large-scale loss of life, and to many people ranks as one of the most tragic events in Indian history.

Nevertheless, India has survived the transition to independence and has succeeded in preserving its own culture while at the same time incorporating innovations and technological development from the West.

Akbar (1542-1605), the greatest Mughal emperor: he established a society in which all faiths were treated with respect and his reign marked a brief respite from religious strife.

The Mahabharata is the world's longest work of literature, and one of its oldest. It still has a powerful influence on Indian life and culture.
In this extract, the five heroic brothers, about whom the story revolves – Yudhishthira, Bhima, Arjuna, Sahadeva, and Nakula – are being instructed in the art of warfare by their teacher, Drona:

"One day Drona, desirous of testing the comparative excellence of all his pupils in the use of arms, collected them all together after their education had been completed. And before assembling them together, he had caused an artificial bird, as the would-be aim, to be placed on the top of a neighbouring tree. And when they were all together, Drona said unto them.

'Take up your bows quickly and stand here aiming at that bird on the tree, with arrrows fixed on your bowstrings; shoot and cut off the bird's head, as soon as I give the order. I shall give each of you a turn, one by one my children.'

...Then Drona, that foremost of all Angira's sons, first addressed Yudhishthira saying, 'O irrepressible one, aim with thy arrow and shoot as soon as I give the order. Yudhishthira took up the bow first, as desired by his preceptor, and stood aiming at the bird. But Drona in an instant, addressing the prince standing with bow in hand said, 'Behold, O prince, that bird on top of the tree.'

Yudhishthira replied unto his preceptor saying, 'I do.' But the next instant Drona again asked him, 'What does thou see now, O prince? Seest thou the tree, myself or thy brothers?'

Yudhishthira answered, 'I see the tree, myself, my brothers, and the bird.'

Drona repeated his question, but was answered as often in the same words. Drona then, vexed with Yudhishthira, reproachingly said, 'Stand thou apart. It is not for thee to strike the aim.'

Then Drona repeated the experiment...but the answer in every case was the same as Yudhishthira's, viz, 'We behold the tree, thyself, our fellow pupils, and the bird.'

...When everyone had failed, Drona smilingly called Arjuna, and said unto him, 'By thee the aim must be shot; therefore turn thy eyes to it. Thou must let fly the arrow as soon as I give the order.'

Thus addressed, Arjuna stood aiming at the bird as desired by his preceptor with his bow bent. An instant after, Drona asked him as in the case of the others,

'Seest thou, O Arjuna, the bird there, the tree, and myself?'

Arjuna replied, 'I see the bird only, but not the tree or thyself.'

Then the irrepressible Drona, well pleased with Arjuna, the instant after, again said unto that mighty car-warrior, 'If thou seest the vulture, then describe it to me.'

Arjuna said, 'I see only the head of the vulture, not its body.'

At these words of Arjuna, the hair of Drona's body stood on end from delight. He then said to Partha (Arjuna) 'Shoot.' And the latter instantly let fly his arrow, and with his sharp shaft speedily struck off the head of the vulture on the tree and brought it down to the ground."

From the Mahabharata, translated by Kisari Mohan Ganguli

Africa

North Africa

North Africa was part of the Roman Empire and afterwards became absorbed into the world of Islam. It fell victim to European colonialism in the nineteenth century, and although now politically independent, it is still economically dependent on its European neighbours.

Even though North Africa has always been part of the Mediterranean world, extensive trans-Saharan trading links have ensured that it is connected to the rest of Africa – and also ensured that Africa was connected to the outside world.

West Africa

Prior to the eighteenth century, West African cities were situated inland and all trade was conducted across the Sahara desert. The arrival of European ships brought about an end to this way of life: centres of population moved to the coast and local rulers became involved in the infamous transatlantic slave trade.

Modern West Africa does not appear to have been able to escape from the legacy of European colonial rule. The region is beset by religious and political divisions that have made it impossible for its people to enjoy its wealth and fertility in peace and security.

Idia, mother of King Oba Esigic.
West Africa is an ancient centre of civilisation and culture. The bronze
'Benin Heads' originate from an area which is now part of Nigeria.

East Africa

East Africa has a diverse culture, made up of traditional African elements, combined with strong Arabic, Portuguese and British influences dating back to the

Swahili Proverbs:

Nimekula asali udogoni, utamu ungali gegoni. I ate honey in my childhood, and its sweetness is still in my tooth.

Mtoto umleavyo ndivyo akuavyo. As you bring up a child, so he will be.

Mstahimilivu hula mbivu. A patient man will eat ripe fruits.

Akili ni mali. Ability is wealth.

Aisifuye mvua imemnyea. He who praises rain has been rained on.

region's colonial past. There has also been a long history of trade with India which has had an effect upon the region's languages and customs.

South Africa

The temperate climate of Southern Africa made it the one area of Africa attractive to European settlers. Dutch Protestants emigrated to South Africa where they established farms and homes. World politics brought their descendants, the 'Boers', into conflict with the British Empire which wanted to gain a monopoly on South African gold and diamonds, and protect the major routes to India.

After the Boer Wars, South Africa became a self-governing dominion of the British Empire but local white politicians had a strong prejudice against the native population and when the country gained full independence, they instituted a system of apartheid that segregated black people from white people. The system effectively guaranteed wealth and comfort for the white population and poverty and deprivation for the people of other races.

Nelson Mandela

Resistance to the apartheid came to centre around one man – Nelson Mandela – a radical lawyer and leading black politician who had been convicted of treason in 1964 and sentenced to life imprisonment, possibly only escaping the death penalty because of the fear that it might provoke a bloody uprising. The government tried to make the world forget about his existence and allowed him to receive neither visits nor letters while they cemented their policies of racial discrimination.

For many years the South African regime had the tacit support of the United States and Europe but gradually the opprobrium of being the world's most racist regime began to stick, and the white population of South Africa found itself isolated from the rest of the world and facing increasing resistance at home.

At this point rumours started to circulate that Nelson Mandela was ill and might not have long to live. Suddenly a man who had spent the past twenty-five years in a high security prison became the most powerful person in the country. The government realised that if he were to die in captivity, the country could be overwhelmed by a wave of riots and bloodshed.

Nelson Mandela refused to negotiate conditions for his release and in a remarkable turn around of events, government ministers were forced to pay court to him in his prison cell. He walked free from gaol on his own terms and became president of South Africa four years later in 1994.

Instead of the predictable programme of revenge, Nelson Mandela's government sought reconciliation between the different racial groups of South Africa. The possibility of amnesty was extended to everyone who had committed political crimes in the apartheid era and Nelson Mandela demonstrated his own commitment to democratic government by voluntarily relinquishing power at the end of his term of office.

South America

Spanish colonialists destroyed the ancient civilisations of South and Central America and in their place established colonial governments modelled upon European feudal society: the local population was reduced to a state of slavery and when it became depleted by disease, more slaves were purchased from Africa.

Vast amounts of gold and silver were plundered from the ancient cities of the region and shipped back to Europe, where they were used to finance wars and prop up inefficient and repressive regimes.

Manco Capac, the legendary founder of the Inca dynasty.

Independence

The Napoleonic wars of Europe, at the beginning of the nineteenth century, seriously disrupted the administration of the Spanish and Portuguese South American colonies and this encouraged the ruling elites in these colonies to declare independence.

Rather than bringing better conditions to the local population, independence only served to preserve unscrupulous and corrupt dictators in power and isolated the region from the modest freedoms that were being won by people in Europe.

Problems were exacerbated by the power enjoyed by the Catholic Church in the region. The Church was very slow to recognise the benefit of education and, up until relatively recently, was happy to see most of its adherents kept in a state of illiteracy, dependent upon the local priest for anything that involved reading and writing.

The people in South America are still struggling to come to terms with this legacy of poor education and bad government, and the task has been made even more difficult by the presence of their overwhelmingly powerful neighbour, the United States. American business has long viewed South America as a region to be exploited for its raw materials and cash crops.

Political and economic instability continue to make life precarious for the majority of South Americans, but it is a region blessed with abundant natural resources and is relatively free from the bitter religious and ethnic disputes that scar the lives of people living in so many other parts of the world.

Japan

Japan's separation from the mainland resulted in it developing independently from its largest neighbour, China, and although there was a certain amount of cultural exchange, relationships between the two countries have usually been marked by mistrust and hostility. Japan proved readier than China to adopt new, Western ideas and underwent a process of industrialisation during the nineteenth century. It exploited the chaos resulting from the collapse of the Chinese empire and by the start of the 1939-45 war had occupied large areas of mainland China – often behaving more ruthlessly than the European colonialists at their worst.

Jealous of British and French influence in the Far East, Japan allied itself with Adolf Hitler in the 1939-45 war. Japanese forces displaced Britain from all its Far Eastern colonial possessions and launched a pre-emptive strike against the American fleet at Pearl Harbour in Hawaii, which precipitated American entry into the war. At first, this did not check Japanese military successes: America lost control of its bases in the Philippines and the Pacific islands and it appeared that even Australia might be under threat.

Japan developed a unique cultural tradition over thousands of years of stable government.

However, when the full weight of the American economy was directed towards military production, the Japanese forces found that they were overstretched and that they had won an empire they could not hold.

America recaptured its lost bases island by island, and after the surrender of Germany, was able to concentrate all its resources on the war against Japan. An unprecedented invasion of Japan by British and American troops seemed inevitable, even though it was expected to result in enormous loss of life.

Instead of launching the invasion, the American president decided to use a new weapon: the atomic bomb. Two bombs were dropped, one on Hiroshima and one on Nagasaki, both of which were cities full of ordinary men, women and children. Japan surrendered unconditionally and was de-armed. Since the war, Japan has ceased to be involved in military activities.

People are still struggling to come to terms with these events: it was immediately apparent that the widespread use of nuclear weapons would inevitably result in the end of civilisation, and possibly the end of life on the planet, but whether this can best be avoided by maintaining a 'balance of power' between states armed with nuclear weapons, or by the destruction of all such weapons, is still the subject of fierce debate.

History and the Family

History tends to focus upon wars, battles and politics, but normal human life does not revolve around these things: if it did there would soon be no people left to recount anything that took place in the past. Genuine success cannot be measured by the rank that someone has achieved in the army, the amount of money they have amassed, or the number of honours that they have been awarded.

In terms of history, a successful human being is one who leaves the world a better place than they found it and although this is not something that can be said about many of the 'great' historical figures it does apply to huge numbers of 'ordinary' people who have enabled human societies to grow and prosper over the millennia.

Ordinary activities such as housework are now commonly regarded as second-rate and synonymous with failure and drudgery. This is not logical: bringing up children, caring for old people, cooking, cleaning, and growing food are the things that allow human life to continue from one generation to the next. A civilised society values these activities above everything else and organises itself so that the majority of people are able to pass their lives in this way.

The history of Western society is firstly one of warfare, in which the strongest and most aggressive elements in society are able to win power for themselves, and, more recently, materialism, in which the people with the most money are most highly regarded. Neither of these is conducive to family life, and it is not surprising that the care of the elderly, the care of the sick and, above all, the care for and education of the young has fallen into neglect.

A clearer understanding of history might help young people to see that raising a family is one of the most challenging and most important of all activities, and the idea that it should take second place behind money or a career, simply does not make sense.

Conclusion

Everyone has a choice about what they learn from history. There have been many examples of human greed, stupidity and cruelty and if one focussed exclusively upon these, one could be excused for thinking that there was no hope for the human race, but there have also been societies in which honesty and integrity have been paramount and there have been people who have succeeded against great odds in improving the world in which they have lived, and if one chooses to take these as one's inspiration then anything seems possible.

Moreover, an objective study of history shows that whereas the ancient world throws up many examples of both the best and the worst of human nature, the past few hundred years provide very few examples of anything of which people can be truly proud. Understanding this fact helps to prevent one from feeling too superior to people who lived in ancient times and opens up the possibility of learning from them, rather than simply viewing their lives and work as an interesting curiosity.

Educational Resources

Teachers often fail to recognise that people learn from everything in their environment and from everything that happens to them. This means that it is far more important for someone to have a rich environment in which to live and work, than to be provided with a set curriculum and a set of coursebooks. Failure to acknowledge this fact, over a long period of time, has led to schools providing a very poor environment in which to learn.

The ideal situation is one in which a young person has constant access to older people with whom they can talk things over; there should be plenty of books around that they can consult; they should be able to spend large parts of the day outside, learning from Nature; and they should have lots of materials to hand with which they can paint, draw and make things. There should be a well-stocked kitchen, so that they can cook; and a garden, so that they can grow fruit and vegetables. If, in addition to all this, someone has the use of a television and a computer, then they are pretty well set up to learn in a balanced and well-coordinated way.

It is the need for a proper balance in the resources available that is often overlooked when people discuss what is good and what is not good for children: neither television nor computer games are necessarily bad when they take up only a small part of a full and active life, and the same could be said for school. On the other hand, things such as reading, writing, and studying from books, which are generally worthwhile, can lose their value when not balanced by other activities.

People who are lucky enough to grow up in a secure home, surrounded by a variety of interesting and stimulating things, will turn any new experience to their advantage and will learn from it. This is not simply a question of money: material possessions on their own cannot create a good learning environment – the presence of caring adults, access to the world of Nature and having time to pursue your own interests are the things that make the difference.

Continued from page 25

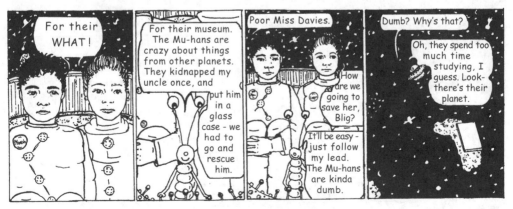

People

People have always been, and always will be, the most important learning resource. In essence, education *is* one generation passing on to the next generation the things that they have learnt over the course of their lives.

At one time, all of this transfer of information was done orally, and even though we now have books and computers, people still learn most from the interaction that takes place directly between one person and another.

This is not simply about learning from what someone is telling you, it is about learning from how they say it, how they behave, the emotions they express, the degree of certainty they have, the way they look while they are talking – it is a myriad of indefinable things that could never be contained in a book or on a computer screen. Human communication is a non-stop, three-dimensional, multi-sense learning experience that stretches everyone involved to the limit.

This is the learning resource that is most undervalued and which goes almost unrecognised in our society. For most adults, it comes as a complete surprise that they are themselves a source of almost endless wonder to children and young people. The things that they have done, stories from their childhood, people they have known, places they have been to – these are all links to another age, as far as a young person is concerned, and they cannot help but be interested by them.

A lack of meaningful communication with adults is the greatest sensory deprivation that can be imposed upon a child, because it cuts them off from all the knowledge that they need in order to make sense of their lives.

No amount of books, televisions, computers, or technological wizardry can compensate for proper human communication: above everything else, people need other people if they are to develop into well-balanced and successful adults.

> "Penye wazee haliharibiki neno."
>
> "Where there are old people, nothing goes wrong."
>
> *Swahili Proverb*

Parents

The most significant people in a young person's life are their parents. Obviously, everyone wants to be a perfect parent, but sometimes it is our very ideas about how a parent ought to behave that cause the most problems.

Probably the most important attribute of a good parent is being able to change when you realise that you are making mistakes.

Some points that my own experiences have taught me to be important include:

- **Not Taking Oneself Too Seriously** – It is easy to fall into the trap of thinking that you always have to be right and have an answer to every question. In the long run, all this achieves is that you make yourself appear ridiculous to your own children.

- **Listening to One's Children** – Parents sometimes let their ideas about how things ought to be prevent them from seeing how things actually are. If you make a point of listening to your children – and taking what they say as seriously as if you were saying it yourself – you stay in touch with what is really happening to them in their lives.

- **Making Time to Be With One's Children** – The difference between being a good parent and not being a good parent may come down to the amount of time that a parent actually spends with their child. Children grow up quickly and spending time with them is not something that can be put off till later.

- **Being Honest** – Honesty is a very engaging quality; for instance, it is better to explain to your children the anxieties that you have about them following a particular course of action than to simply tell them that they aren't allowed to do it.

- **Being Willing to Learn** – You don't have to stop learning just because you have grown up. You can learn things just as readily as your children can, and when *you* learn, it makes it easier for them to learn as well.

- **Doing Plenty of Cooking** – Cooking is insufficiently valued as one of the main attributes of a good parent. It is no coincidence that many people talk about their mother's cooking throughout their lives, and even though this may seem too simple to be true, children and young people who are fed well are more content and have a more positive outlook on life, than those who are not.

Teachers

A good teacher has the potential to change the course of a young person's life.

Good Teachers: One of the chief attributes of a good teacher is that they like people; it is not possible to teach unless you have some empathy with the person being taught, and a good teacher always cares about their pupils. This is what creates the conditions in which learning can take place.

A good teacher also has enthusiasm for their subject. Teaching is essentially a process in which the teacher communicates this enthusiasm to the pupil.

Good teachers are not confined to schools and do not necessarily have any qualifications. Anyone can be a good teacher: friends, relatives, neighbours, the local piano teacher, the Girl Guide leader, a local craftsman, an employer – anyone who takes an interest and who is keen to communicate something that they have learnt.

Bad Teachers: Bad teachers are not really teachers at all – they are people doing a job that they don't enjoy.

Unfortunately, this applies to the majority of school teachers who are not free to teach their subject the way that they would like to teach it and therefore have no enthusiasm for what they are doing.

Bad teachers develop bad habits – they become bullies – with the result that instead of creating an interest in their subject, they put their students off.

This is one of the disservices that schools perform: they confine young people to classrooms with people who have lost faith in what they are doing, thereby restricting the amount of time that they can spend in the wider world which is full of people who could inspire them in so many ways about so many things.

Friends

Most people have been to school, and when they remember the experience the only good thing that comes to mind is the friends that they made there. This can lead people to think that friends are an important part of the educational process – which is illogical.

If you meet people at school who you like and who you get on with then you have been lucky, and perhaps it provides a good reason for going to school – but it doesn't mean that you are going to get an education there.

Another side to school friendships is that you have little choice but to try to make friends with people in your own class, even if you don't like them. This means that if they all smoke, take drugs, drink alcohol and commit crimes, then you have to as well. This isn't having friends.

It might be helpful to draw a wider definition of friendship. Why should young people only have friends who are the same age as themselves? Why shouldn't they be able to have friends of all different ages and different sections of society?

If the idea is that one learns about 'growing up' with one's friends, then how much better if at least some of one's friends were older and able to give a wider perspective on the whole process. There is no reason why young people shouldn't be friends with their parents, their grandparents, their teachers and their neighbours as well as with people of their own age. It cannot be good for young people if the only people with whom they can talk about important issues are their classmates – in such circumstances it is almost inevitable that they will come to wrong conclusions, make disastrous mistakes, and be taken in by the most unscrupulous elements of society. A system that fails to make all the experience gained by previous generations fully available to the young is a very bad system indeed.

This is another disservice that schools perform: they disrupt the natural balance, and make young people put too much emphasis on making friendships with people of their own age at the expense of making friends with people in general.

> "The friends thou hast, and their adoption tried,
> Grapple them to thy soul with hoops of steel;
> But do not dull thy palm with entertainment of
> each new-hatched, unfledg'd comrade."
>
> *Shakespeare, Hamlet, Act I, Scene III*

155

Books

After people, books are still the best source of information and ideas. They are as important now as they were before the onset of the technological revolution, and an understanding of the true value of books is vital to a good education.

- **Books at School** – People do not have proper access to books at school, and even if they did, they would not have time to use them – the school day is too regimented.
- **Books in the Library** – Public libraries give everyone access to a wide range of books and are an invaluable public service. They provide a good starting point for anyone who wants to improve their own education but they do have one serious drawback – when you find a really good book, you have to give it back. A good book is not something that you read once and then never look at again, it is something that you return to many times. You cannot do this with library books. This means that a library does not replace the need to buy books for yourself – it introduces you to books that, if possible, you then go out and buy.
- **Books in the Home** – It is the books in your home that will have the biggest effect upon your education because they are there whenever you want them. Books that you grow up with become absorbed into your personality.

It *is* a privilege to be surrounded by well-stocked bookshelves but, ultimately, it is the quality of the student that determines how much use is made of the available material.

History is full of people who have grown up in relative poverty and who have had access to only one or two books, but they have taught themselves to read, have mastered the contents of these books and have gone on to become both learned and wise. There is no reason why you should end up with an inferior education if you do not have enough money to buy lots of books: the important thing is to make the best possible use of the books that you do have.

A Home Library

These are the sorts of books that, if possible, your home should contain.

- **Reference Books** – Dictionary, thesaurus, world atlas, road maps, books of facts and encyclopaedias (second-hand encyclopaedias are often very inexpensive, and although they are out of date on topical questions, they still contain masses of useful pictures and information).

- **Wildlife Guides** – Identification guides for flowers, trees, birds, mushrooms, mosses, insects, life on the seashore etc.

- **Literature** – Generally, if a work of literature is worth reading once, it is worth reading again. It is therefore better to buy these books rather than borrow them.

- **History** – The more good history books you have, the better.

- **Gardening** – You cannot learn to garden from a book, but the more gardening books you have, the more likely you are to come across ideas and tips that are helpful in your own garden.

- **Recipe Books** – Lots of recipe books means lots of recipes which means that you will never run out of ideas of things to cook.

- **Art Books** – Collect books that contain good-quality reproductions of old masterpieces: you can use them for copying from and also for studying the techniques of the best painters. Books about how to use different media – oils, watercolours, pen and ink, pastels, etc. – are also useful.

- **Craft Books** – Embroidery, sewing, knitting patterns, woodworking, toy-making, kite making, origami, building, etc. etc. The more books you have, the more things you can do.

- **Languages** – Simple language courses, dictionaries, phrase books, and foreign language literature.

Buying Books

Before you become serious about books, it is easy to imagine that you can just go down to the local bookshop and find a book on any subject that you want. The reality is not so simple: you have to be very determined and very persistent in order to build up a good collection of books.

The Modern Book Trade

The first thing to understand is that the modern book trade is not about good books, it is simply about making money. This means that the majority of books in the shops have little real value. They are designed to have a short-term appeal linked to television personalities, sports stars and celebrities. They are often packaged so that they look attractive but they have no serious content – and this applies particularly to books marketed to young people.

So-called educational books are amongst the worst offenders. Any book written with a particular course or examination in mind can be guaranteed to be neither interesting nor factually correct. Very few academic books contain anything that has not already been covered, much more intelligently, in works that have been around for hundreds of years.

This huge volume of really bad books makes the pursuit of knowledge at least as difficult now as it was in former times when people were not faced with a surplus but with a shortage of printed material.

It is no longer sufficient to have enough money to buy a new book, one has to have the discrimination to avoid spending the money on books that turn out to be of no use at all.

Sometimes, however, in spite of itself, the system does throw up a book that is inspired, intelligent, well-crafted, beautiful, witty or thought-provoking and that is what makes bookshops enjoyable – searching out the good books hidden amongst all the others.

Second-Hand Books

Once you become a connoisseur of good books, you will find that you start to gravitate towards second-hand book shops and to any stalls selling second-hand books that you can find.

The sometimes dull appearance of a collection of second-hand books can disguise their many advantages:

- **They are Cheaper** – Providing you don't buy limited editions or antiquarian books, second-hand books are considerably cheaper than new books.
- **They are Better Quality** – Second-hand copies of classic novels, history books, etc., tend to be printed on better-quality paper and to have a better binding than affordable modern editions. This is because nowadays marketing and distribution costs take up a disproportionate amount of the cover price of a book, while in the past, production costs took priority.
- **They are More Interesting** – When you buy an old edition of a book, you have the added advantage that the introduction, the footnotes, the illustrations, etc. date from the period in which the book was printed. Sometimes these can be as interesting as the text of the book itself, because they give an insight into the way things were viewed in the past.
- **They are Better Books** – Educational standards were much higher fifty years ago than they are today and this is reflected in the books that have survived from that time. One is more likely to find foreign language literature, classical literature, good collections of poetry, intelligent history books, etc., in a second-hand book shop than in any collection of new books.
- **They Sell Books that are now Out of Print** – Books regularly go out of print. Publishers can only afford to keep a certain number of titles in stock at any particular time and the fact that a book goes out of print does not necessarily mean that it is not a good book. The stock of a second-hand book shop tends to reflect the relative popularity of books over the past few decades and gives you a chance to buy titles that were popular for a while but are now out of print. Some of these books are well worth reading.

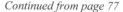

Continued from page 77

Money

People worry that if they do not have enough money their children's education will suffer, but education is not a commodity, and money, on its own, cannot purchase learning. When used unwisely, money can even do more harm than good.

> "In teaching there should be no class distinctions."
>
> *Confucius, The Analects*

Using Money Wisely

Having money can allow you to spend more time with your children; it can enable you to select a good school (if you can find one); to buy lots of good books; to live in a nice house with a big garden; to buy musical instruments and to pay good teachers to give your children private lessons.

It is possible for rich children with wise parents to have a good education, but, in practice, this proves to be the exception rather than the rule.

Using Money Badly

Most people who have money get it by working hard. This work usually takes them away from the home and means that they cannot spend as much time with their children as they would like. When this happens it is all too easy for a gulf to open between parents and children, even though they are living in the same house. Parents who find themselves in this situation sometimes try to use their money to compensate for the lack of attention that they give their children.

Instead of helping, this tends to make the children feel guilty and confused: they think that they ought to be grateful for all the things that are being bought for them, but feel just as dissatisfied as ever. Unless steps are taken to remedy the situation, (which probably involves parents making more time to be with their children) it can deteriorate into mutual recrimination with parents blaming the children and children blaming the parents for a breakdown in communication.

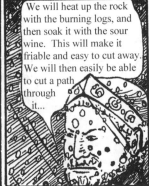

Not Having Money

Thankfully, not many people in Europe and America live in real poverty – whatever obstacles we do have to face, not many of us are caught up in a daily struggle against cold and hunger, and nearly all of us have a roof over our heads.

Thus the poverty that we suffer is relative poverty, compared to the material well-being of others. Being poor in this way does not inevitably lead to a lack of education. On the contrary, many of the best writers, artists, scientists and scholars have come from very humble origins. Some things are more important than others, and it is within the scope of most people to provide their children with the most important things for most of the time. If this means occasionally giving up the less important things, then it should be worth it.

The most important things are a home to live in, good food, time spent together, freedom to experience the world of Nature and some good books. Children that have all of these could never be considered disadvantaged. They will grow up to be as well balanced and successful as anyone else.

Growing up in a loving home but without much money can even have advantages. It teaches a child to understand the value of money and how to get the most out of that which they have. They learn to be resourceful and start looking for ways to make money for themselves from a younger age.

Making Compromises for Money

Most of us are brought up to believe that you have to make compromises in order to earn money. This attitude is severely challenged when one becomes a parent: the compromises that one accepts for oneself are harder to accept when they mean that you are not able to care for your child properly. Becoming a parent causes many people to re-evaluate how they lead their lives and what they are prepared to do in order to make a living.

How a parent chooses to live is the most powerful lesson that they teach their children. Children know whether or not their parents are happy and this is far more important to them than knowing that their parents are rich.

Schools

Schools ought to be one of the best educational resources available. The basic idea of a school is so good – a well-financed institution, staffed by specially-trained academics who are dedicated to imparting knowledge to young people, housed in a building that contains all the latest specialist equipment and resources. It should be a dream come true for young people in search of knowledge and training.

It is hard to see how it has all gone so badly wrong and why, in the majority of cases, young people can learn more by not going to school than they can by going.

The underlying problem with most schools is that they have allowed themselves to become impersonal. Small schools do better than big schools and schools do well when teachers and pupils have a good relationship with each other. Some private schools are better than publicly-funded schools because the teaching staff are directly responsible to their pupils' parents instead of to a large bureaucracy.

Perhaps some young people do derive benefits from going to school, but nowadays it is naïve, and almost irresponsible, for a parent to think that a school can take care of all their child's needs – and this is a sentiment with which even the majority of schoolteachers would agree.

Schools would be much more effective if they could be radically changed to meet the needs of changing times: compulsory schooling could be abandoned; exams could be forgotten; young people could be free to come and go as they pleased; and everything to do with education could be taken out of political control. Simple changes of this sort would make secondary schools much more pleasant to work in and much more pleasant to attend.

If teachers were allowed to devise their own courses, the best ones would be well attended and the bad ones would have no students at all. This would be more in keeping with the true spirit of education and would introduce an element of automatic self-regulation into the school system, which would benefit everyone involved.

However, until such reforms are implemented, parents and young people have little choice but to accept that modern schools are not a useful educational resource.

It is an excellent path our men have built – even the elephant can get down.

Italy at last! The grass is green again.

Praise be to Zeus!

We have finally reached Italy, my prayers have been answered. Before the year is out I shall be dining in Rome!

In fact Hannibal lost two thirds of his army in the Alps, and all but one of the elephants. Despite this loss he defeated the Romans in numerous battles, and came near to capturing Rome herself. But he failed to follow up his advantages, and after 15 years of fruitless fighting was compelled to return to Carthage. He was there finally defeated at Zama by the Roman general, Scipio Africanus.

THE END

The Garden

A garden is an educational resource of almost unlimited potential. There is a fundamental difference between learning about things from books, and seeing them for yourself. That is not to say that there is anything wrong with book learning but it is important that there be the correct balance between theory and practice. For the vast majority of children growing up in industrial countries the balance has been tipped too far in favour of book-based learning, and, through no fault of their own, they lack the real, hands-on experience that would enable them to make sense of their education.

A garden can go a long way to redressing the balance, because it allows you to:

- Experience Nature at first hand.
- Become familiar with the plants that grow in the area.
- See the effects of the changing seasons.
- See the impact that man can have on his environment.
- Appreciate the difference between working *with* Nature and *against* Nature.
- Experience how much work is involved in the growing of top-quality food.
- Taste food the way it ought to taste – straight from the ground.
- Experience at first hand how plants convert air, water and sunlight into actual matter.
- Recognise the local bird life.
- Grow flowers.
- Grow herbs.
- Plant and look after trees.
- Experience beauty in the way that can only be created by Nature itself.

Looking after a garden is better than any science lesson, and it is better than any number of lectures about good food and a healthy lifestyle. It is also a good antidote to things like computer games and television which prey upon the boredom experienced by young people when they are trapped in a modern home with nothing to do.

Not everyone has a garden but it is worth going to considerable lengths to try to find an allotment or a patch of ground on which you can work. Gardening is probably the best antidote to the ills of the modern education system.

This is nice and fresh!

The Kitchen

As with the garden, people do not look upon their kitchens as being a major educational resource – but in reality people could learn far more about a whole range of subjects in a kitchen than they ever could in a classroom, no matter how good the teachers or the facilities available.

For example, the use of weights and measures in cooking provides a direct and practical introduction to mathematics – by following recipes, young people are able to learn how to use both the metric and the imperial system, and they can learn about fractions, decimals, ratios, and centigrade and Fahrenheit scales of temperature. Cooking food also gives a much better understanding of chemistry than can be achieved in a laboratory; it provides children with an intuitive understanding of the effect of heat, it teaches them how to combine ingredients to achieve a desired result, it introduces them to the action of yeast, the action of baking powder and the preserving effects of vinegar, sugar, and freezing, amongst a range of other things.

Cooking also teaches people to appreciate the difference between good and bad food. Schools are able to provide young people with information about calories, food additives, balanced diets, etc., but if, at the end of a school day, someone is feeling tired, frustrated, or dissatisfied they will still go out and buy themselves a packet of crisps and a fizzy drink. Someone who has spent their afternoon in the kitchen cooking with fresh ingredients is not subject to the same temptations.

Furthermore, cooking is not a skill that can be acquired overnight; it is something that takes years of practice to perfect, and it is difficult to see any good reason for people not starting to acquire it when they are young.

The fact that many children spend twelve or more years in the school system and

at the end of it are not able to cook, is a more severe indictment of the system than people care to acknowledge. Exam passes and qualifications become meaningless if they are not accompanied by the skills that have been passed down from generation to generation. Of these skills, cooking must be considered to be amongst the most important.

Computers

Computers are not essential to education – people have been educating themselves to the highest standards, without the aid of computers, for thousands of years – but if you can afford one, they do add an extra dimension to the work that you can do in the home.

Computers as an educational resource:

- **As a source of information**
    - **CD ROMs:** Encyclopaedias on CD ROMs contain all the information that used to take up a dozen large volumes of print. The information is not as accessible on a screen as it is in a book, but it is much more affordable.
    - **The Internet:** The internet can be a very useful resource for an independently-motivated person, studying at home. Features that are particularly useful are the large number of historical documents that can be accessed online; the ease with which you can locate pictures of people, places and things; the fact that you can download copies of plays and short pieces of literature; access to news from different areas of the world; foreign language sites; recipes; etc.
- **As a Tool** – A computer lets you do things that at one time would have required expensive, specialist equipment. Printing, word processing, image editing, designing publications, video editing, preparing web pages, etc. can all be done on an ordinary computer. This book has been written, designed and prepared for press on a home computer.
- **As a Self-Teaching Aid** – The best way to learn about computers is to use them. The rapid development in technology has a constant levelling effect on the world of work and this means that people who have been in employment for many years, or who have well-established businesses, can easily find themselves being overtaken by a young person, working from home, who has grasped the implications of a new piece of technology better than they have.

Free Time

Free time is of fundamental importance to education. People learn, they are not taught, and in order to learn they need to have space and time to themselves.

Some young people have very little free time. Every day is taken up by travelling to school, being at school, travelling home and doing their homework. At weekends, they are too tired for academic or creative interests and consequently, they learn hardly anything at all – especially during term times.

Some of the pressure placed on young people's time is unnecessary:

- **Homework** – Homework does not make sense. If teachers think that children can do the work at home, then why make them go to school at all? People who go to work don't have homework to do when they get home – and they are being paid for what they do. Everybody needs a break, even from good things: if things are going well at school, it's good to have a break from them in the evenings, but if things are going badly, then you *definitely* need a break in the evenings. There is no way in which homework can be justified; everyone has the right to use their free time in whichever way they choose and neither teachers nor parents should be allowed to take that right away from young people.

- **After School Activities, Clubs, Extra Lessons** – Many of the activities arranged for young people are very good in themselves but become oppressive when taken in conjunction with an onerous school timetable. Children who don't go to school can enrol in as many different activities as they want and still have plenty of time to themselves, but children who do go to school need to guard their free time more carefully.

Free time is being at home, not feeling exhausted by all the things that you have been made to do, and being free to decide what you want to do for yourself –

painting, drawing, gardening, cooking, reading, writing, making something or simply doing nothing at all.

Television

Television comes pretty low on the list of useful educational resources. It is possible to argue a case for television being a source of entertainment but its educational potential has always been exaggerated.

Maybe it can be used as a ball

I don't think so Judith, there is an intelligent-looking man behind that glass – perhaps he would like to chat!

Part of the reason why people have become so dependent on television is that modern living conditions are so barren. If someone is cooped up inside a house with no one to talk to and nothing to do, then the television represents the most interesting thing in their environment and it makes sense for them to watch it, but this is not the same as saying that they enjoy watching television or that it has any real intrinsic value.

Part of the problem is probably due to the nature of television itself: watching it is a passive process; it doesn't allow any interactivity, it goes at its own pace and you cannot slow it down or speed it up. This is very different from a book, which you can read at your own convenience, and carry round with you. The book has to adapt to your agenda, but when you watch television you have to adapt to its agenda. Given that learning is an active process in which the student has to play the leading role, the television is bound to be a poor teacher.

It is of course a mistake to try to make young people watch less television: people should be allowed to do what they want to do, providing it does no harm to anyone else. If someone watches a lot of television it is because they have nothing better to do or because it provides a good way of switching off from the stress caused by a day at school. When something better is available, television automatically loses its appeal.

This is the ten o'clock news

HELLO, MY NAME IS ANAXAGORAS!! Answer me, answer me, answer me, ANSWER ME!!!

It has no manners. Leave it alone—it doesn't merit our company

Trees

I think that I shall never see

A poem lovely as a tree,

A tree whose hungry mouth is prest

Against the Earth's sweet, flowing breast;

A tree that looks at God all day,

And lifts her leafy arms to pray;

A tree that may in summer wear

A nest of robins in her hair;

Upon whose bosom snow has lain;

Who intimately lives with rain.

Poems are made by fools like me,

But only God can make a tree.

Joyce Kilmer

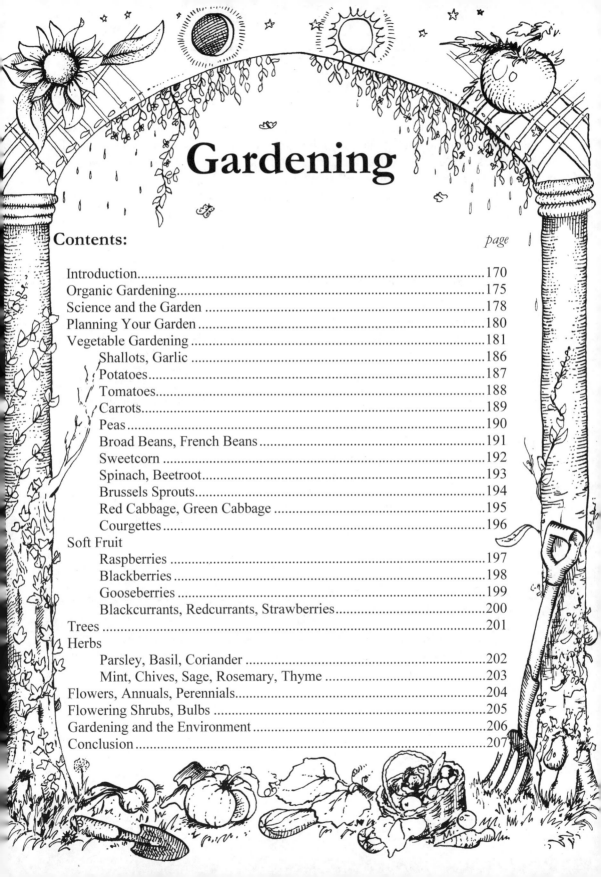

Gardening

Contents: *page*

Gardening

Gardening is sometimes included in the educational curriculum, but it is rarely taken seriously, in fact it has even become something towards which 'less able' students are directed and has to take its place at the periphery of the timetable, in space left free by 'more important' subjects.

This is a misguided approach. In a society in which people have only limited access to the world of Nature, they can learn more from gardening than from anything else:

Art: Nothing that people have created comes close to matching Nature for beauty – the more time you spend surrounded by flowers and trees, and the sun and the sky, the greater will be your appreciation of true beauty. The garden supplies a constant supply of beautiful things to draw and paint.

Growing Your Own Food: Until you make a serious effort to grow a significant amount of your own food, you cannot have any real idea about the processes that are keeping you alive.

Science: Science is about understanding Nature. The only way to understand Nature is to immerse yourself in it. A gardener knows more about Nature than a scientist can ever do.

The Environment: A garden is the world in miniature: treat it well and it will prosper; treat it badly and it will wither. A good gardener understands how the environment should be cared for.

Respect for Others: There is an assumption running through almost every aspect of our education system, that Western people are superior to those people who live simpler lives in other parts of the world. Gardening teaches us to respect the skills of the millions of people who are able to feed themselves and their families simply from the produce of their own gardens.

Health: Gardening is good for your health: it is a good source of exercise; it encourages you to go outside; and it provides you with healthy food.

Enjoyment: Human beings have not been designed to sit indoors. When you have a chance to spend time in the world of Nature, you realise that modern systems of entertainment – television, computer games, etc. – are poor substitutes for the real thing.

> "The goal of life is to live in agreement with nature."
> Zeno

Gardening and School

Everyone has to try to maintain a good balance in their daily life – even if they go to school. Attending school is a stressful activity: pupils spend most of their time indoors and nearly all the time doing things that other people are telling them to do. It is essential that they spend as much of their free time as they can out of doors doing what *they* want to do. Working in their own garden provides the ideal opportunity for this.

No one is capable of working in the way that is expected of school children: it is not possible to be at school all day and to then spend every evening doing homework. Being in the garden is one of the best ways of putting everything to do with school out of one's mind and re-establishing mental equilibrium.

Gardening and Young People

For one reason or another, it is now some time since gardening has been seen as either fashionable or radical by young people. It is an activity, and a cause, that has been increasingly ignored by successive generations, to the point that it is now often regarded as the exclusive preserve of old people.

In fact, the right to have a garden is the most basic of all human rights, and by allowing themselves to be deprived of a patch of ground to cultivate, people are accepting a dangerous dependency upon supermarkets, food distributors and big business – it only requires food distribution systems to be suspended or disrupted for a few days and there would be nothing to eat. This state of affairs is not compatible with a free society, and everyone, especially young people, could be more active in reasserting their right to have a garden.

> "Adopt the pace of nature; her secret is patience."
>
> Ralph Waldo Emerson

Gardening as a Source of Inspiration

Irrespective of what work you do, time spent in the garden is always beneficial. It forces you to slow down to the pace of Nature, which helps to put everything into the correct perspective, and enables you to see your way round problems in new and innovative ways.

> "If you would be happy your whole life long,
>   Become a gardener."
>
> Old Chinese Proverb

What do You Need?

Land

It is possible to have a garden even in a confined, built-up space, by using pots and containers, but it is much better if you can obtain some land. Depending on where you live this may vary from being a very easy to a very difficult task: if your home does not have a garden attached, you may have a neighbour or relative who will let you care for their garden; the local council may have allotments to let; there may be community gardening projects available or a local landowner may rent you a patch of ground.

Even though we live in an age in which many people seem willing to accept that they do not themselves have a patch of ground to cultivate, everyone is generally very supportive of a young gardener in search of a garden and will do whatever they can to help.

Ideally, your garden should be free from serious pollution; if possible, it should not be right beside a major road, and it should be reasonably secure – it is very disheartening when a garden is vandalised.

Do not be put off by rough ground or by a plot that has been overrun by weeds: land that has not been cultivated for a while should be reasonably free of garden chemicals and, in addition, it provides you with the opportunity to create a new garden for yourself.

How Much Land?

It is better to start with a small plot – 3 ft x 10 ft (1 m x 3 m) for example – than to take on something that you cannot look after properly. If space permits, you can then extend your garden each year, as you get a clearer picture of how you want it to develop. Unused areas can be mown and the cuttings used as a mulch, or composted.

Eventually, a garden about 30 ft x 30 ft (10 m x 10 m) should allow you to grow most things that you could want to grow, without involving too much work.

Time

Gardening requires time – at least a few hours per week for most weeks of the year. Proper gardens cannot be made overnight; each garden is a unique and living work of art created by the gardener working in partnership with Nature. If you want to enjoy gardening you have to spend as much time in your garden as possible. This enables you to pull up weeds as they appear and to work with the plants as they are growing. Once you allow things to get out of hand, it can take days of hard work before order is restored, and gardening then ceases to be a pleasure.

Tools

It isn't necessary to have many tools, but those which you *do* have should be of good quality. Cheap tools can be a false economy, because they are usually poorly designed and break easily.

Second-hand gardening tools are widely available and they often combine good quality with affordability.

The basic tools that most gardeners use are:

- Spade
- Garden fork
- Dutch hoe
- Pair of secateurs
- Trowel
- Dibber
- Rake
- Wheelbarrow
- Draw hoe
- String
- Gloves
- Watering can

A draw hoe is one of the most useful tools in the garden. It can be used to break up the soil and to dislodge large weeds.

A Dutch hoe is useful for weeding between rows of vegetables in summer.

A watering can and a trowel are essential in even the smallest garden

A length of string wrapped round two sticks is invaluable when it comes to marking out the vegetable rows.

Power Tools: Modern gardeners make much use of power tools. Some of these, such as lawn mowers, are very useful but others, and this may include hedge trimmers, chainsaws, and a host of electrical gadgets, serve only to deprive the gardener of the enjoyment to be derived from doing jobs by hand.

What is perhaps worse is the way in which the use of power-operated tools tends to give a uniform appearance to a garden, thereby taking the edge off its natural beauty.

What Can You Grow?

People who have grown up in a modern city suburb could be forgiven for thinking that a garden is simply a patch of grass surrounded by shrubs and garden furniture. In fact, the garden provides you with an opportunity to grow a whole range of things including vegetables, fruit, flowers, herbs, and craft materials, in addition to allowing you to create a space for peace and relaxation.

- **Vegetables** – Vegetables were once the major component of everyone's garden but growing good vegetables requires a greater level of skill and patience than that demanded by most other activities and perhaps that is why it has gone out of fashion. Each vegetable requires special conditions and the right sort of care, but all the hard work is rewarded when you are able to pick your own vegetables from your own garden.
- **Herbs** – If you intend to cook properly, you *have* to grow your own culinary herbs, such as thyme, sage, parsley, rosemary, etc. You can also grow medicinal herbs for use in remedies or to make herbal teas. Traditional herbalists used plants native to their locality and now that there are less of these wild herbs in the countryside, it makes sense to grow them oneself. They give a wild, natural look to a garden and they often have delicate flowers which in some ways are more beautiful than those of highly-bred garden plants.
- **Soft Fruit** – Where space permits, soft fruits, such as raspberries, gooseberries, strawberries, redcurrants, blackcurrants, etc., are some of the easiest things to grow in the garden.
- **Flowers** – Flowers can be grown to create a beautiful flower garden, or they can be grown in beds for cutting, for flower arrangements or drying, or they can simply be grown amongst the vegetables to add colour and variety. They can also be grown in pots, window boxes, and hanging baskets.
- **Trees** – You should only plant trees if you think that they have a reasonable chance of being left to reach maturity. Planting native trees, such as oaks or beech, makes a genuine and significant contribution to improving the local environment. Even if you do not have room for a tree of this size, most gardens have space for at least one fruit tree – apple or plum trees are the most popular.

Perhaps we should get a garden!

- **Shrubs** – There is a wide selection of garden shrubs that can be grown for their flowers, the colour of their leaves or the colour of their winter twigs. Many shrubs provide berries and shelter for wildlife and they can be used as a hedge or screen around your garden.

Organic Gardening

Whatever type of garden you decide to have, you should aim to make it organic.

Compromise

There is a tendency to believe that it is not worth sticking to ideals and that doing what you know to be right is impracticable. This applies to gardening. Most people do not want to use chemicals such as pesticides, herbicides, fungicides and fertilisers in their gardens. They know that they are bad for the soil, give rise to inferior produce and are harmful to wildlife, but when the crunch comes and they are confronted by a particular garden pest, they may decide to put their principles to one side and use a toxic chemical to kill it.

When people are prepared to compromise in this way, they never have a chance to experience the true joys of gardening. A garden that is never treated with artificial chemicals, or worked by heavy machinery, gradually evolves into a living entity, complete in itself – plants, birds, insects, and everything in the garden somehow manage to work with the gardener to create a garden that is both beautiful and able to grow the finest quality produce.

Health in Nature

Health has to be nurtured in the garden, just as it has to be nurtured in life. Pests and diseases attack unhealthy plants; when you use chemicals to kill the pests, you are keeping the unhealthy plants alive and you end up with a sickly garden.

Sometimes the plants are unhealthy because of abnormal weather conditions, in which case the organic gardener simply has to accept failure; sometimes plants are unhealthy because they are too highly bred, in which case the organic gardener reverts to older varieties; sometimes plants are unhealthy because of poor soil and this is the area in which the organic gardener can help.

Chemicals and fertilisers are bad for the soil – the more you use, the worse the soil gets, so the more you have to use and so on. It is a vicious cycle that takes all the fun out of gardening. Organic gardening reverses this process – you nourish the soil so that the plants become stronger, which is good for the soil and the plants get even stronger and so on and so forth.

Healthy Food

When you make a serious effort to grow your own vegetables without the assistance of added chemicals, you begin to appreciate the amount of work that is required to grow good food. You soon realise that none of the food in the shops – not even things labelled organic – could have been grown to the standards that you can apply in your own garden; it would not be economically viable.

Even with all the advances in technology, growing your own plants in your own garden is still the only way of ensuring a plentiful supply of healthy food.

Soil

Gardening is essentially about providing plants with good soil in which to grow. There are many different types of soil – clay, sandy, chalk, etc. – but they all need to be treated in more or less the same way. The principal objective is to ensure that there is as much organic plant material near the surface of the soil as possible. The best way to achieve this is to disturb the soil as little as possible and to apply plenty of mulch.

Mulch

Mulching involves covering the surface of the soil to protect it from the atmosphere. (Leaving the surface of the soil exposed has various disadvantages: it allows weeds to germinate freely, it allows the soil to dry out, which inhibits the activity of worms and bacteria near the surface, and it can result in the roots of garden plants being deprived of water.) Making sure that the soil is covered with a thin layer, 2″ to 3″ (5 cm to 8 cm), of organic plant material, i.e. a mulch, prevents all these problems. Sometimes people use plastic sheeting for this purpose, but an organic mulch has the advantage of feeding the soil at the same time as preventing weed growth and evaporation – the organic material is broken down and integrated into the structure of the soil by the creatures living in the ground.

Different types of mulch:

- **Grass Cuttings:** Providing that a lawn has not been treated with chemicals, its cuttings make an excellent mulch. They should be spread straight away because a large pile of grass cuttings left even for one night starts to decompose and soon becomes unusable.

- **Weeds:** If you weed regularly, you can pile up the uprooted weed plants on the surface and use them as a mulch. Don't use plants that have gone to seed because the seeds will fall on the ground, germinate and cause you further problems. Some plants, such as docks and nettles, readily spread through their roots – when you are clearing a patch of ground of well-established weeds, do not use them as a mulch, but compost them instead.

- **Comfrey:** You can grow plants specifically for use as a mulch; comfrey leaves, for example, make a good mulch, and once the plants have become established, they can be cut two or three times per year.

- **Compost:** Instead of digging compost into the soil, spread it on the surface – especially over the winter months. This helps to concentrate the nutrients from the compost in the top few inches of the soil where they are most useful.

- **Wild Area:** If you have space, you can keep part of your garden wild – if you don't touch the vegetation through the spring and summer months (thereby providing a haven for birds and insects) and then cut it in the autumn, you can use it to mulch the following year's potato bed. The potatoes won't be troubled by the weed seeds in the mulch.

Compost

A compost heap allows you to recycle all the organic plant matter that cannot be used directly as a mulch; this can include large weeds, household vegetable waste, leaves, twigs, and hedge clippings (provided they are cut up into small pieces). You should be able to recycle everything that your garden produces.

The Compost Heap

People sometimes make the mistake of hiding the compost heap in an obscure corner of the garden. It is better to site it somewhere where it is easily accessible and gets a reasonable amount of sun and rain.

You do not need to make a compost bin: you can simply pile up the accumulating garden debris for a couple of months and then turn it over with a garden fork once or twice at monthly intervals. This will produce compost that can be spread on vegetable and flower beds in the autumn and winter.

If you prefer to use a compost bin, you must take care not to restrict the air supply to the compost – it is tempting to keep adding more and more things to the top of the bin with the result that the contents become compacted at the bottom. The bin should be emptied every few months and the contents left to stand for a few weeks to complete the process of decay. When emptying the bin try to 'turn' the contents so that the newest material goes to the bottom of the heap and the material from the bottom of the bin goes to the top.

Animal Products

At one time, organic gardeners made considerable use of animal products – especially farmyard manure. Modern methods of animal husbandry make this no longer desirable – even manure is now contaminated with the chemicals and drugs that have been administered to the animals and it may be linked to the transmission of farm-related diseases.

If you have a good relationship with a local stables or organic farmer, you may be able to obtain a supply of good-quality, organic manure but it is always difficult to be certain that they are working to the same standards as yourself.

On balance it is best to try to maintain your garden as a closed system, producing its own organic plant matter to nourish its own soil.

Science and the Garden

Science should be learnt through practical experience, observation and experimentation. Every significant scientific process is taking place in the garden, and in order to be successful, the gardener *has* to observe and experiment. The garden is, therefore, the ideal place in which to learn science.

Scientific Processes

The basic process upon which all life ultimately depends is the capture of sunlight by plants; plants are able to combine the sun's energy with carbon dioxide, which they get from the air, and water, which they take up through their roots, to make a form of sugar (glucose). This process is known as photosynthesis:

water + carbon dioxide + sunlight $\longrightarrow$ **sugar + oxygen**

When the sugar is broken down to its constituent parts, the energy stored within it is released. All living things are dependent on this energy and the process through which it is released is known as respiration:

sugar + oxygen $\longrightarrow$ **energy + water + carbon dioxide**

The oxygen required for respiration comes from the air.

There are some bacteria that are able to revert to another form of respiration when air is lacking. It is less efficient and produces toxic by-products:

sugar $\longrightarrow$ **energy + acid + gases**

This process of fermentation should be avoided in the garden – the acids that are produced inhibit plant growth and eventually become toxic even to the bacteria themselves. It is responsible for the creation of acid soils.

It is therefore clear that one of the gardener's main tasks is to ensure that all parts of the plant receive a plentiful supply of air. Plant roots, in particular, suffer if the soil is not well-aerated.

Good soil aeration is most easily achieved by mulching: the mulch encourages worms and insects to come to the surface of the soil and, by so doing, they open up passageways through the earth through which air can flow.

Nitrogen

Plants and animals need nitrogen in order to make proteins. There is no shortage of nitrogen itself – the air is eighty per cent nitrogen – but neither plants nor animals can use it in this form. Plants are dependent upon soil bacteria which are able to use the nitrogen in the air and which then release nitrogen-containing compounds into the soil. These compounds dissolve in the water that is in the soil, and the plants take them up through their roots. Animals get their nitrogen by eating plants (or other animals).

It is therefore essential that your garden soil provides good conditions for bacteria. Synthetically-produced nitrogen compounds are the main components of the artificial fertilisers upon which modern agricultural practices are based, but we now know that they inhibit the activity of the all-important soil bacteria. (They also alter plant growth patterns making them more susceptible to disease.)

The organic gardener ensures a good supply of nitrogen by natural means:

- All plant material contains nitrogen – mulches and compost applications therefore replenish nitrogen levels in the soil in a natural way.

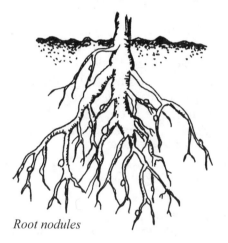

Root nodules

- The bacteria which are able to take nitrogen from the air (nitrogen-fixing bacteria) thrive in well-aerated soil, rich in organic matter.
- Some plants, notably legumes (peas, beans, clover, etc.) have nodules in their roots that contain these nitrogen-fixing bacteria. The plant supplies the bacteria with nutrients and in return receives a plentiful supply of nitrogen compounds from the bacteria. Growing these plants increases nitrogen levels in the soil – the organic gardener rotates crop production so that each area of the garden produces a crop of legumes every three or four years.

Minerals

Plants need small amounts of minerals such as potassium, phosphates, sulphates, iron, magnesium, etc., all of which occur naturally in the soil. They are more easily absorbed from well-aerated soils rich in organic matter, than from waterlogged or depleted soils. Some plants, such as comfrey, have deep roots and are particularly efficient in taking up minerals. These plants can be grown specifically to be used as a mulch, thereby making these minerals available to other plants.

Each plant demands different things from the soil; growing different plants in the same place each year prevents the soil from becoming exhausted.

Science and Understanding

To the gardener, the science of life is not a theory but a practical experience. It requires an understanding that does not depend solely on logic and analysis but also on an ability to feel how things work – sometimes in a way that cannot be put into words. This understanding is rewarded in the form of a beautiful garden, good crops, and a sense of harmony with Nature. The blight that seems to follow in the wake of modern science would suggest that scientists do not have as good an understanding of how Nature really works, as they imagine. It is important to bear this in mind when studying science.

Planning Your Garden

Start Small

It is best to start small and build up the cultivated area of your garden year by year as your knowledge and experience develop. If you start with a single bed 3 ft by 10 ft (1 m by 3 m) you will be able to keep it weed-free and productive without any difficulty. Unused areas of a garden can be cut or mown and the cuttings composted or used as a mulch: build up layers of mulch on areas that you plan to bring into cultivation in the following year, as this improves soil fertility at the same time as clearing the area of weeds.

Plan things Year by Year

If you could see into the future, you would be able to lay out your garden plan before you started, plant everything in the right place and then just watch it all grow.

Things rarely work out like this – it takes time to get to know your garden; you find that you have planted things in the wrong place; you discover new plants that you want to grow; your personal tastes change; and the garden itself starts to develop a personality that you could not have envisaged at the outset.

It is therefore best to plan out the garden one year at a time. Each year you can decide, in the light of previous experience, such things as:

- Which vegetables and flowers you intend to grow.
- Whether you are going to bring any new areas under cultivation.
- Whether to move any well-established plants.
- Whether you are going to plant any new trees or shrubs.
- Whether you are going to build any paths, walls or other features in the garden.

If you allow yourself to be guided by experience and change your plan for the garden, year by year, it will gradually develop a character of its own, much better than anything that you could have envisaged at the outset.

Garden Plan 1

Vegetable Gardening

The principal reason for growing vegetables is to produce food for the kitchen. It is therefore sensible for the gardener to work with the cook – or for the cook to be the gardener, as there are few things more disheartening than growing food that no one eats. If you grow the vegetables that are already popular and in demand in your household, then your produce is unlikely to suffer this fate.

The following pages outline the basic principles of successful vegetable gardening. It is important to remember that local conditions have a big effect upon the way in which vegetables grow: late frosts, strong winds, dry spells, day length, soil type etc., all have to be taken into account in order to succeed in getting a really good crop and these can only be learnt about through working in a particular garden for several years. This means that you should not follow the instructions in any book too literally and that you should never be discouraged – things in the garden tend to get better, rather than worse, with each successive year.

Varieties

Separate varieties of the same vegetable can differ greatly from each other in the way that they are grown, their appearance and their taste. It is therefore advisable to read the seed packet, or the seed catalogue, carefully, every time that you buy seeds, to make sure that you select the variety most suited to your own needs. Traditional varieties are generally more suited to organic gardening than modern varieties.

F1 Seeds are produced by a genetic cross that increases the vigour of the plant but makes them produce infertile seeds: using F1 seeds may increase your yield but you will not be able to save seed from these crops for sowing the following year.

F1 seeds are particularly popular for vegetables such as sweetcorn and tomatoes, which are being grown at the limit of their climate range.

No Digging

Traditional vegetable gardening involved back-breaking digging and heavy applications of manure. It is possible to adopt a more subtle approach which, in the long run, yields better results with less work and is better for the garden itself:

- Lay out your vegetable garden in beds separated by paths – this reduces the amount that you walk on the productive area of the garden and hence prevents soil compaction.

- Ensure that the soil surface on the beds is always well mulched – this prevents the soil from drying out and encourages a rich ecosystem to develop in the top two or three inches of the soil.

- At least twice a year – before you plant seeds and after you harvest the crop – work the top few inches with a hoe or a rake. This clears the bed of weeds and ensures a good distribution of organic matter without damaging the organisms that live in the soil.

Vegetable Beds

Beds should be wide enough for you to be able to reach the centre without having to stand on the bed, i.e. about three feet (1 metre). Their length is determined by the size of the garden. You also have to give some consideration to the paths between the beds. If you leave them as they are, they will have to be mown and must be at least the width of your lawnmower. This has the advantage of providing more mulching material but involves a lot of work and the beds are under constant attack from weeds spreading from the paths. In the long term, it is worth paving the paths – the simplest method is to use a single line of breeze blocks placed end to end. This provides a very thin path, but it is wide enough to walk on and impervious to weeds.

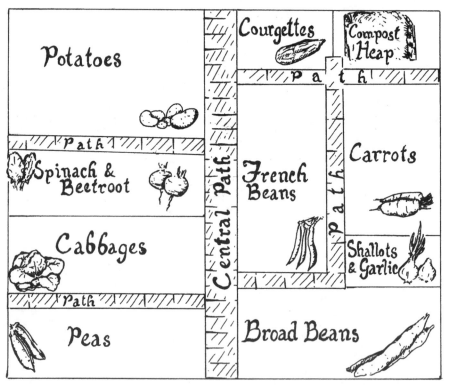

Garden Plan 2: Showing an arrangement of vegetable beds. The vegetables grown in each bed would change from year to year in accordance with your pattern of crop rotation.

Crop Rotation

Crop rotation is an essential part of organic vegetable gardening. Vegetables are very demanding plants, and growing the same crop in the same area two or three years running exhausts the soil, and allows a build-up of the insects and fungi that attack that specific crop. The following suggested crop rotation involves the vegetable garden being divided into four:

Year 1: Brassicas - cabbages, Brussels sprouts, cauliflower, radishes, turnips, swedes, etc.

Year 2: Potatoes or onions

Year 3: Carrots, parsnips, spinach, beetroot, etc.

Year 4: Legumes - peas, broad beans, French beans, etc.

Alternatively, if you do not want to grow brassicas, you could try the following:

Year 1: Potatoes

Year 2: Onions, garlic, and leeks

Year 3: Legumes - peas, broad beans, French beans, etc.

Year 4: Beetroot, spinach, carrots

In practice, things don't usually work as smoothly as this: sometimes an area of the garden has two or three crops in the same year or you may want to grow a mixture of different plants in the same area – but it is advisable to follow the principle of crop rotation wherever possible.

Garden Plan 3: The arrows suggest a possible sequence for crop rotation.

Practical Tips

Planting Seeds in the Ground

One of the most important aspects of growing vegetables from seed is the preparation of the 'seed bed'. In order to germinate successfully, seeds need light, crumbly soil, that is free from weeds. It should retain water, but should not be waterlogged. This is achieved by mulching the soil in the months prior to sowing the seeds, in order to stifle the weeds and to help build up the organic matter near the soil surface. When it is time to plant the seeds:

- Rake off the mulch and put it to one side (it can be used to mulch round the plants once they have grown to a reasonable size, or can be used elsewhere in the garden).

- Remove any stones and weeds that remain on the bed.

- Rake the surface to break the soil down to a fine tilth.

Making a seed drill.

- Mark out a straight line with a piece of string.

- Make a furrow with the edge of a hoe or with a stick. The furrow should be of the depth indicated on the seed packet, and is known as a seed drill.

- Plant the seed, taking care not to let seeds fall on either side of the drill that you have prepared.

- Use your hands to carefully replace the earth over the seeds. Pat it down with your hands or with the flat part of a hoe, so that the soil is tightly packed around the seeds.

Sowing the seeds – space them according to the instructions on the packet.

- In dry spells, water with a fine spray to ensure that the seed bed does not dry out.

Planting Seeds in a Tray

- Line the bottom of a tray with newspaper.
- Fill the tray to within ½" (1 cm) of the top with potting compost.
- Sprinkle the seeds over the surface.
- Cover with a layer of potting compost.
- Water with a fine spray.
- Keep in a warm, sunny position.

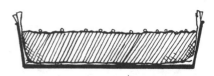

Seed tray

Planting Seedlings

Plants that are grown in seed trays, under cover, or in a specially-prepared seed nursery (an area in a sheltered spot with well-worked soil suitable for raising seedlings) can be transplanted to their final growing position once they have a few proper leaves. Plants can also be bought from a nursery or garden centre.

- Use a trowel to dig up the plants from their original position. Be careful not to damage the roots.
- Separate the plants by carefully pulling them apart, once again being careful to keep the roots of each plant as intact as possible.
- Use a trowel to make a hole large enough to take the roots of one of the plants.
- Place the plant in the hole.
- Fill the hole with water and then carefully push the soil back into the hole. Pat down the soil to ensure good contact between the roots and the earth.
- Repeat with all the other plants.

Planting with a trowel

Notes:

1. Try to ensure that the roots do not dry out while you are in the process of transplanting – only dig up a few plants at a time, and keep the plants that you have dug up out of the sun, or cover them with a damp cloth.
2. Plants are vulnerable to attacks by birds for a few weeks after they have been transplanted and, where this proves to be a problem, they can be covered with wire or plastic netting.

Thinning

Thinning involves pulling up young seedlings that are growing too close together, in order to give those that you leave in the ground enough space to mature properly.

It is something that new gardeners are sometimes reluctant to do – especially if they had difficulty in getting the seed to germinate in the first place.

However, when vegetables are grown too closely together the plants compete against each other for light, water, and space with the result that none of them grow well and the total crop is greatly reduced.

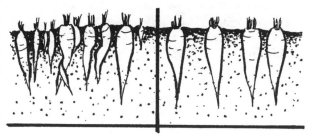

Carrots grown too close together tend to be small and are often crooked. Properly-spaced carrots are larger and of uniform shape.

Shallots

Shallots are a member of the *allium* family that also contains onions, leeks and garlic. They can be used in the same way as onions but are easier to grow. They are a traditional crop that does not lend itself to commercial production – this explains why they have become less common in recent years.

Planting

Shallots are planted early in the year – in January, February or March. The bulb is planted so that its tip is just protruding above the surface of the earth.

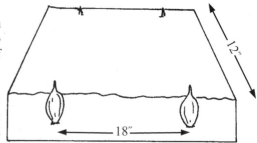

Maintenance

If planted early, the shoot of the shallot will emerge before weeds have a chance to germinate and this makes them an easy crop to care for. Weed and mulch (with grass cuttings, etc.) once or twice when they are still small. The mulch will help to prevent the ground from drying out but the plants should be watered during any long dry spells that occur in early summer.

Harvesting

Each shallot forms a clump of several separate shallot bulbs. These can be harvested once the leaves have died back in late summer. The shallots must be thoroughly dry before they are stored.

Shallots can be woven together with raffia and hung up in the kitchen to be used over the winter.

	J	F	M	A	M	J	J	A	S	O	N	D
Planting		▓	▓	▓								
Harvesting								▓	▓			

Some of the crop should be saved for planting the following year. With careful management, it should not be necessary to buy new bulbs after the first couple of years.

Garlic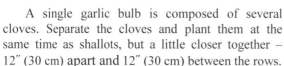

A single garlic bulb is composed of several cloves. Separate the cloves and plant them at the same time as shallots, but a little closer together – 12″ (30 cm) apart and 12″ (30 cm) between the rows.

You are unlikely to be able to grow garlic bulbs as big as those in the shops (unless you are living in a very sunny location) but small, home-grown garlic bulbs cannot be beaten for taste.

Garlic sometimes flowers, in which case snip off the flower stalks at the top. The plants will still produce garlic cloves in the usual way.

Save some of the crop for planting the following year.

	J	F	M	A	M	J	J	A	S	O	N	D
Planting		▓	▓	▓								
Harvesting								▓	▓			

Cut the flower off the garlic.

  Easy   *Medium*   *Advanced*

Potatoes

The ideal is to be able to grow enough potatoes to last the whole year: true connoisseurs are reluctant to eat any shop-bought potatoes because of their inferior quality.

Planting

Buy certified seed potatoes (organic if possible): these are potatoes that have been grown in areas that are free of aphids and which are therefore relatively free of the infections that they carry. These infections are not harmful but they do reduce the yield.

From January or February onwards, store seed potatoes in shallow trays on a window sill; they will develop little green buds prior to planting.

Planting has to be timed so as to avoid the young shoots being exposed to late frosts (which do not kill the plant but delay its development by several weeks). In most areas this means planting in April.

The ground should be well prepared: ideally it should have been heavily mulched over the previous winter and will therefore be weed free. Dig trenches about 6″ (15 cm) deep and 2 ft 6″ (80 cm) apart. Plant the potatoes 12″ (30 cm) apart in the trench, with at least one bud pointing upwards; cover over with soil.

Maintenance

Young shoots should be protected from late frosts by covering them on cold nights with sheets of newspaper, polythene or straw.

The plants need to be kept free of weeds, the soil should be kept moist and the developing potatoes must not be allowed to extrude from the earth. This is achieved by earthing-up the plants and by mulching, which should be done at least twice over the first couple of months.

Earthing-up the potato crop: potatoes that protrude into the daylight turn green and should not be used.

Harvesting

You can start to harvest your crop as soon as the potatoes are big enough to eat (which you can check by carefully removing the soil from the base of the plant).

Dig up the whole crop when the leaves and stems die back. Potatoes should be kept in the dark in a cool, dry place. They can be stored in cardboard boxes. Check the boxes from time to time and remove any potatoes that are going mouldy.

Save some small potatoes for planting the following year. Buy new seed potatoes every three or four years.

	J	F	M	A	M	J	J	A	S	O	N	D
Planting			▨	▨	▨							
Harvesting							▨	▨	▨			

Recipes:
Vegetable Feuilleté *page 222*
Potato Patties *page 227*

Tomatoes

Tomatoes are a relative of the potato but they are more sensitive to frost and cold. They can be grown outdoors against a south-facing wall or indoors in a greenhouse, conservatory or close to a south-facing window.

Planting

Tomatoes are very demanding plants – they require rich soil, warmth and plenty of sunlight. They need several months of uninterrupted growth in order to produce ripe tomatoes and that is why they are started off as early as possible, in pots, and then transplanted to their final growing position when the weather permits.

You can either buy tomato plants or grow your own from seed. If you are growing from seed, plant one seed per 3½″ (9 cm) pot, filled with potting compost. Keep the pots indoors, in the warmest, sunniest spot that you have and do not let them dry out.

Transplant to their final position when the first flower buds can be seen. They should not generally be placed outdoors before the beginning of June. Give them the richest soil that you possibly can – mix plenty of compost into your tomato bed and regularly mulch round the plants.

Maintenance

Tomato plants grow prodigiously and then suffer problems from mildew and mould because air cannot circulate around the leaves. This can be counteracted by staking up each plant, to prevent the main stem from falling over, and by vigorous pruning: allow four flower stalks to develop and then snip off the top of the plant and all side shoots as they grow, and also cut off the lower leaves. This forces the plant to put all its resources into the production of the fruit and also ensures a free flow of air around the plant.

The roots of the plants should be kept moist but the fruit and leaves should be kept as dry as possible. Make sure that the tomatoes themselves do not rest on the ground.

Pinch off side shoots as soon as they appear.

Harvesting

Pick the tomatoes as they become ripe. If you are left with a lot of green tomatoes when the first frosts threaten outdoor plants, pick them all and bring them indoors. Store them in a cool, dark, drawer or box which contains at least one ripe tomato or other piece of fruit: the ripe fruit gives off gases that encourage the tomatoes to ripen.

	J	F	M	A	M	J	J	A	S	O	N	D
Planting		▦	▦	▦								
Harvesting						▦	▦	▦	▦			

Peppers, Aubergines and Chilli Peppers are in the same family as tomatoes and can be grown in a similar way – especially if you have room in a greenhouse or conservatory. They do not need to be pruned. They yield their fruit later than tomatoes.

Recipe: Green tomato chutney *page 226*
Moroccan Aubergine Salad *page 230*

Mmm! We don't have these in Athens!!!!

  Easy Medium 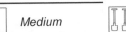 Advanced

Carrots

Carrots are one of the most popular of all vegetables and they are easy to grow – the only serious problem is the activity of carrot fly larvae.

Planting

Do not sow carrots too early – cold, waterlogged soil results in poor germination. April and May are good months for sowing carrots in most areas but late sowings can also be made in June and July.

Carrots grown in heavy, compacted soil will divide to become 'leggy': to avoid this, sow your carrots in areas that were previously used for potatoes – a crop which breaks up heavy soils.

Carrots are usually sown in drills 6″ (15 cm) apart *(page 184)*. Sow the seeds thinly – if you sow them too thickly, it may be difficult to thin the seedlings without causing root disturbance; if you sow them *too* thinly, however, you may have large gaps in the rows. The germination rate depends on the weather and the soil temperature, and carrots should, therefore, be sown more thinly as the season progresses.

Maintenance

Carrot fly are attracted to the smell given off by carrot plants when their roots are disturbed. Weeding and thinning should therefore be done on wind-free days.

Carrot seedlings are small and can easily be choked out by weeds, which means that you must weed them soon after they get their first proper, feathery, leaves. They can be thinned at the same time: leave about 2″ (5 cm) between plants.

Thin carrot seedlings so that there is 2″ between plants.

When they are bigger, you can hoe between the rows and mulch round the plants. Earth up the plants so that the top of the carrot is not exposed to the air. This gives some protection against the carrot root fly and stops the carrots turning green. Water the plants during dry spells.

The most effective way of countering the carrot fly larvae is to prevent carrot flies from laying eggs on your plants. One way of doing this (or at least reducing it) is to cover your carrot bed with fleece (sold by garden centres) throughout the growing season.

Harvesting

Carrots can be pulled up and used any time after 3 to 4 months of growth. The leaves start to die back in the autumn but the carrots can be left in the ground and dug up as you need them. Cover over with straw or compost to prevent the tops being damaged by frost: the carrots should survive in good condition until late November or December.

	J	F	M	A	M	J	J	A	S	O	N	D
Planting			░	░	░	░	░					
Harvesting								░	░	░	░	░

Recipe:
Winter vegetables

page 220

Parsnips are a relative of the carrot but they are more hardy, less susceptible to carrot root fly and easier to grow. Plant them in February or March, thin the seedlings so that they are 4″ (10 cm) apart and start to harvest after the first frost. They can be left in the ground until February of the following year. Frost improves the flavour.

Peas

Planting

Timing is important in the sowing of peas – too early and the seeds will rot in the ground, particularly in heavy, waterlogged soils, too late and the young plants will struggle to grow in dry conditions and could be affected by mildew in the height of summer. In most areas April is the best month for sowing peas.

Peas prefer rich soil and the pea bed should, ideally, be prepared several months in advance. It should be heavily mulched over the winter, hoed and raked in the spring and then mulched again.

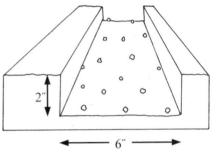

Sow the seeds in trenches about 2″ (5 cm) deep and 6″ (15 cm) wide: sprinkle the peas in the trench so that they are 2″ - 3″ (5 - 8 cm) apart. Carefully cover with soil.

If you want more than one row of peas, they must be quite far apart: about 3 feet (1 metre).

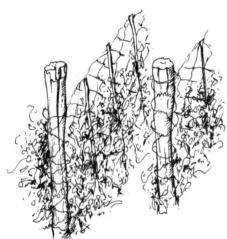

Chicken wire can be used to make a strong, easy-to-construct framework for climbing plants such as peas.

Maintenance

Germinating peas are attractive both to birds and to mice and need to be protected with wire or plastic netting. Alternatively, cut up plastic, 1½ litre, bottles into rings, 2″ - 3″ deep, and place the rings over the pea seedlings as they emerge – this prevents attacks by both birds and mice and protects the seedlings from cold winds.

Peas are climbing plants and must be supported by a framework of some sort – sticks, wire netting, plastic netting or string. This should be constructed when the plants start to produce tendrils.

Harvesting

Pick the peas as they become ripe, i.e. when they are still small and sweet. Surplus peas can be frozen. Some pods can be left on the plants to mature. They should then be picked, dried and stored for sowing the following year.

	J	F	M	A	M	J	J	A	S	O	N	D
Planting												
Harvesting												

Recipes:
Peas *page 219*
Freezing vegetables
page 218

Runner Beans are another traditional favourite. The plants are frost sensitive and require a framework at least six feet high to climb up, but the extra effort is rewarded by a copious crop lasting for several weeks in the summer.

  Easy   *Medium*   *Advanced*

Broad Beans

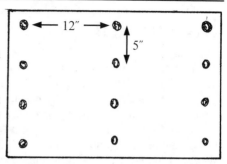

Broad beans provide one of the earliest crops in the garden.

Planting

If you have reasonably mild winters, plant broad beans in a sheltered spot in the autumn – late October or November – otherwise plant them when the weather starts to improve in the New Year, that is to say in February or March.

Seeds can be planted individually by making a hole for each seed with a dibber or small stick, 5″ (12 cm) apart, in rows 12″ (30 cm) apart. Make a hole about 1″ (2 cm) deep, drop the seed in, and cover over with soil.

Maintenance

Seeds and seedlings can be protected with rings made out of plastic bottles (as described under peas); place the ring over the seed immediately after planting. Weed and mulch round the plants once or twice during the spring and, if your garden is subject to winds, support the plants with stakes. Broad beans are susceptible to blackfly but, providing the seeds were planted early enough, the beans should mature before blackfly appear in the garden – snip off any growing tips on which you see blackfly.

Harvesting

Pick the beans when they are still small and tender, and cook them straight away; waiting until the next day results in a loss of taste. Surplus beans can be frozen.

	J	F	M	A	M	J	J	A	S	O	N	D
Planting		▓	▓							▓	▓	
Harvesting							▓	▓				

French Beans

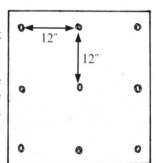

French beans are easy to grow and highly productive. Select a stringless, non-climbing variety.

Planting

French beans are frost sensitive and the seeds do not like cold, wet soil. They should be planted in early summer – late May or June – in well-prepared soil. They can be planted with a dibber, allowing about 12″ (30 cm) around each plant in all directions.

Maintenance

Weed round the young seedlings and mulch. Water in dry weather.

Harvesting

Depending on the variety, pick the beans when they are 3″ to 6″ (8 to 15 cm) long. Regular picking, every 2 to 3 days, will ensure a steady supply of beans up until the first frost.

	J	F	M	A	M	J	J	A	S	O	N	D
Planting					▓	▓						
Harvesting							▓	▓	▓			

Recipe:
French Bean Pickle *page 223*
Freezing Vegetables *page 218*

Sweetcorn

Planting

If it is to yield a good crop, sweetcorn needs to get off to an early start. In colder areas this is achieved by planting the seeds in small, 2″ (5 cm), pots in late spring – late April/early May.

Keep the pots in a warm, sunny place (they can be moved outside during the day), and transplant the seedlings into their final position as soon as the weather permits: i.e. after the last frost. The young plants can be protected by rings cut from plastic bottles. Sweetcorn should be planted in a block, 18″ (45 cm) apart, rather than in rows, as this improves the pollination of the grains on the cobs.

Maintenance

Remove the plastic rings when the young plants are 6 to 12″ (15 to 30 cm) high, weed and mulch. Water during dry spells. If it gets off to a good start, sweetcorn requires very little work.

Harvesting

It can be quite difficult to judge when the crop is ready for picking. The grains have to have time to fill out, but if they are left too long they lose their sweetness. Feel the cobs every few days and when they fill out and become firm, they should be ready.

The crop tends to ripen at more or less the same time. Any surplus can be frozen.

After the cobs are harvested, the rest of the plant can be chopped up and added to the compost heap or used directly as a mulch.

Recipe:
Corn on the Cob *page 219*
Freezing vegetables
              page 218

	J	F	M	A	M	J	J	A	S	O	N	D
Planting				▓								
Transplanting					▓							
Harvesting								▓	▓			

Cereals

Each of the world's civilisations has been based upon the cultivation of a particular crop: **Maize**, of which sweetcorn is one variety, was the staple crop of American civilisations before the arrival of Europeans.

Wheat: European, Middle Eastern, and North African civilisations were based upon the cultivation of wheat. Until recently, most people tried to grow enough wheat to last through the year and there is no reason why you should not include wheat in your crop rotation. There are a number of simple flour grinders available that would allow you to grind your own grain to get fresh flour for baking.

Oats, Rye, and Barley are easier to grow than wheat but they are not as versatile in cooking.

Rice is the world's principal food crop. It requires hot, humid conditions and does best in tropical and sub-tropical regions.

      Easy   *Medium*   *Advanced*

Spinach

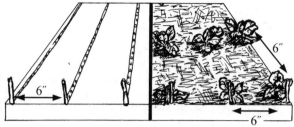

Planting

Spinach is prone to bolting (flowering) which results in the loss of the crop. The risk of this happening can be minimised by growing it as a winter crop or by sowing it very early in the spring.

Select a sheltered position and sow spinach seeds in late summer/early autumn – September. Sow thinly in rows ½" (1 cm) deep, 6" (15 cm) apart.

Maintenance

Weed regularly and thin the plants so that they are 6" (15 cm) apart. In cold areas the plants may need some protection for the winter months: they can be covered with straw or fleece. Remove the covering in the spring.

Harvesting

Using scissors, cut leaves off the plants from early spring onwards. Winter-grown spinach provides something from the garden at a time when produce is scarce.

Recipes:
Spinach   *page 219*
Catalonian Spinach and Onion Flat-
bread   *page 234*
Vegetable Feuilleté   *page 222*

	J	F	M	A	M	J	J	A	S	O	N	D
Planting								▨	▨			
Harvesting		▨	▨	▨	▨							

Beetroot

Beetroot is one of the easiest root crops to grow. It does not suffer from any specific pest and will grow on soil that has not been particularly well prepared.

Planting

Plant beetroot in late spring or early summer – in April or May. Sow thinly in rows ½" (1 cm) deep, 6" (15 cm) apart.

Maintenance

Weed regularly and thin the plants when they have two or three proper leaves, leaving 4" (10 cm) between plants. Mulch round the plants after a few weeks. Beetroot are prone to splitting when subjected to periods of alternating rain and drought, so the soil should be kept moist.

Harvesting

Start picking as soon as the beetroot are about 1½" (4 cm) in diameter. Harvest any remaining crop in late autumn before the arrival of heavy frosts.

	J	F	M	A	M	J	J	A	S	O	N	D
Planting				▨	▨							
Harvesting								▨	▨	▨		

Recipe:
Boiled Beetroot   *page 220*
Pickled Beetroot   *page 220*
Beetroot Rice   *page 224*

Leaf beet and Swiss chard are relatives of beetroot and are grown in the same way. They can be used in place of spinach in most recipes.

Brassicas

Brassicas – the cabbage family – are amongst the oldest and most widely grown vegetables. Given proper management it is possible to pick brassicas from the garden all year round, but each of them has its own special requirements and it may take a few years of trial and error before you are able to get a good crop from your garden.

Cabbage plants are very demanding on the soil and, in addition, are susceptible to soil-borne diseases: these factors combine to make it imperative that brassicas are not grown on the same patch of ground more than once every three years.

Cabbage seeds are usually sown either indoors, in a seed tray, or in a small seed bed which is weed free, warm, and sunny. The plants are transplanted to their final growing position when they are big enough to be moved.

Caterpillars: All brassicas are very susceptible to caterpillar attack: big plants can be devoured in the course of a few days. The best organic solution is to inspect all your cabbage plants regularly during the summer months (especially when there are a lot of cabbage white butterflies around) and to remove the clutches of eggs that have been laid on the underside of the leaves. If you miss the eggs, you will probably still be able to catch the tiny caterpillars that emerge from them before they have a chance to spread out and destroy your crop: this is an unpleasant but necessary job. Covering the plants with plastic netting helps to reduce the number of eggs that the butterflies are able to lay on them.

Plants grown over winter are much less affected by caterpillars than those that mature during the summer months.

Brussels Sprouts

Planting

Plant seeds in a sunny, weed-free position in mid-summer and transplant the seedlings to their final position in August (alternatively, buy plants ready for planting out). The plants need plenty of room so leave 2 feet (60 cm) round the plants in every direction. Stamp down the soil round the plants – firm soil is believed to yield compact sprouts.

Maintenance

Mulch round the plants to keep them free of weeds. Don't worry if they tip over under the influence of the prevailing wind: they will suffer less damage in winter gales if they are closer to the ground.

Harvesting

Pick the sprouts off the stems as they become ready – from November to January. This is often a bitterly cold job but one that is well worth the effort. Most people consider that the sprouts taste better after they have been exposed to at least one hard frost.

Picking Brussels sprouts

	J	F	M	A	M	J	J	A	S	O	N	D
Planting						▓	▓					
Transplanting								▓	▓			
Harvesting	▓										▓	▓

   Easy   *Medium*   *Advanced*

Red Cabbage

Planting

The red cabbage bed should be prepared well in advance; during the winter, mulch it heavily with your best compost but do not dig over or disturb the soil.

Plant the seeds in the spring (March or April), in a seed tray, and keep them indoors in a sunny position. Transfer the seedlings to their final growing position when they each have two or three proper leaves. Leave about 18″ (45 cm) around each plant in every direction.

Maintenance

Mulch round the plants, keep them free of weeds, and water in dry spells. Pick off caterpillars as they appear.

Harvesting

Pick the plant when a firm heart has developed in its centre, and discard the outer leaves. Red cabbage is relatively reluctant to flower, providing the bed is kept moist, so the mature plants can be left in the ground for several weeks and picked as required.

Recipe:													
Red Cabbage with Pine Nuts		J	F	M	A	M	J	J	A	S	O	N	D
page 223	Planting			▓	▓								
	Transplanting				▓	▓							
	Harvesting								▓	▓	▓		

Green Cabbage

There are many different types of green cabbage:

Summer cabbages: Summer cabbages should be grown in the same way as red cabbages (described above). They are generally very susceptible to caterpillar attack and need to be checked every few days. Many varieties are prone to flowering instead of forming a firm heart - especially if they are allowed to dry out.

	J	F	M	A	M	J	J	A	S	O	N	D
Planting			▓	▓								
Transplanting					▓	▓						
Harvesting								▓	▓	▓		

Winter cabbages: Winter cabbages should be grown in the same way as Brussels sprouts. Their outer leaves can be damaged by heavy frosts and it is best to use them in early winter - December or January. Some varieties are prone to flowering in early spring.

	J	F	M	A	M	J	J	A	S	O	N	D
Planting						▓	▓					
Transplanting							▓	▓				
Harvesting	▓										▓	▓

Spring cabbages: Spring cabbage seeds should be planted outdoors in the summer (July) and the seedlings planted out six to eight weeks later in September. In colder areas they will need to be protected over the winter months with a covering of straw, fleece or a cloche.

Remove the covering in the spring and the plants will grow rapidly to produce a plentiful supply of spring greens.

	J	F	M	A	M	J	J	A	S	O	N	D
Planting							▓					
Transplanting									▓			
Harvesting			▓	▓								

Courgettes

Courgettes are young marrows but, whereas marrows are traditionally grown on trailing plants, courgettes are usually grown on 'bush' varieties that have a compact pattern of growth.

Planting

Young courgette plants are very sensitive to cold; if you plant them out too early, cold spells of wind and rain will make them wither and die – even when there isn't a frost. On the other hand, if you plant them out too late, you will not get a very large crop.

For this reason, courgettes should be started off indoors in 3½" (8 cm) pots, in a sunny position. Do not plant them out until they have at least two proper leaves (very small plants are susceptible to slug damage) and the weather is warm.

Courgettes do best in very rich soil and they can even be planted directly into a compost heap, providing that it is reasonably well rotted down.

In the right conditions, the plants will grow rapidly and take up a lot of space: allow 3 or 4 feet (1 to 1.2 metre) between plants.

Maintenance

The plants need to be looked after carefully for the first few weeks: weed, mulch and water them during dry spells. After the first month they require little further maintenance.

Harvesting

Courgette plants produce male flowers and female flowers. The courgettes develop at the base of the female flowers. Female flowers may not appear until a few weeks after the first male flowers.

Courgettes develop rapidly and can be picked at any time after they are 4" or 5" (10 to 12 cm) long. They should be cut off with a knife, or carefully twisted off. Picking the courgettes while they are small encourages more to develop.

			J	F	M	A	M	J	J	A	S	O	N	D
Recipe:														
Italian-Style Courgettes	Planting					▓	▓							
page 228	Transplanting								▓					
	Harvesting									▓	▓			

Other plants in the same family:

Pumpkin: grown in exactly the same way as courgettes, except that they are grown on trailing plants and should therefore be given a great deal of room.

Cucumber: even more sensitive to cold than courgettes. Best grown in a cold frame or in a greenhouse.

Melon: requires as much heat as possible; needs to be grown in a greenhouse or conservatory, with plenty of sun.

Gourds and Squashes: ornamental gourds can be grown outdoors. Squashes need heat and sunlight.

Soft Fruit

If you have a permanent garden (as opposed to a plot of land that you have only been given for a year or two) it is definitely worth establishing a good selection of soft fruit plants.

Raspberries

Planting

Any gardener who has a vigorous raspberry patch will be happy to give you a few plants either in the spring or in the autumn. Alternatively, buy plants from a plant nursery (these will have been selected to give larger fruit and a higher yield than the average garden raspberry). Plant them in a line, leaving 2 feet (60 cm) between plants.

Maintenance

Drive a wooden or metal stake into the ground at each end of the row, fix wires between the stakes, and tie the raspberry plants to the wire. In late summer cut out all the canes that have fruited that year and thin out the new canes so that they are about 1 foot (30 cm) apart. Weed round the canes and mulch heavily with whatever material you have available. Mulch again in the spring.

Harvesting

The fruit should be harvested as it ripens – for a few weeks in mid-summer you can pick raspberries every day.

Propagation

Raspberries self-propagate vigorously, producing new canes from their roots in an area of up to 6 to 8 feet (2 to 3 metres) around the main plants. These small plants can be dug up – thereby severing their connection with the parent plant – in the spring or the autumn and planted in the area to which you want to extend your raspberry bed. Unwanted plants have to be cut down.

Planting young shrubs and trees:
1. Dig a hole approx 1 ft x 1 ft x 1 ft (30 cm x 30 cm x 30 cm).
2. Pour in a bucket of water.
3. Place the plant in the hole, taking care to spread out the roots as much as possible.
4. Gently fill in the hole with compost or good topsoil, holding the stem of the plant to keep it above the surface.
5. Stamp down the soil round the plant to ensure that there is good contact between soil and roots. Make sure there is a slight depression round the plant, to make watering easier.
6. Prune the plant, so that the shoots do not make too much demand on the roots while they are becoming established. (Ideally, at the time of planting, the part of the plant above the ground should be no bigger than the part below the ground.)
7. Water regularly, especially if a week passes without rain.
8. It takes at least 12 months for a plant to become established in a new site. Take especial care to water newly-transplanted plants during dry spells.

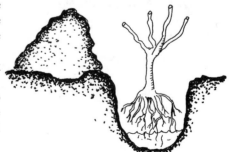

Planting a shrub

Blackberries

Blackberries require a little more work than raspberries. Instead of producing canes, they produce runners that have to be kept under tight control – otherwise your garden will turn into a bramble patch. Thornless varieties with large fruit are available from nurseries.

Planting
Start off with one or two plants. Plant them about 6 feet (2 metres) apart. Blackberries can be grown against a wall or fence, providing it faces south or west.

Maintenance
It is essential for the blackberry runners to be tied up. If the plants are growing beside a wall, fix wires to the wall; if they are growing in the open, construct a framework along which they can be trained.

The runners grow rapidly in early summer and should be tied up every couple of weeks. Allow each plant to develop 6 to 8 runners and cut off any extra ones.

The runners flower and produce fruit in their second year. After the fruit has been harvested, the old runners should be cut off and removed, to allow space for the following year's growth. Mulch round the plants regularly.

Harvesting
Blackberries ripen in late summer.

Propagation
Propagate by layering (see below) or by taking cuttings *(page 199)*.

Layering:
Layering is a very effective method of propagating trees and shrubs that produce branches or runners hanging close to the ground.

1. Select a branch or runner that is close to the ground and weigh it down with a small stone, so that the stem is pressed against the soil but the growing tip extends beyond the stone.

2. Leave the stone undisturbed for at least one year – the stem should produce roots where it is in contact with the ground. Hard-wooded shrubs should be left for two years.

3. Cut the branch linking the new plant to the parent.

4. Remove the stone and transplant the new plant to its final position.

Layering

  Easy   *Medium*   *Advanced*

Gooseberries

Gooseberries are a traditional English garden plant. They are hardy, easy to grow and produce fruit in abundance. There are many varieties that produce fruit of varying size and sweetness.

Planting

Plant gooseberry plants 4 feet (1 m 30 cm) apart in an open, sunny position.

Maintenance

Keep the gooseberry patch free of weeds by careful hoeing and applying as much mulch as you can spare. Gooseberries have a shallow root system which is easily damaged by over-vigorous hoeing.

If the plants get too large, prune the older branches in the summer, after harvesting the fruit.

Harvesting

Gooseberry plants have sharp spines and care has to taken when harvesting. All the fruit can be left on the plant and harvested at the same time. If it is to be used for jam making, it can be picked while it is still hard, but should be left to go soft and sweet if it is to be used for pies and tarts, etc. – in this case the fruit may need to be protected from birds.

Propagation

Propagate by layering or by cuttings.

Cuttings:

Many trees and shrubs can be propagated by cuttings. If possible, have a cuttings bed in a damp, sheltered spot of the garden, or in the corner of a greenhouse, in which you can plant cuttings as soon as you take them.

The best time to take cuttings from woody plants is in the autumn, other plants produce roots more readily and cuttings can be taken from them throughout the summer.

1. Cut, or break off, side shoots that are 6 - 12″ (15 - 30 cm) long: try to select shoots with new, vigorous growth. Take as many cuttings as you can, as only a proportion of them will survive.

2. Strip off all the leaves except for those growing at the tip of the cutting.

3. Using a dibber, or small stick, make a separate hole for each cutting. Put the cuttings in the holes, leaving just a few inches exposed above the ground. Pack soil back into the holes around the cuttings.

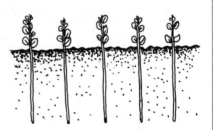

4. Never let the ground dry out and protect it from direct sun and heavy frost. Keep it free of weeds.

5. Do not disturb the cuttings for at least a year.

6. Transplant them when they have started to grow vigorously.

There should be more of the cuttings below ground than above.

Blackcurrants and Redcurrants

Blackcurrants are easy to grow and produce fruit for making jams, jellies and tarts in mid-summer. Redcurrants are less sweet than blackcurrants, and they are traditionally used for making jellies.

Planting
Over a long period of time, redcurrant and blackcurrant plants lose their vigour and the crop starts to decline. It is therefore best to start off with disease-free plants from a nursery or garden centre. Plant them 4 feet (1 m 30 cm) apart in an open, sunny position.

Maintenance
Keep them weed-free: hoe round them regularly, being careful not to damage the roots, and keep them well mulched. If the plants start to get too big and bushy, prune off the old stems after harvesting.

Harvesting
Pick the fruit as it becomes ripe. Redcurrants in particular are attractive to birds. The crop can be protected by covering the bushes with a net while the berries are ripening.

Propagation
Propagate by taking cuttings *(page 199)*.

> *Recipe:*
> Berry Muffins   *page 242*
> Blackcurrant Jam   *page 245*

Strawberries

Strawberries need a weed-free bed in a sunny location.

Planting
If possible, buy plants in the autumn and plant them about 12″ (30 cm) apart, in their final position – this should ensure that you get a crop the following year.

Maintenance
Weed regularly and apply plenty of mulch. In the summer, mulch with straw, if you have any, as this will keep the strawberries from touching the ground (fruit that touches the ground tends to rot in wet weather and is often attacked by slugs). You can put a cloche over the plants in the spring if you want to get an earlier crop.

Harvesting
Pick the fruit as it becomes ripe. It may be necessary to protect the fruit from birds and squirrels with a net.

Propagation
Strawberry plants produce copious amounts of runners. Runners produce roots and shoots at points where they touch the ground. Select the runners that you want to keep (cut off all the rest); weigh them down with a small stone, so that the roots can become established; and in the autumn cut the runner and transplant the new plant to its final position. In this way, you can make a new row of strawberries each year. Dig up older plants when they start to produce less fruit (after three or four years).

Cutting off a strawberry runner.

    Easy   *Medium*   *Advanced*

Trees

Native Trees

Gardens have always been associated with the presence of ornamental trees but now a case can be made for every gardener planting at least one native tree somewhere in their garden – modern agricultural techniques have led to the devastation of the tree population so it is now up to gardeners to maintain at least a small population of the trees that are so important to the local flora and fauna.

Study your local area and work out which trees should naturally be growing there. If you have space, plant one of the species of trees that would have been dominant in your region, such as oaks or beech; if you do not have much room plant one of the species that would have lived beneath the main canopy of the forest – such as birch, hazel, hawthorn or holly.

Oak

As well as providing a focal point for your garden, these trees will attract birds and wildlife. Spring-flowering bulbs will thrive if planted around their trunk, and the trees will provide shade in the summer.

Planting

Whether grown from seed or from cuttings, trees are not usually planted in their final position until they are three or four years old. Plant in the usual way but try to make a large depression round the trunk so that water is retained when you water during dry spells.

All trees need to be looked after for the first one or two years since it takes them this long to establish a strong root system. This is particularly true of ornamental trees and fruit trees; they cannot be vigorously pruned on planting and this makes them susceptible to being dislodged by strong winds: if a tree's roots move in the ground its ability to take up water from the soil is impaired, and it becomes susceptible to drought. The problem can be reduced by attaching the tree to a firm stake (make sure that you use a plastic or rubber tie because string or rope can rub through the bark).

Fruit Trees

Apples, pears, plum, and cherry trees were at one time a feature of every garden. If possible, purchase your tree from a specialist nursery which is able to advise you on the size that the tree will reach. Old varieties are preferable to modern ones – they take longer to mature but require less maintenance. Ideally, try to let the tree achieve its natural shape, but if there is not sufficient room for this to happen, prune the tree each autumn – use sharp secateurs and cut the branches cleanly to reduce the chances of infection.

Fruit trees that are not pruned produce fruit of varying sizes, but this need not be seen as a disadvantage.

Herbs

Grow your herbs as close to the kitchen as possible. If you do not have a garden beside your home, consider growing herbs in pots or in window boxes. Herb plants require quite a lot of looking after and it is better to have a small, carefully-tended herb bed than a large one that gets out of control.

Annual Herbs

Many culinary herbs have to be grown from seed every year:

Parsley

Parsley is one of the most widely-used herbs in cookery. If you experience difficulty in getting the seeds to germinate, buy plants and, instead of pulling them up at the end of the season, allow them to flower and produce seeds. Collect some of the seed for planting the following year and leave the rest on the plant. Seedlings will grow up around the old plants in the following spring. These seedlings can be transplanted to a new position without difficulty.

	J	F	M	A	M	J	J	A	S	O	N	D
Planting				▓	▓							
Harvesting	▓	▓						▓	▓	▓	▓	▓

A dozen good parsley plants should be sufficient to supply any family kitchen.

Basil

Basil is a vital ingredient of many Mediterranean recipes. It *can* be grown outdoors but it grows best under cover. The seedlings are prone to being attacked by slugs when they are small and can be protected with rings cut from plastic bottles. Basil leaves can continue to be picked from the plants even when they are flowering.

	J	F	M	A	M	J	J	A	S	O	N	D
Planting			▓	▓	▓							
Harvesting						▓	▓	▓	▓	▓		

Coriander

Fresh coriander is an essential ingredient in Indian cooking. Coriander is a tough plant that has no difficulty growing outdoors but it does tend to flower as soon as it has reached a reasonable size. Leaves from flowering plants can still be used but once the flower has formed, the plant stops making new leaves. To ensure a continuous supply of coriander you must make successive sowings throughout the spring and summer.

Leave a few flowering plants to self seed and your herb bed will always have a few coriander plants springing up of their own accord.

Anaxagoras! What are you doing with my parsley soup?

What else Judith, but decorating the tomb of my ancestor? It is a custom among us Greeks.

	J	F	M	A	M	J	J	A	S	O	N	D
Planting			▓	▓	▓	▓	▓	▓				
Harvesting						▓	▓	▓	▓		▓	

Perennial Herbs

Mint

Mint has very vigorous roots that spread rapidly, growing just beneath the surface of the soil. For this reason, mint plant roots have to be contained by a barrier of bricks or similar material to stop them spreading over the whole herb bed.

The tops die down each winter and grow up again in the spring. The first leaves of the year are generally considered to be the best.

There are different varieties of mint – peppermint, spearmint, lemon mint, etc. Keep them separate from each other if you want them to retain their individual characteristics.

Chives

Chives are in the same family as onions and shallots but are grown for their leaves rather than their bulbs. The leaves can be cut for salads early in the year, when the garden is not yielding many crops. Later on the distinctive chive flowers make an attractive feature in the herb bed.

Weed the chives once or twice a year as they can become choked with grass.

Sage, Rosemary, and Thyme

Sage, rosemary, and thyme have similar requirements to each other. They thrive best in a sunny, well-drained position where they are protected from high winds. They can be bought as individual plants and replaced every three or four years.

There are several different varieties of thyme and they can be grown for their attractive flowers as well as for their aromatic leaves.

Drying Herbs

Collect the herbs on a dry day. The plants should be mature but, if possible, not flowering. Tie the plants in small bunches of 7 to 10 stems and hang them upside down in a warm place, such as an airing cupboard or a well-heated room. Crumble the leaves when they are brittle, and store them in a dark, air-tight container.

(In the case of lavender, it is the flower stalks that are picked. Cut the stalks just before the flowers open, tie them together in small bunches and hang them up to dry.)

Recommended Books:
A Modern Herbal, Margaret Grieve, Dover

Flowers

There are hundreds of different types of flowers that you can grow in the garden. The following list describes some traditional favourites that are relatively easy to grow and which make a good starting point for any flower garden.

Annuals

Annuals are plants that have to be planted from seed each year, and which die back after flowering; many of the most attractive garden flowers are annuals. Some of them are more resistant to cold than others and it is best to be guided by instructions on the seed packet as to sowing and transplanting times.

Candytuft, Marigolds, Poppies and Cornflowers

Some garden annuals – such as cornflowers, poppies, marigolds, and candytuft – are closely related to wild plants that, before the advent of modern farming, grew abundantly in the fields and hedgerows. These thrive when sown directly into their final flowering position. Leave a few of them to set seed after flowering, collect some of the seed and leave the rest on the plant. These flowers should grow up of their own accord the following year.

Sweet Peas

Sweet peas do best when they have a long growing season and should therefore be started off as early in the year as possible. Sow them in a pot in early spring and keep them indoors, on a sunny window sill. Transplant them to their final position once the weather becomes warm (April or May). Either train them up a south-facing wall or fence, or construct a framework up which they can climb. Sweet pea plants will provide cut flowers for the house throughout the summer – the more you cut them, the more they will bloom.

Aster, Petunia

Aster and petunia are grown in the same way. Both are sensitive to frost and should therefore be started off in a seed tray indoors. The young plants can be planted out after all

danger of late frosts has passed and the soil has had a chance to warm up; they should be watered copiously for the first few weeks. Once established, both aster and petunia flower prolifically and have a long flowering season, providing colour in the garden, for many weeks.

Herbaceous Perennials

A bed of herbaceous perennials provides masses of very striking flowers for very little work. Perennials are plants that flower in the summer and then die back in the winter – to grow up again the following spring. They include **Lupins, Red-hot Pokers, Delphiniums,** and **Chrysanthemums**.
The bed needs to be weeded once or twice a year and well mulched over the winter. The plants will gradually spread to fill the bed and will have to be dug up and split into smaller clumps every few years.

Flowering Shrubs

Roses

Roses are the most popular flowering shrub. They can be grown from cuttings taken in the autumn or bought as plants. Climbing roses give a traditional, cottage atmosphere to a garden, especially when combined with **Honeysuckle**. They need a framework up which to grow, but are otherwise easy to care for. They do not need regular pruning, and, in fact, will not flower if they are cut back too severely.

Bush varieties, on the other hand, do best if they are pruned every year. Flowers appear on the new growth produced each year and the plant should therefore be cut back every spring. This process is very demanding on the soil, and bush roses must, therefore, be kept well nourished: mulch around them with compost in the winter and grass cuttings in the summer.

A Shrubbery

A shrubbery is a very attractive feature particularly when it is beside a lawn or at the edge of the garden. Once it has become established it will require very little maintenance, and will provide shelter and food for birds, insects, and other small animals.

When you buy shrub plants, try to work out how big each of them will eventually grow and how they look in the different seasons of the year, and then position them accordingly in your shrubbery: put the small shrubs at the front and the tall ones at the back, keep a balance between those that lose their leaves in the winter and those that keep them, etc.

Designing a shrubbery is a difficult task – there are so many factors to take into account: the colours of the flowers, the colours of the berries, the way the leaf colour changes with the seasons, the colour of the twigs in winter, and the pattern of growth – and you are bound to put some plants in the wrong place. Young shrub plants can, however, be moved and many of them are relatively easy to propagate by taking cuttings, or by layering.

For the first few years, weed and mulch round the plants and water them in dry weather. Eventually they should start to look after themselves – the leaves they shed will act as a mulch, and weeds will have difficulty growing in their shade.

Bulbs

Bulbs are able to flower at unusual times of the year because the bloom is produced from the reserves stored in the bulb rather than directly from nutrients produced by the leaves. **Snowdrops, Crocuses,** and **Daffodils** flower early in the year providing a welcome sign that winter is coming to an end.

Bulbs are often grown under trees but they can also be planted in the lawn or in flower beds. Their leaves should be left for as long as possible after the flower has bloomed, because it is these leaves that produce the nutrients which replenish the bulbs and allow them to flower again the following year.

A Place to Sit

It should never be forgotten that, in addition to all its other attributes, a garden provides the perfect place for peace and relaxation.

Depending on the size of your garden, you can have a lawn, a pond, a sheltered arbour, a bench under a tree, or a little corner in which you can sit and be part of the natural world.

Gardening and the Environment

Nowadays, young people are given a great deal of information about environmental issues. Much of what they hear relates to global concerns and can often leave them feeling overwhelmed – there is very little that an individual can do about global warming, the destruction of tropical rainforests, and holes in the ozone layer – however, there are serious environmental issues closer to home which are often glossed over and which everyone can do something to alleviate.

Modern farming methods have proved to be an unmitigated environmental disaster. They have led to the uprooting of hedgerows, the felling of trees, the depletion of bird and insect populations and the disappearance of wild flowers. To all intents and purposes the countryside has been reduced to an industrial wasteland, depopulated even of the people who have cared for it and moulded it for hundreds of years.

By creating a garden, especially an organic garden, you are actually doing something to reverse this process. You will find that, as each year passes, the fertility of your soil will increase, there will be more insects, a greater variety of wild plants, more birds visiting the garden, and the trees that you plant will flower and produce seed. Your garden will act as a sanctuary in which the local flora and fauna can survive until conditions once again become favourable for them in the surrounding countryside, and, if enough people were to follow your example, and enough gardens were created, there would no longer be an environmental problem in your area.

Coal tit.
Tits nest in holes in trees. If
you do not have mature trees
in your garden, you can hang up nestboxes for them to use.

Conclusion

One of the major problems associated with our education system is its lack of flexibility. Perhaps, a few years ago, there was a valid reason for trying to increase the literacy or the scientific knowledge of the population as a whole, but, for reasons that may or may not be the responsibility of the education system itself, there is now an urgent need for the priority to be shifted towards introducing young people to the world of Nature.

All life, including human life, depends on Nature; the traditional approach to education with its emphasis on languages, mathematics, literature, science, etc., is based upon the assumption that the student is already grounded in a thorough understanding of the natural world. Given the fact that this is increasingly not the case, the first priority of education should now be to ensure that the student has an opportunity to experience the world of Nature every day, three hundred and sixty-five days per year.

Gardening is the only activity that allows this to happen. Even when surrounded by the harshest urban environment, a garden remains a perfect piece of Nature in every respect, and can teach a willing student everything that they need to know about the processes of life. The only condition is that the student has to be allowed to take responsibility for that garden – it has to become their own.

By great good fortune, gardening is not only an activity of paramount educational importance, but it is also immensely rewarding. It can be recommended to a young person without fear of causing the alienation and disappointment that attends so many aspects of education today.

Of all smells, bread;
of all tastes, salt.

George Herbert (1593 - 1633)

Cooking

Contents:

Cooking

Somehow, cooking has managed to gain a second-class status within the education system, making it suitable only for those young people who are not clever enough to pursue academic subjects. It is difficult to explain how or why this can have happened. The ability to cook is one of the most sought-after skills in the job market and opens up possibilities of well-paid employment virtually anywhere in the world.

More importantly, the ability to cook is fundamental to the quality of life. Good food, prepared from fresh ingredients, is a source of health and pleasure, and there is virtually no way in which it can be obtained unless it is prepared by yourself or by someone in your home.

No matter how successful or wealthy you become, if you lack the ability to cook good food for yourself, your quality of life may still be very poor.

Cooking should, therefore, be an integral part of everyone's education, and, if necessary, should even take precedence over other activities that are traditionally considered educational.

The Food Industry

Although there are some good points about the food industry – it has developed a distribution system that makes it easy to obtain ingredients relatively cheaply and easily from around the world – it does need to be treated with extreme caution.

In general, it must be a serious mistake to treat food as though it is an industrial product, and all factory processes, mechanised production techniques or factory farming methods, must surely be robbing food of much of its inherent value. The huge array of processed and pre-prepared foods – including crisps, sweets, chocolates, soft drinks, biscuits, tinned foods, frozen foods, and chilled foods – that appears on supermarket shelves, seems to offer an alternative to cooking for yourself, but its long-term effects upon health are unknown. Furthermore, processed foods lack the variety and subtlety of taste that exist in things that you have cooked yourself.

> "Foods must be in the condition in which they are found in nature, or, at least, in a condition as close as possible to that found in nature."
>
> *Hippocrates (460 BC)*

The Solution

The solution is simple: it is to start cooking your own food from fresh ingredients, organic if possible. You can begin cooking at eleven or twelve-years old, and there is no reason why young people should not do all the cooking for the family, especially if their parents work long hours and cannot cook for themselves.

Recipes

Cooking is a creative process and it takes time and practice to get it right. Everyone has occasional disasters when they are learning to cook (and when they are an experienced cook), but that is part of the learning process.

Cooking is something that you have to learn by practical experience, usually through a process of trial and error; if you know someone who can cook and you can work with them, they will be able to give you help and assistance, but ultimately everyone has to develop their own style of cooking and this takes time and practice.

The recipes in the following section have been written with a view to appealing to cooks of varying experience and varying tastes.

Balanced Meals

There are different culinary traditions in different parts of the world, but they all have one thing in common: balanced meals. A balanced meal contains carbohydrate, such as rice, pasta, potato, or bread; protein, such as beans, nuts, cheese or eggs; and fresh vegetables which are particularly rich in minerals, vitamins and fibre. When preparing meals it is important to respect this tradition. Balanced meals are not only more satisfying to eat but they are also healthy. It is eating unbalanced meals, especially those lacking in fresh fruit and vegetables, that can cause people to gain weight and to develop associated health problems.

One of the most difficult things about cooking a meal is getting all the separate dishes ready at the same time: even with careful planning, this is something that you may not be able to achieve the first time that you cook a new meal. One solution is for each member of the family to cook a different dish; providing you can synchronise your activities, this can be a very enjoyable way of working together.

Internet Recipes:

One of the most practical aspects of the internet is the way in which it allows people to share recipes. If you find that you suddenly have a surplus of produce from the garden, or a special meal to prepare, searching the internet can rapidly provide you with a list of new recipes and suggestions. These recipes have the advantage over recipe books and magazines in that they are being recommended by ordinary people who have, perhaps, used them many, many times. The internet is also able to offer a much wider choice than could be included in any collection of books – there are now thousands of sites offering recipes of every conceivable description, most of which can be downloaded free of charge.

In Greece our food is our medicine and our medicine is our food—delicious balanced meals!

But it's not easy to make them balanced!

The Kitchen

It is not necessary to have a large, elaborately-equipped kitchen in order to cook for yourself and your family: ideally you will have a cooker with an oven, a sink, a surface to work on, and all or most of the utensils listed below, but none of these things are essential. Many of the world's best-loved recipes have been developed by people cooking over a fire in the open air, and, in reality, most things can be cooked in the very simplest of kitchens, with a minimal amount of equipment.

Kitchen utensils:
- Wooden chopping boards
- Knives
- Saucepans – enamelled cast-iron or stainless-steel pans if possible (try to avoid using aluminium utensils, because there is a risk of aluminium compounds getting into the food)
- Cast-iron frying pan
- Non-stick frying pan
- Wok – a steel wok will last longer than a non-stick wok
- Sieve
- Colander
- Mixing bowls
- Wooden spoons
- Pestle and mortar
- Baking trays
- Oven gloves
- Cake tins
- Bread tins
- Measuring spoons, measuring cups
- Hand-held electric blender
- Wire rack
- Griddle

Ingredients

If you do a lot of cooking, you will need to keep some basic ingredients always in stock.

Herbs

Try to grow your own herbs, close to the kitchen door or in a window box, if possible. Freeze or dry any surplus in the summer for use during the winter. The most commonly used herbs are:

- Parsley
- Thyme
- Mint
- Basil
- Rosemary
- Sage
- Oregano
- Coriander
- Dill

Spices

- Chilli powder
- Cumin powder, cumin seeds
- Turmeric powder
- Cinnamon powder, cinnamon sticks
- Coriander powder, coriander seeds
- Garam masala
- Paprika powder
- Ginger

You also need a ready supply of salt, sugar, flour, baking powder, and yeast.

In addition to these basic ingredients, you need the specific ingredients for each recipe – vegetables, beans, rice, flour, pasta, etc. If possible, buy organic ingredients and ingredients that have not been held in storage for long periods of time. Whole-food shops and natural food stores may be a better source of such ingredients than the local supermarket.

Fresh, organic ingredients are not necessarily more expensive than the equivalent processed foods, but, even when they are, it is important to keep a sense of perspective and to remember that you cannot put too high a price on really good food.

Safety in the Kitchen

Cooking involves using fire to change the property of food; everyone knows that fire is dangerous and cooking is therefore a potentially dangerous activity. Furthermore it involves the use of knives which are also intrinsically dangerous. It is imperative to consider safety at all times while you are cooking.

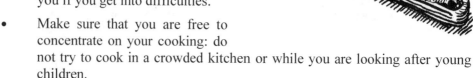

- If you are an inexperienced cook, do not cook while you are alone in the house – make sure that there is a responsible person at home who will be able to help you if you get into difficulties.

- Make sure that you are free to concentrate on your cooking: do not try to cook in a crowded kitchen or while you are looking after young children.

- Familiarise yourself with your cooker: make sure that you know how to turn the oven, and all the different rings, on and off. If it is an electric cooker, make sure that you know where the mains switch is.

- Have a fire blanket close to the cooker: practise taking it out of its bag and ensure that you know how it works.

- Don't leave pan handles sticking over the edge of the cooker.

- Use oven gloves when taking things in and out of the oven.

- Be careful when you use knives: when chopping, keep the blade as far away from your fingers as possible. Do not leave knives lying about, especially in the presence of young children.

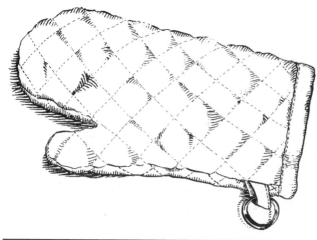

- If you use electrical items, such as a hand-held blender, make sure that you know how they work; do not let them get wet; and do not leave electrical leads hanging over the edge of work surfaces.

- Try to tidy up as you go along.

Glossary of Cooking Terms

Bring to the Boil .... To heat water over a high heat, in a pan with a lid on, until the water is bubbling vigorously and giving off steam.

Dice .... To cut vegetables into dice-sized cubes.

Dough .... A mixture thick enough to be rolled or kneaded.

Drain .... To allow excess water to run off vegetables, grain, etc., by placing them in a sieve, or colander, over a sink.

Dry Roast .... To cook nuts etc. using no oil.

Fry .... To cook food in a small amount of oil.

Grease .... To coat a tin with oil or some kind of fat.

Knead .... To pummel and stretch dough with the heel of the hand for 8 – 10 minutes.

Knock back .... To knead a yeast dough for a second time, after leaving it to rise, to ensure an even texture.

Purée .... Fruit or vegetables sieved, cooked, or blended to a smooth pulp.

Roast .... To cook food in an oven in an open tray or pan.

Rub in .... To rub fat and flour together between the fingers of both hands, until they combine to form a dry mixture, resembling breadcrumbs.

Season .... To add flavouring (usually salt and pepper) to a dish.

Sauté .... A quick way of cooking food in a little oil, over a high heat.

Simmer .... A low boil, in which the surface of the water bubbles gently.

Work in .... To gradually add an ingredient to dough, batter, etc.

Note:

1 teaspoon = 5 ml   1 tablespoon = 15 ml

There is a set of conversion tables on *pages 336 and 337*.

All recipes are for 4 – 5 people.

Preparing Vegetables

- **French Beans**
  Wash the beans and cut off both ends. Long beans can be cut in half.

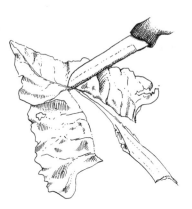

- **Spinach**
  Wash spinach leaves carefully to remove earth and any insects that may be on them, then carefully cut out and discard the central rib of each leaf. Also remove any brown parts of the leaves.

- **Parsnips**
  Cut off both the top and bottom of the parsnip, being careful to remove all brown or soft areas – the top of the parsnip can be damaged by frost towards the end of winter. Parsnips tend to become tough and fibrous close to the root tip and it does no harm to remove 3″ – 4″ (7 cm – 10 cm) of the thin, tapering part of the root.

  The parsnip can then be either scrubbed or peeled.

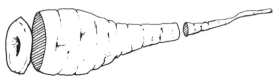

- **Carrots**
  Cut off the top and bottom of the carrot. Early carrots can then be scrubbed and used.

  Later in the season it is advisable to peel the carrots so that any carrot root fly larvae damage can be seen and removed.

- **Tomatoes**

Remove the stalk that attached the tomato to the plant. Cut the tomato into quarters and carefully cut out the fibrous part in the centre.

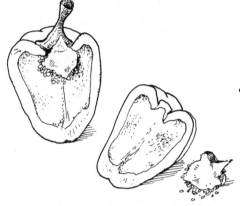

- **Peppers**

Cut the pepper in half and remove seeds and the stalk that attached it to the plant. The pepper can then be cut up and used.

- **Onions**

Cut off the top of the onion and the roots at the base. The outer skin can be peeled off by hand, leaving the onion to be cut either into rings or pieces, according to the recipe.

When they are cut, onions give off a fine spray that gets into the eyes and makes them water. This can be so acute that it becomes painful and can make it impossible to continue. The problem is reduced by using a very sharp knife and working quickly. If you have to cut up a large amount of onions, try wearing glasses.

- **Garlic**

Prise the garlic bulb apart with your hands. Select the clove that you want to use, and cut off its base. It should then be possible to peel off and discard its outer skin.

The clove can either be squeezed through a garlic press or chopped up with a sharp knife.

Sautéed Vegetables

*Sautéeing vegetables requires more skill than
simply boiling them, but it is worth the extra effort.*

Ingredients:
One of the following:

> Carrots, cut in rings or strips
> Broad beans and peas, shelled
> French beans cut in halves
> Brussels sprouts, outer leaves
> removed, cut in halves
> Cabbage, thinly sliced
> Courgettes, sliced

1 tablespoon olive oil

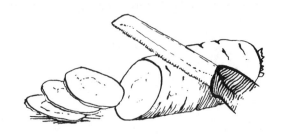

Method:

1. Pour the oil into a cast-iron saucepan and heat.
2. Add the vegetables and stir with a wooden spoon for two or three minutes.
3. Add enough water to cover the bottom of the pan, cover with a lid and keep on a high heat.
4. Remove the lid and stir every two or three minutes. Add more water if the vegetables start to stick to the pan. Turn off the heat when the vegetables are cooked but still firm. Ideally, there should be no water left in the pan at this point.
5. Serve hot.

Freezing Vegetables

Vegetables should be 'blanched' before being frozen: this helps to preserve their taste and colour. The aim is to heat the vegetables up to 100°C and to then cool them down as quickly as possible.

Ingredients:

> Vegetable for freezing: broad beans, peas, French beans, etc.

Method:

1. Bring a large pan of water to the boil.
2. Prepare a bowl of ice-cold water (this is done by adding ice cubes to cold water).
3. Add the vegetables to the pan of boiling water. Keep the heat turned up high, bring the water back to the boil, and boil for 1 minute.
4. Drain the vegetables through a colander. Rinse with cold water.
5. Tip the vegetables into the bowl of ice-cold water and stir them round with your hand to cool them down as quickly as possible. Leave for 3 minutes.
6. Strain the vegetables through the colander.
7. Put the vegetables in plastic bags and place them in the freezer.
8. Tie up the plastic bags, when the vegetables are thoroughly frozen – i.e. on the following day.

  Easy   *Medium*   *Advanced*

Corn on the Cob

Ingredients:

Corn on the cob (1 per person)
½ teaspoon salt

Method:
1. Half fill a large pan with water, add the salt and bring to the boil.
2. Remove husks and silk from the cobs, then add the corn cobs to the boiling water.
3. Bring water back to the boil and boil vigorously for 5 minutes.
4. Drain and serve.

Peas

Fresh peas, picked when young and cooked straight away, are one of the sweetest delicacies from the garden.
Method:
1. Bring a small pan of water to the boil, and add the peas.
2. Boil for two or three minutes, then taste the peas to see if they are cooked.
3. Strain through a colander and serve hot.

Spinach

It is not too difficult to have fresh spinach from the garden throughout the year. When cooked properly it is one of the tastiest and most versatile of all vegetables. The secret of success is to use as little water as possible.

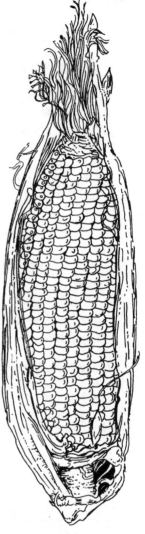

Method:
1. Wash each leaf carefully and then shake it to remove excess water.
2. Rib each leaf *(see Preparing Vegetables page 216)*.
3. Add 2 tablespoons of water to a large pan, and add the spinach. Place a lid on the pan, and cook over a high heat.
4. Remove the lid and stir every 30 seconds. The spinach should collapse to a fraction of its original size. If it starts to stick to the pan, add a little more water; if there is too much water, remove the lid, heat vigorously and stir until all the liquid is boiled off.
5. The spinach should be cooked in 4 – 5 minutes.
6. Serve hot.

Boiled Beetroot

Ingredients:

Beetroot, fresh from the garden, with the leaves twisted off

Method:

1. Carefully rinse the beetroot to remove earth, taking care not to break the skins, and put them in a large pan of water. Bring to the boil.
2. Turn down the heat slightly and boil for 30 minutes.
3. Turn off the heat and allow the pan to cool down.
4. Discard the water and peel the beetroot.

Pickled Beetroot

Ingredients:

Boiled beetroot

Organic vinegar – cider or other vinegar

Method:

1. Slice the beetroot.
2. Fill a clean jar with the slices (the jar should have a screw-top lid).
3. Pour vinegar into the jar until all the beetroot is covered.

If stored in the refrigerator, beetroot pickled in this way will last for several weeks.

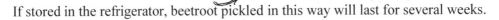

Winter Vegetables

A winter recipe containing parsnips, celeriac, and carrots, flavoured with brown sugar and cardamom.

Ingredients:

12 oz (350 g) carrots

12 oz (350 g) parsnips

12 oz (350 g) celeriac

¼ pint (150 ml) olive oil

4 cardamom pods, lightly crushed

1 tablespoon soft brown sugar

Salt and pepper

Method:

1. Peel all the vegetables and cut off the ends *(see page 216)*. Cut them into chunks.
2. Pour the olive oil into a roasting tin and heat in the oven for a couple of minutes. Remove, and add the vegetables, turning them so that they are well coated in oil. Roast them in the oven at 200°C (400°F) Gas Mark 6 for 30 minutes, turning the vegetables again twice during cooking.
3. Add the crushed cardamom pods and sugar to the vegetables, turning them to coat evenly. Return to the oven and bake for a further 30 minutes, until well browned and completely soft, but not disintegrating.
4. Season with salt and pepper and transfer to a serving dish.

Summer Pasta Salad

A Mediterranean-style salad.

Ingredients:

Dressing:
6 tablespoons olive oil
2 oz (150 g) sun-dried tomatoes, drained
2 fl oz (50 ml) vinegar
1 garlic clove, finely chopped

Pasta:
1 lb (450 g) pasta shells
8 oz (225 g) halved cherry tomatoes
8 oz (225 g) tofu or feta cheese, cut into
   ½" cubes
1 oz (25 g) fresh basil leaves, thinly sliced
2 teaspoons dried oregano
20 – 25 black olives (chopped)

Method:
1. Fill a large pan two thirds full with water, cover with a lid and bring to the boil.
2. Meanwhile, blend dressing ingredients in a blender or food processor until they form a smooth paste. Transfer to a small bowl and set aside.
3. Add a teaspoon of salt and the pasta to the boiling water. Cook until tender, stirring occasionally. Drain well and transfer to a large serving bowl.
4. Add the dressing to the pasta and toss to coat. Leave it to cool (about ¼ hour) then mix in the cherry tomatoes, tofu, basil, oregano and olives. Season to taste and serve.

Green Salad with Walnut Dressing

Traditional lettuce salad. Amounts can be varied according to the size of the salad.

Ingredients:
A medium-sized lettuce
3 tablespoons olive oil
½ teaspoon wine or cider vinegar
½ teaspoon soya sauce or ¼ teaspoon salt
Freshly ground black pepper
½ oz (15 g) walnuts, finely chopped

Method:
1. Wash the lettuce and drain it in a colander. Chop and put it in a bowl. Set aside.
2. In a small jug or glass mix together the olive oil, vinegar, soya sauce, and pepper. Add the chopped walnuts, stir well, and pour over the lettuce.
3. 'Toss' the lettuce by stirring it with your fingers or a wooden spoon – take care not to crush it – and serve.

Vegetable Feuilleté

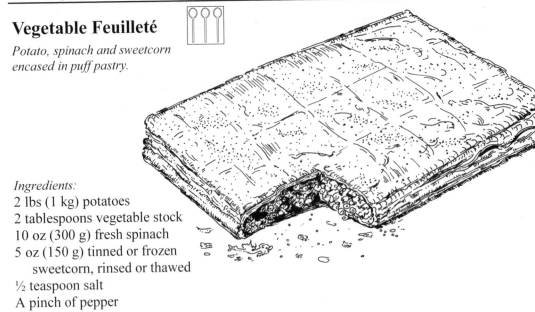

*Potato, spinach and sweetcorn
encased in puff pastry.*

Ingredients:
2 lbs (1 kg) potatoes
2 tablespoons vegetable stock
10 oz (300 g) fresh spinach
5 oz (150 g) tinned or frozen
    sweetcorn, rinsed or thawed
½ teaspoon salt
A pinch of pepper
A pinch of grated nutmeg
One 13 oz (370 g) packet frozen puff pastry, thawed
Poppy seeds

Method:
1. Fill a large pan two thirds full with water. Add a pinch of salt, and bring to the boil.
2. Wash, peel and chop the potatoes. Add them to the boiling water and cook until soft. Drain.
3. Mix the vegetable stock with the potatoes and mash well.
4. Prepare the spinach *(see page 216)*. Chop and cook for about 3 minutes in 2 tablespoons water, until it has wilted. Drain well.
5. Mix the spinach, sweetcorn, salt, pepper and grated nutmeg into the mashed potato.
6. Roll out the pastry thinly and cut in half. Place one half on a lightly-oiled, flat baking tray.
7. Pile the potato mixture onto this half, flattening the mixture out to within ¼" (½ cm) of the edge.
8. Place the other half of the pastry on top, pressing the edges firmly together. Make 3 small slits in the pastry to allow steam to escape when cooking.
9. Sprinkle poppy seeds over the pastry.
10. Cook in a preheated oven at 220°C (425°F) Gas Mark 7 for about 20 minutes or until the pastry is golden brown and well risen. Serve hot or cold.

Easy   Medium   Advanced

French Bean Pickle

Based on a Botswanan recipe, this highly-spiced pickle is the perfect answer to a bumper crop of French beans.

Ingredients:

2 lb (1 kg) French beans, trimmed
2 tablespoons salt
16 fl oz (450 ml) corn oil
1 tablespoon turmeric
1 teaspoon ground fenugreek
2 teaspoons garam masala
1 green chilli, seeded and chopped

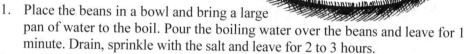

Method:

1. Place the beans in a bowl and bring a large pan of water to the boil. Pour the boiling water over the beans and leave for 1 minute. Drain, sprinkle with the salt and leave for 2 to 3 hours.
2. Heat 2 tablespoons of the oil in a saucepan and lightly fry the spices. Add remaining oil and heat, stirring often, for 3 – 4 minutes. Turn off the heat.
3. Pack the beans into a large jar with the green chillies. Pour the oil and spices over them. Leave to cool and seal with an airtight lid.
   The pickle will keep for several months.

Red Cabbage with Pine Nuts

A simple but tasty way to cook red cabbage.

Ingredients:

1 medium/large red cabbage
2 tablespoons olive oil

¼ pint (150 ml) vegetable stock
2 tablespoons balsamic vinegar
2 oz (50 g) pine nuts

Method:

1. Halve the red cabbage, remove the white core and slice each half thinly. Rinse in a colander and drain.
2. Add the oil to a large, ovenproof, casserole dish and heat for half a minute, over a medium heat. Tip in the shredded red cabbage, stir, and cover with a lid.
3. Cook for 4 – 5 minutes. Remove the lid and pour the vegetable stock into the pan. Stir again, replace the lid and cook in the oven at 190°C (375°F) Gas Mark 5 for about 30 minutes or until the red cabbage is soft.
4. Meanwhile dry roast the pine nuts in a pan, until they just start to colour. Put to one side.
5. Remove the casserole dish from the oven and add the balsamic vinegar to the red cabbage. Mix well.
6. Sprinkle the pine nuts on top just before serving.

Beetroot Rice (Chakanda Chawal)

A quick and unusual recipe for rice, based on an authentic Indian dish.

Ingredients:

Rice:
3 cups water
½ teaspoon salt
2 cups white rice, washed and drained
2 tablespoons sunflower or sesame oil

Vegetables:
2 tablespoons sunflower or sesame oil
1 teaspoon mustard seeds
1 teaspoon freshly-ground black pepper

½ teaspoon cumin seeds
1 green chilli, chopped (optional)
2 onions, chopped
A few curry leaves
1 large cooked beetroot, diced
½ teaspoon salt
½ teaspoon turmeric powder
Juice of 1 lemon
10 cashew nuts, chopped

Method:

Rice: 1. Put water on to boil with ½ teaspoon salt.
2. Meanwhile, heat the oil in a large heavy-bottomed pan. Add rice and stir over a low heat until the water in the other pan starts to boil.
3. Turn off both heat sources. Add the water to the rice. **This has to be done very carefully: the water may boil furiously and should be added only a little at a time.** Cover with a lid.
4. Place in the oven and cook at 160°C (325°F) Gas Mark 3 for 15 minutes.

Vegetables: 1. In a medium-sized frying pan heat 2 tablespoons of oil and fry the mustard seeds, pepper, cumin seeds and chilli for 1 – 2 minutes. Add the onions and curry leaves and fry over a low heat until the onions start to brown. Stir in the beetroot, salt, and turmeric and fry for a further few minutes.
2. Add the beetroot mixture to the cooked rice, stir well and sprinkle with lemon juice.
3. Dry roast the cashew nuts in a small frying pan for 1 – 2 minutes and sprinkle them over the rice.

Curried Avocado

Ingredients:
2 large (or 3 small) avocados, quartered and peeled
2 limes (zest and juice)
2 tablespoons sesame oil
1 clove garlic, finely chopped

1 onion, finely chopped
1 green chilli, finely chopped
1 tablespoon mustard seeds
1 - 1½ tablespoons medium curry paste
1 tablespoon coriander leaves (optional)
½ teaspoon salt

Method:
1. Cut the quartered avocados lengthwise into ¼" (½ cm) slices and sprinkle with the juice and zest of the limes. Set aside.
2. Heat oil in a cast-iron frying pan. Add the garlic, onion, green chilli, and mustard seeds. Cover and cook over a low heat.
3. When the mustard seeds begin to pop, stir in the curry paste and cook (uncovered) for another minute.
4. Add the avocado slices to the pan, and turn off the heat. Sprinkle with the chopped coriander leaves and salt. Serve immediately.

Vegetable Curry

This traditional Nepalese curry is an ideal way to use vegetables from the garden.

Ingredients:
2 lbs (1 kg) potatoes, cubed
5 medium carrots, diced
8 oz (225 g) French beans
4 tablespoons sunflower or
   sesame oil
2 medium onions, chopped
1 bay leaf, broken
½ teaspoon black pepper
2 – 3 garlic cloves, chopped
1½" (4 cm) piece of ginger,
   finely chopped
½ teaspoon turmeric
2 teaspoons coriander seeds
1 tablespoon cumin seeds

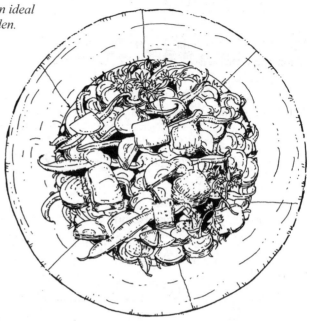

Method:
1. Wash and peel the potatoes and carrots, and chop them into smallish chunks. Top and tail the French beans *(see Preparing Vegetables page 216)*.
2. Heat the oil in a large, heavy-bottomed pan and fry the onion until golden. Add the bay leaf, black pepper, garlic, ginger, and turmeric, and fry for about 30 seconds.
3. Add the potatoes and stir well to cover with the spice mixture. Fry for 2 – 3 minutes.
4. Add the carrots, French beans, coriander seeds and cumin seeds and 1½ cups of hot water.
5. Cover the pan with a lid and simmer over a low heat until the vegetables are tender. Season to taste and serve with rice.

Note: The vegetables in this recipe can be varied according to season and availability.

Lentils and Spinach (Sag Dal)

Tasty red lentils and spinach, flavoured with a variety of different spices.

Ingredients:

10 oz (300 g) masur dal (red lentils)
½ teaspoon tumeric
1 teaspoon salt
½ teaspoon paprika or chilli powder
1 lb (450 g) spinach

2 tablespoons oil
1 onion, chopped
1½ teaspoon black mustard seeds
½ teaspoon cumin seeds
1 teaspoon garam masala

Method:

1. Wash the lentils and place them in a pan. Cover them with a lid and leave to soak for at least an hour.

2. Pour 3 cups of water into a heavy-bottomed pan and bring to the boil. Add the drained lentils, turmeric, salt and paprika, and simmer until cooked.

3. Wash and finely chop the spinach *(see Preparing Vegetables page 216)* and cook over a medium heat until wilted (9 – 12 minutes).

4. Heat the oil in a small pan and fry the onion, mustard seeds and cumin seeds until golden. Stir into the cooked dal, and add the spinach and garam masala.

5. Cook for another 5 minutes, stirring from time to time to prevent sticking. Check the seasoning and serve hot.

Green Tomato Chutney

Makes 2 jars approx. of chutney

A good way to make use of unripe tomatoes, this chutney is delicately spiced and goes well with Indian curries.

Ingredients:

1 lb (450 g) green tomatoes, chopped
1 large onion, chopped
1 large apple, chopped
½ pint (275 ml) vinegar (brown or cider vinegar)

8 oz (225 g) soft brown sugar
4 oz (125 g) sultanas
¾ teaspoon dry mustard powder
½ teaspoon ground cinnamon
pinch cayenne pepper

Method:

1. Combine all the ingredients in a large saucepan.
2. Stir over a low heat, without boiling, until the sugar is dissolved.
3. Bring to the boil and simmer, uncovered, stirring occasionally, for 1 – 1½ hours, or until the mixture is thick.
4. Let the chutney stand for 10 minutes, and then pour it into clean dry jars.
5. Place rounds of greaseproof paper on the surface of the chutney. When cold, screw on the lids and store in a cool place.

Note: At the final stage of the simmering, when the chutney is thickening, stir frequently to ensure that it doesn't stick to the bottom of the pan and burn.

  Easy *Medium* *Advanced*

Chapatis

These classic Indian flat breads are
traditionally made three times a day.

Ingredients:

12 oz (350 g) chapati or wholemeal flour
1 teaspoon salt
7 fl oz (200 ml) water
2 teaspoons vegetable oil

Method:

1. Sift together the flour and salt. Add the water and mix to a soft dough.
2. Add the oil and knead for 5 – 6 minutes. Cover with a damp tea towel and leave to rest for half an hour.
3. Divide the dough into 12 equal pieces and shape each piece into a ball.
4. Take one ball. Press it into a large round with the palm of your hand, then roll it out on a floured board into a 5″ (13 cm) chapati. Repeat with the other balls.
5. Heat a griddle or heavy-based frying pan for a few minutes until it is hot. Take one chapati and place it on the griddle. Turn it over when the top begins to bubble (about 1 minute) and cook for a further 30 seconds.
6. Remove from the pan and butter one side immediately. Fold in a tea towel to keep warm, while cooking the remaining chapatis. Serve warm.

Potato Patties

Small Indian rissoles flavoured with lemon, garlic, and spices.

Ingredients:

1 lb (450 g) potatoes
½ teaspoon salt
2 onions, finely chopped
2 green chillies (optional)
2 medium garlic cloves

½ teaspoon cumin seeds
Juice of ½ lemon
1 tablespoon gram (chickpea) flour
1 – 2 oz (25 – 50 g) flour
2 – 3 tablespoons frying oil

Method:

1. Fill a large pan with water and bring to the boil over a high heat.
2. Wash, peel and quarter the potatoes. Boil with ½ teaspoon salt until tender.
3. Meanwhile, grind the onions, chillies, garlic, cumin seeds, lemon juice and gram flour to a paste, using a pestle and mortar or a blender.
4. Drain and mash the potatoes. Add the spice paste and enough flour to make a soft dough.
5. Shape mixture into round balls, press flat into patty shapes and roll in flour.
6. Heat 1 tablespoon of the oil in a frying pan and fry 3 or 4 patties at a time. Turn from time to time, until the patties are golden on both sides. Carefully remove and set on kitchen paper to drain. Add more oil to the pan with each batch.

Italian Rice

An easy-to-make Italian rice dish. Arborio rice gives it a more authentic taste.

Ingredients:

14 oz (400 g) fresh spinach leaves
1 onion
1 garlic clove
1¼ pints (750 ml) vegetable stock

1 oz (25 g) butter or margarine
8 oz (225 g) arborio rice
½ teaspoon salt
¼ teaspoon freshly ground black pepper

Method:

1. Trim the spinach *(see Preparing Vegetables page 216)*. Chop roughly, wash and leave to drain. Finely slice the onion and garlic.

2. Pour the vegetable stock into a small pan and bring to the boil. Meanwhile, melt the butter in a medium-sized heavy-bottomed pan and add the onion and garlic. Cook for 4 – 5 minutes, until the onion is soft.

3. Add the rice, salt and pepper to the larger pan, and cook over a low heat for 2 – 3 minutes, stirring all the time. Pour the vegetable stock into the rice, cover the pan with a lid, and cook in the oven at 160°C (325°F) Gas Mark 3 for 13 – 16 minutes.

4. Place the spinach in a large pan, add two tablespoons water, and cook for 2 – 3 minutes over a high heat until the spinach is reduced to a third of its original volume. Drain the spinach and press out the water with a wooden spoon.

5. Remove the rice from the oven. Check to make sure it is cooked, and stir in the spinach. Season to taste and serve immediately.

Italian-Style Courgettes

A delicious side dish. Quick and easy to prepare.

Ingredients:

4 medium courgettes
2 tablespoons olive oil
1 teaspoon dried parsley

½ teaspoon oregano
¼ teaspoon freshly-ground black pepper
¼ teaspoon sea salt

Method:

1. Cut the courgettes into thick rounds.

2. Heat the oil in a large cast-iron frying pan, then add the courgettes and sauté over a high heat until they are lightly browned. Turn them gently every two or three minutes to prevent burning.

3. Turn off the heat and add the herbs and seasoning.

4. Stir and serve.

Panini All'Olio (Italian Olive Oil Buns)

Rustic Italian buns with a melt-in-your-mouth texture. Makes 12 buns

Ingredients:

- 1 lb (450 g) strong plain white flour
- 2 teaspoons salt
- 1 teaspoon fast-action dried yeast
- 4 tablespoons extra-virgin olive oil
- 8 fl oz (240 ml) warm water

Method:

1. Sift the flour and salt into a large bowl.
2. Add the yeast, olive oil and water, then mix to a soft dough.
3. Knead for 8 – 10 minutes until smooth and elastic (add more flour if the dough is too sticky). Lightly oil the bowl and cover with a tea towel. Leave to rise in a warm place for an hour.
4. Knock back the dough and divide into twelve equal pieces. Shape into rolls as in notes 1, 2 and 3, below.
5. Leave the buns to rise for 20 – 30 minutes.
6. Preheat the oven to 200°C (400 °F) Gas Mark 6 and bake the buns for 15 minutes. Take them out of the oven and stand them on a wire rack to cool.

Note 1: Tavalli (twisted spiral rolls):
Roll each piece of dough into a strip about 12″ long and 1½″ wide (30 x 4 cm). Twist each strip into a loose spiral and join the ends to make a circle. Place on a well-greased baking sheet and brush with olive oil.

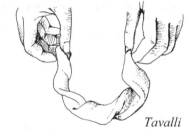

Tavalli

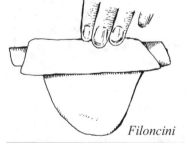

Filoncini

Note 2: Carciofi (artichoke-shaped rolls):
Shape each piece of dough into a ball, place on a well-greased baking sheet and brush with olive oil.
After they have risen, snip deep cuts in them with scissors.

Carciofi

Note 3: Filoncini (finger-shaped rolls):
Flatten each piece of dough into an oval and roll to a length of about 9″ (23 cm). Roll it up and cut in half. Place on a well greased baking sheet and brush with olive oil.

Middle Eastern Stew

A simple way to prepare carrots, potatoes and chickpeas.

Ingredients:
1 lb (450 g) potatoes
4 large carrots
4 tomatoes
1½ tablespoons olive oil
2 teaspoons ground cumin
1 teaspoon turmeric
2 large onions, chopped
14 oz (400 g) can chickpeas, rinsed and drained

Method:
1. Wash and peel the potatoes and carrots, and cut into ½" (1 cm) chunks. Wash and dice the tomatoes.
2. Heat the oil in a large, cast-iron pan over a medium heat. Add the spices and fry for a few moments.
3. Add the onion. Cook, stirring frequently, until softened – about 5 minutes.
4. Add the vegetables and just enough water to cover. Bring to the boil, cover with a lid and simmer gently until the vegetables are tender – 20 to 25 minutes.
5. Add the chickpeas, and season to taste. Simmer over a low heat for a further 5 minutes. Serve warm with Middle Eastern Flat breads. *(See page 231)*

Moroccan Aubergine Salad

Ingredients:
2 large aubergines, each about 12 oz (350 g)
2 teaspoons salt
4 tablespoons olive oil
2 garlic cloves
1 onion
4 ripe tomatoes
¼ teaspoon turmeric
½ teaspoon ground coriander
Pinch of ground cinnamon
Pinch of paprika
Lemon zest and juice of ½ lemon
1 to 2 tablespoons chopped coriander

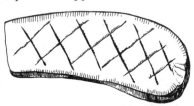

Method:
1. Trim and wash the aubergines, then halve them lengthwise. Score a deep criss-cross pattern over the surfaces, sprinkle with the salt and set aside for 30 minutes.
2. Rinse the aubergines and pat dry with kitchen paper. Place them in a roasting tin, brush the cut surfaces with 2 tablespoons of the olive oil and roast in an oven at 230°C (450°F) Gas Mark 8 for 45 – 50 minutes, brushing occasionally with oil. Remove from the oven and set aside to cool slightly.
3. Finely chop the garlic and onion, and dice the tomatoes. Cut the aubergines into small cubes. Heat the remaining oil in a large frying pan, add the garlic and onion and fry for 5 minutes. Next add the tomatoes, spices and lemon zest and fry for 1 minute. Cover the pan with a lid and simmer for 5 minutes. Stir in the aubergine, coriander, and lemon juice. Season to taste and remove from the heat. Serve warm or cool.

    Easy   Medium   Advanced

Middle Eastern Flat Bread

An interesting griddled bread that requires little preparation. For a complete meal, serve with Middle Eastern stew. Makes 12 breads.

Ingredients:
10 oz (300 g) plain white flour
6 oz (175 g) gram (chickpea) flour
1 teaspoon salt
2 teaspoons ground cumin
2 teaspoons fast-action dried yeast
½ teaspoon sugar
8 – 10 fl oz (250 – 300 ml) warm water

Method:
1. Sift the flours into a large bowl and mix in the dry ingredients. Make a well in the centre and gradually work in the warmed water to form a soft dough. Add flour if the mixture is too sticky.
2. Knead for 8 – 10 minutes until the dough is smooth and elastic.
3. Grease the bowl, cover, and leave to rise in a warm place for 1 – 1½ hours.
4. Knock back the dough and divide into 12 equal pieces. Roll each piece out to a small oval about 3″ x 6″ (7.5 x 15 cm) and place on floured baking trays.
5. Sprinkle with a little water, cover loosely, and leave to rise for a further 15 minutes.
6. Preheat a lightly-oiled griddle or cast-iron frying pan. Cook a few of the flat breads at a time, for 1 – 2 minutes – until they are lightly puffed up. Flip them over and cook for another minute.
7. Transfer to a tray or wire rack, cover with a tea towel and keep warm while cooking the remaining flat breads. Serve as soon as possible.

Hummus

Traditional Middle Eastern dip, delicious eaten with flat breads.

Ingredients:
1 14 oz (400 g) can chickpeas
2 medium garlic cloves, chopped
Juice of one lemon
3 tablespoons tahini (sesame paste)

4 tablespoons olive oil
¼ teaspoon black pepper
Salt
4 fl oz (125 ml) water
¼ teaspoon paprika

Method:
1. Drain the chickpeas and mash until they are fairly smooth.
2. Add the garlic, lemon juice, tahini, oil, and seasoning.
3. Blend in a blender or food processor and add enough water to make a smooth paste.
4. Spoon into a serving dish. Drizzle with olive oil, sprinkle with paprika, and serve.

Red Bean Chilli

A simple Mexican dish. If available, use black beans instead of red.

Ingredients:

3 large tomatoes
1 green or yellow pepper
3 large shallots
3 tablespoons olive oil
6 oz (175 g) sweetcorn
¼ teaspoon chilli powder

1 teaspoon ground cumin
1 teaspoon fresh oregano, chopped
6 fl oz (170 ml) water
2 x 14 oz tins red (or black) beans
Salt
Freshly-ground black pepper

Method:

1. Dice the tomatoes and the pepper. Chop up the shallots.
2. Heat the oil in a large, heavy-bottomed pan and add the shallots. Cook for 2 minutes over a medium heat, stirring constantly.
3. Add the sweetcorn and pepper to the pan, turn down the heat and cook for a further 2 minutes.
4. Add the chilli powder, ground cumin, oregano, water, beans and tomatoes. Stir well.
5. Partially cover pan with a lid and simmer gently for 20 minutes. Season with the salt and pepper, and serve.

Chilli Sauce

Fiery hot sauce using dried jalapeño chillies; the amount can be varied according to taste.

Ingredients:

24 dried jalapeño chillies
8 fl oz (225 ml) red wine vinegar
Juice of one lemon
2 tablespoons sugar
1 tablespoon salt
1 shallot
1 garlic clove

Diagram 1

Method:

1. Cut chillies in half and remove the seeds and stem *(see diagram 1)*.

2. Bring a small pan, about two thirds full of water, to the boil. Remove from heat.

3. Drop chillies in boiling water and leave for 30 seconds.

4. Drain chillies and place in a blender with the remaining ingredients. Combine till smooth, then transfer to a jar.

 Easy   *Medium*   *Advanced*

Salsa

An appetising salsa using avocados, tomatoes, and pepper, and flavoured with fresh coriander and chilli.

Ingredients:

1 small green pepper, diced
1 small shallot, sliced
4 tomatoes, diced
2 ripe avocados, peeled and
  stoned. *(Diagram 1)*.
2 tablespoons coriander leaves
1 garlic clove
1 red chilli, seeded and chopped
3 tablespoons olive oil
2 tablespoons lemon juice

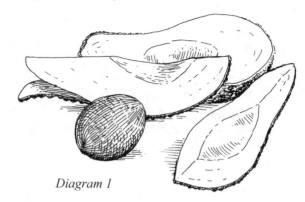

Diagram 1

Method:

1. Dice the avocados and combine with the pepper, shallot and half the tomatoes in a large bowl.

2. Blend the remaining tomatoes, coriander, garlic, chilli, lemon juice and olive oil until they form a thick purée.

3. Add the purée to the vegetables and stir well. Season with salt and leave to stand for half an hour before serving.

Tortillas

An adaptation of the famous corn tortillas of South America; serve these wheat tortillas with bean chilli and salsa.

Ingredients:

8 oz (225 g) plain white flour
¾ teaspoon baking powder
1 teaspoon salt
3 tablespoons vegetable oil
¼ pint (150 ml) warm water

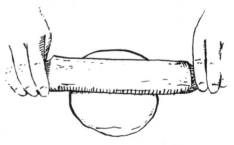

Diagram 1

Method:

1. Sift the flour and baking powder into a bowl. Add the salt.

2. Rub in the oil, stir in the water and knead lightly to form a soft dough.

3. Cover with a tea towel and leave to rest for 15 minutes.

4. Divide into 12 equal pieces and shape into balls. Roll out on a floured surface into 6″ – 7″ (15 cm – 18 cm) rounds *(see diagram 1)*.

5. Heat a griddle, or heavy-based frying pan, and place one tortilla on it. Cook for 1 – 2 minutes, turning over when the surface starts to bubble. The tortilla should remain flexible. Remove from the griddle and wrap in a tea towel to keep warm. Cook the remaining tortillas in the same way.

Catalonian Spinach and Onion Flatbread

A pizza-style flatbread topped with spinach, caramelised onion, balsamic vinegar and pine nuts.

Ingredients:
Base:
7 oz (200 g) plain white flour
2 oz (50 g) corn meal
1½ teaspoons fast-action dried yeast
1 teaspoon salt
½ teaspoon sugar
7 fl oz (200 ml) water
2 teaspoons olive oil

Topping:
1 oz (25 g) sultanas
3 teaspoons olive oil
2 onions, thinly sliced
1 teaspoon salt
1 lb (450 g) fresh spinach, trimmed and
  rinsed *(see page 216)*
1 oz (25 g) pine nuts
2 tablespoons balsamic vinegar
¼ teaspoon freshly-ground black pepper

Method:
Base:
1. Sift the flours, yeast, salt, and sugar into a medium-sized bowl.
2. Heat the water in a saucepan until lukewarm. Add the water and oil to the flour. Mix well. The dough should be quite soft.
3. Turn onto a floured surface and knead for 5 – 8 minutes.
4. Return the dough to the bowl, cover with a tea towel, and leave to rise in a warm place for 25 – 30 minutes.

Topping:
5. Place sultanas in a small bowl and cover with hot water. Leave for 20 minutes.
6. Heat 2 teaspoons of the olive oil in a medium-sized frying pan. Add the onions and ½ teaspoon salt. Cook for 20 – 25 minutes over a medium heat. Stir often. (If necessary, add a little water to prevent burning.) Set aside.
7. Cook the spinach in a large saucepan, over a high heat, in the water that clings to its leaves after rinsing. Stir often, until the spinach is reduced to a third of its original volume. Drain in a colander and squeeze out excess moisture. Return to the saucepan and add remaining ½ teaspoon salt.
8. Dry roast the pine nuts in a small frying pan until lightly golden (3 – 4 minutes).
9. Drain the sultanas and add to the onion mixture with the balsamic vinegar and black pepper.
10. Sprinkle a large baking sheet with corn meal. Roll out the dough to a 16" x 12" (40 cm x 30 cm) rectangle, transfer to the baking sheet, and turn the edges under to form a crust. Brush with 1 teaspoon oil. Scatter the spinach over the base, top with the onion mixture and sprinkle with the pine nuts.
11. Bake in oven at 200°C (400°F) Gas Mark 6 for 10 – 15 minutes, until the underside of the base is crisp and golden. Serve hot or warm.

Easy Bread

A very simple no-knead recipe that makes three hearty brown loaves.

Ingredients:

2 pints (1.2 litres) water
1 packet fast-action dried yeast
1 tablespoon muscovado sugar or molasses
2 lb (900 g) wholemeal flour
1 lb (450 g) plain white bread flour
1 tablespoon salt

Method:

1. Heat the water in a saucepan until luke-warm. Pour ¼ pint (150 ml) of it into a small bowl.
2. Sprinkle the dried yeast over the surface. After a couple of minutes stir in the sugar. Leave for 10 minutes.
3. Sift the flour and salt into a very large bowl.
4. Thoroughly grease three 1 lb loaf tins and leave in a warm place.
5. Make a well in the centre of the flour and stir in the yeast mixture and remaining water with a wooden spoon. Carefully work the sides into the middle and mix for two minutes, with the spoon. The dough should be slippery.

Diagram 1

6. Divide among the prepared tins *(diagram 1)*, cover with a plastic sheet and leave to rise in a warm place until the dough has risen to within ½″ (1 cm) of the top of the tins: this should take 30 – 40 minutes.
7. Meanwhile preheat the oven to 200ºC (400ºF) Gas Mark 6. Bake for 40 minutes until the loaves are chestnut brown and sound hollow when tapped on the base. Turn out and cool on a wire rack.

Bagels

This classic Jewish bread is poached in boiling water. For variety, try topping with sesame seeds, crushed garlic or linseed. Makes 12 bagels.

Ingredients:
1 lb 4 oz (600 g) strong plain white flour
1 packet fast-action dried yeast
2 teaspoons brown sugar
1 tablespoon salt
½ pint (275 ml) warm water
Poppy seeds

Method:

1. Sift the flour into a medium-sized bowl and add the yeast, sugar and salt.

2. Pour in the warm water and combine to make a soft dough.

3. Knead for 7 minutes then cover with a tea towel, and leave to rise in a warm place for 40 minutes.

4. Turn the dough out onto a floured surface and form into a long roll. Using a sharp knife, cut it up into twelve equal pieces. *(Diagram 1)*

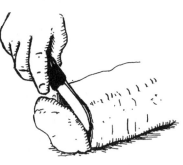

Diagram 1

5. Shape each piece into a circle. Insert your thumb into the centre of each one to create a hole *(diagram 2)* and place them on a floured tray. Set them aside, and leave them uncovered for another 30 minutes.

6. Fill a large pan two-thirds full of water and bring to the boil.

7. Preheat the oven to 220°C (425°F) Gas Mark 7.

8. Drop three bagels into the water and boil for 2 minutes. Turn them over and boil for another minute. The bagels should firm and puff up.

Diagram 2

9. Using a slotted spoon, remove bagels from the water and drain for a minute on a wire rack with kitchen paper underneath. Sprinkle poppy seeds over both sides of the bagels.

10. Repeat the process with the remaining bagels, then place them on a greased baking tray and cook for 15 – 20 minutes. When the bagels are light brown on top, remove from the oven and transfer to a wire rack to cool.

　 Easy　 *Medium*　 *Advanced*

Shortbread

Easy-to-make, crumbly shortbread.

Ingredients:

2 tablespoons rice flour
10 oz (300 g) plain flour
2 oz (50 g) icing sugar
8 oz (225 g) margarine or butter

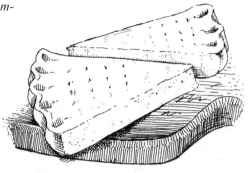

Method:

1. Sift the flours and icing sugar into a large bowl and rub in the margarine or butter with the tips of your fingers.
2. Press together firmly, then lightly knead until smooth, adding more flour if the dough is sticky.
3. Divide the mixture between two greased trays 7″ (18 cm) round.
4. Pinch a decorative edge with floured fingers, cut into 8 wedges and prick with a fork.
5. Bake the shortbread in the oven at 160°C (325°F) Gas Mark 3 for 15 minutes, or until they have come away from the edge of the tin.
6. Cut again and leave to cool on a wire rack.

Apple crumble

A traditional English recipe that can be made with apples or any other fruit or berry that is in season.

Ingredients:

3 medium sized apples
3 oz (65 g) brown sugar
½ teaspoon ground cinnamon
3 tablespoons apple juice or
   water
1 clove
2 oz (75 g) wholemeal flour
3 oz (75 g) rolled oats
2 oz (50 g) margarine

Method:

1. Peel and core the apples. Cut into small chunks and tip them into a greased, medium-sized oven-proof dish.
2. Add 1 oz (25 g) of the sugar, the cinnamon, apple juice, and the clove. Mix well and set aside.
3. Sift the flour into a medium-sized glass bowl and add the oats and the remaining 2 oz (50 g) sugar. Add the margarine and cut it into small pieces. Rub the margarine into the flour and oats until the mixture is dry and slightly lumpy.
4. Sprinkle the topping over the apple and cook in the oven at 190°C (375°F) Gas Mark 5, for 20 minutes or until the topping is lightly browned and the apple mixture is bubbling around the sides of the dish.
5. Remove from the oven and allow to cool slightly before serving.

Chocolate Chip Cookies
Makes 20 – 24

Authentic American cookies – chunky, chewy, and packed with chocolate chips and walnuts.

Ingredients:
2 oz (50 g) walnuts
4 oz (125 g) chocolate chips (or a
    bar of chocolate chopped up)
8 oz (225 g) unbleached white or
    wholemeal flour
2 teaspoons baking powder
½ teaspoon salt
½ teaspoon cinnamon
8 oz (225 g) muscovado or soft,
    light brown sugar
4 fl oz (120 ml) sunflower oil
1 teaspoon vanilla essence
4 tablespoons water

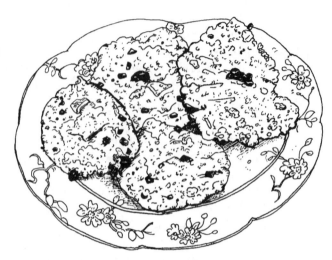

Tip: Cookies will work better if all the ingredients are at room temperature.

Method:
1. Chop up the walnuts (and chocolate, if necessary).

2. Sift the flour into a large bowl. Add the baking powder, salt, cinnamon, walnuts and chocolate chips. Make a well in the centre and set aside.

3. Add the sugar and oil to a medium-sized bowl and mix well. Add the vanilla essence and water and mix again.

4. Gradually pour the wet mixture into the well in the centre of the dry mixture.

5. Stir until well mixed but be careful not to overwork the mixture.

6. Spoon onto ungreased biscuit trays. Put them in the oven at 180°C (350°F) Gas Mark 4. After 5 minutes switch and rotate the trays (i.e. top to bottom and 180 degree rotation). Bake for another 4 minutes.

7. Check the cookies. If they are still soft, cook for another 2 minutes and check again – continue in this way until the cookies are golden and a little softer than required – they harden as they cool.

8. Take them out of the oven and leave to cool for two minutes. Transfer to a wire rack.

   Easy   *Medium*   *Advanced*

Chocolate Doughnuts

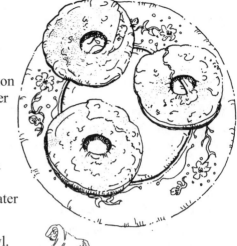

Light, chocolaty doughnuts that are deep fried in hot oil. Best eaten as quickly as possible.

Ingredients:

1 lb (450 g) plain white
  flour
4 tablespoons cocoa
  powder
½ teaspoon salt
2½ teaspoons baking
  powder

1 teaspoon cinnamon
3 tablespoons butter
  or margarine
5 oz (150 g) sugar
1 large egg
½ teaspoon vanilla
  essence
6 fl oz (170 ml) water

Method:

1. Sift all the dry ingredients into a bowl. Set aside.
2. In another, larger, bowl mix the butter or margarine with a wooden spoon and gradually add the sugar. Beat until light and fluffy.
3. Add the egg and vanilla essence and beat well. Alternately add water and the flour mixture, stirring after each addition.

Diagram 1

4. Turn out the dough onto a lightly-floured board and roll to a ¼" (½ cm) thickness *(diagram 1)*. (If the dough is sticky, sprinkle it and the rolling pin with flour.)
5. Cut out doughnuts with a floured doughnut cutter and place them on floured trays. If you do not have a doughnut cutter, an upturned, 3 – 4" (7 – 10 cm) diameter mug can be used to cut out the doughnut and a small bottle top or lid can be used to make the hole *(diagram 2)*.
6. Press together the scraps of dough, roll them out as before and cut out more doughnuts. Repeat this until all the dough is used. Leave the doughnuts to rise, uncovered, for 20 minutes.

Diagram 2

7. Heat about 1" (2.5 cm) of oil in a deep frying pan, a cast-iron saucepan or a chip pan. You can tell whether the oil is hot enough to start frying the doughnuts by dropping in a small piece of dough – if the oil is hot enough the dough will rise to the surface. Fry two doughnuts at a time; they will swell and come to the surface, at which point they can be *carefully* turned over. Remove when both sides are brown and drain on kitchen paper.
8. Sprinkle with icing sugar and store in an airtight tin.

Attention: Deep Frying! Great care has to be taken when deep frying, as it is one of the most dangerous cooking operations. The doughnuts must be lowered very gently into the hot oil, and especial care must be taken not to splash the oil when you turn them over.

Apple Crumble Cake

The bread-like base of this German cake is enhanced by a topping of apples, cinnamon, and sugar.

Ingredients:
Crumble topping:
3 oz (75 g) plain flour
4 oz (125 g) sugar
2 teaspoons cinnamon
6 tablespoons butter or margarine

Cake:
2 fl oz (50 ml) warm water
1 packet fast-action dried yeast
3 oz (75 g) butter or margarine
3½ oz (100 g) sugar
½ teaspoon salt
2 eggs
2 fl oz (50 ml) water
12 oz (350 g) plain flour
2 or 3 large apples, peeled, cored, and sliced

Method:
Crumble topping:

1. Sift the flour into a small bowl, and stir in the sugar and cinnamon.

2. Add the margarine and rub it in with your fingertips until the mixture resembles breadcrumbs (*see diagram 1*). Set aside.

Diagram 1

Cake:

1. Pour the warm water into a small bowl. Sprinkle in the yeast and stir till dissolved. Set aside.

2. In a large mixing bowl, cream together the butter, sugar and salt. Add the yeast mixture, eggs, and water. Stir.

3. Gradually sift in the flour and stir until well blended.

4. Spread in a well-greased 9″ x 9″ x 2″ (20 cm x 20 cm x 5 cm) square tin. Arrange the apple slices on top and sprinkle with the crumble topping.

5. Cover with a tea towel and leave to rise in a warm place until doubled in size (about 1 hour).

6. Bake in the oven at 190°C, (375°F) Gas Mark 5, for 35 – 40 minutes. Cut into pieces when cool.

  Easy *Medium* *Advanced*

Apple Pie

An easy-to-make version of a popular classic.

Ingredients:
Pastry:
5 oz (150 g) plain white or
   wholemeal flour
2 oz (50 g) margarine, diced
1 oz (25 g) sugar
2 tablespoons cold water

Filling:
1 lb (450 g) apples weighed
   before peeling and coring
1 oz (25 g) sugar
½ teaspoon cinnamon powder
4 tablespoons apple juice or water
1 clove (optional)
icing sugar for dusting

Method:
Pastry:

1. Sift the flour into a medium-sized bowl. Add the margarine and rub in until the mixture resembles fine breadcrumbs.

2. Add the sugar and mix well. Pour in the cold water, a little at a time, and mix until the crumbs can be pressed into a ball. If the pastry is wet, add a little more flour.

3. Chill in the refrigerator while preparing the filling.

Pie:

1. Peel quarter and slice the apples. Place the slices in a medium-sized bowl and add the sugar, cinnamon, apple juice, and clove. Mix well.

2. Halve the pastry and roll out one half between two pieces of floured, grease-proof paper. Place in a greased pie-dish and trim, if necessary.

3. Spread the apple filling evenly over the base, then roll out the second piece of pastry in the same way as the first. Place it on top of the apple mixture, and trim to fit the pie dish.

4. Make two slits in the top of the pie, and cook in the oven at 190°C (375°F) Gas Mark 5 for 25 minutes, or until the pastry is lightly browned and firm to the touch.

5. Remove from the oven and sprinkle with icing sugar. Serve hot or cold.

Berry Muffins

Any berry or currant can be used in these delicious, muffins: raspberries, redcurrants, and blackcurrants work particularly well.

Ingredients:
8 oz (250 g) plain flour
5 oz (150 g) brown sugar
3 teaspoons baking powder
1 teaspoon salt
1 teaspoon ground cinnamon

¼ teaspoon grated nutmeg
1 oz (25 g) chopped walnuts
2 eggs, well beaten
5 fl oz (140 ml) water
4 fl oz (120 ml) oil
7 oz (200 g) berries

Method:
1. Sift the dry ingredients into a medium-sized bowl. Stir in the chopped walnuts, and set aside.
2. In a smaller bowl, combine the eggs, water and oil. Pour this wet mixture into the dry mixture and stir until the dry ingredients are just moistened.

   Muffin mixture should not be over-beaten – to make perfect muffins the mixture should be lumpy.
3. Spoon a little mixture into well-greased muffin cups. Scatter the berries over the mixture and top with another spoonful of mix.
4. Bake the muffins in an oven at 190°C (375°F) Gas Mark 5 for 20 – 25 minutes, or until they are golden. When cooked, leave them to cool for 1 – 2 minutes, and then transfer them to a wire rack.

Pecan Balls

Irresistible biscuits that only take a few minutes to make.

Ingredients:
4 oz (125 g) pecans
4 oz (125 g) icing sugar
8 oz (225 g) butter or margarine

1 teaspoon vanilla essence
1 teaspoon ground cinnamon
8 oz (225 g) plain flour

Method:
1. In a food processor or blender, grind the pecans with 1 oz (25 g) of the icing sugar, until very finely ground. Transfer to a mixing bowl.
2. Add the butter, vanilla essence, and cinnamon and mix well, with a wooden spoon. Add the flour and stir until the mixture forms a soft dough.
3. Take rounded teaspoons of the dough and, with floured hands, form them into ¾" (2 cm) balls. Place the balls 1" (3 cm) apart on ungreased biscuit trays.
4. Place the trays in an oven and bake at 160°C (325°F) Gas Mark 3 for 16 – 18 minutes, or until the bottom of the biscuits are lightly browned. Transfer to a wire rack and leave them to cool for about 3 minutes.
5. Sift the remaining icing sugar into a small bowl. Gently roll the warm biscuits, one at a time, in the icing sugar. Leave them to cool completely.
6. Return the biscuits to the wire rack, and when they are completely cool once more roll them in the icing sugar. Store in an airtight biscuit tin.

Pecan Chocolate Cake

Ingredients:

8 oz (225 g) strong plain white flour
1 oz (25 g) unsweetened cocoa powder
½ teaspoon bicarbonate of soda
½ teaspoon salt
7 oz (200 g) brown sugar
4 fl oz (120 ml) vegetable oil
9 fl oz (250 ml) cold water, or chilled
  coffee
1 teaspoon vanilla essence
2 tablespoons cider vinegar

Chocolate Pecan Icing:

1 oz (25 g) pecans (or walnuts)   3 – 4 tablespoons water
1 – 2 teaspoons sunflower oil   ½ teaspoon vanilla essence
2 oz (50 g) black chocolate   6 oz (175 g) icing sugar

Method:

Cake

1. Preheat oven to 110°C (375°F) Gas Mark 5. Line an 8″ (20 cm) cake tin with greaseproof paper.
2. Sift the flour, cocoa powder, bicarbonate of soda, and salt into a large mixing bowl. Add the sugar, mix until the ingredients are combined, and set aside.
3. In a smaller bowl, combine the oil, water or coffee, and vanilla essence. Pour the liquid into the dry mixture and stir until smooth.
4. Add the vinegar and stir briefly. Quickly pour the mixture into the tin and bake for 30 – 35 minutes. The cake is cooked when a knife or skewer inserted into it comes out clean.
5. Remove the cake from the oven and leave for 10 – 15 minutes. Take it out of the tin and leave to cool completely on a wire rack.

Icing:

6. Finely grind the pecans in a pestle and mortar or a blender. Add enough sunflower oil to make a thick paste.
7. Fill a small saucepan with 1 – 2″ of water, set it over a low heat. Put the chocolate in a glass, heat-proof bowl and set this in the pan, making sure that the base does not touch the water *(diagram 1)*. Leave for 4 – 7 minutes until the chocolate has melted.

Diagram 1

8. Mix together the pecan paste, water, and vanilla. Beat in the icing sugar and the melted chocolate. Mix until smooth.
9. Spread the icing over the top and sides of the cooled cake.

Jam Making

Until recently most households made enough jams and preserves from their garden produce to last them for the whole year. There is an art to jam making: only the correct combination of fruit, sugar, water and heat will produce a jam that lasts for several months without deteriorating.

Home-made jam retains the taste of the fruit in a way that factory-made jam does not: they are two different products, having tasted one, you will not want to return to the other.

> **Safety:** *Jam boils at a higher temperature than water and can therefore cause serious burns:*
> - Never leave pan handles sticking over the edge of the cooker.
> - Never leave a pan of jam unattended.
> - Use oven gloves when moving the hot pan.
> - Never let the wooden spoon rest in the pot while the jam is boiling.
> - If the jam should splash onto your skin while it is boiling, wash it off with cold water immediately.

Selecting the Fruit: Fruit for jam making should be dry and not overripe.

Boiling the Jam: When the jam is boiling it will foam and bubble and rise up the inside of the pan. If it looks as if it is going to boil over the top, carefully move the pan away from the heat source for a moment. When the foaming has subsided, replace it on the heat and continue.

If the jam sticks while it is boiling, or if you begin to smell burning, gently remove the pan form the heat source, allow to cool for a moment, pour it into another clean pan and continue with the boiling.

Runny Jam: If, when the jam is cold, it is too runny, you can pour it back into the pan and reheat it for another couple of minutes: some of the water will evaporate and this will help the jam to thicken.

Hygiene: It is important that your jam jars and lids are clean and dry otherwise moulds can develop while the jam is being stored. If you are using old jars, always re-wash in hot water and dry them thoroughly before use.

Storage:
- Place rounds of greaseproof paper on the top of the jam in each jar.
- Wipe off any jam spilt on the outsides of the jars.
- When the jam is cold, screw lids on, label, and store in a dry, cool cupboard.

  Easy   Medium   Advanced

Blackcurrant Jam

This classic recipe uses a lot of white sugar but it is almost completely foolproof – and the jam is exquisite.
Makes 2 jars.

Ingredients:
12 oz (350 g) blackcurrants
½ pint (275 ml) water
1½ lbs (675 g) white granulated sugar

Method:

1. Using scissors or a knife, remove stalks and end tufts from each blackcurrant. Place the fruit in a colander or sieve and wash gently under cold running water. Drain well.

2. Tip berries into a large saucepan together with the water and sugar.

3. Heat gently for 2 to 3 minutes, stirring frequently with a wooden spoon until all the sugar has dissolved.

4. Turn up the heat and bring to the boil. Boil the mixture fiercely for **5 minutes**, stirring occasionally to prevent the jam from sticking to the bottom of the pan and burning.

5. Turn off the heat and let the jam cool for 2 minutes whilst spooning off any scum that has formed on the surface.

6. Carefully ladle or pour the hot jam into the jam jars, to within ¼″ (½ cm) of the top of the jar.

7. Cover the top of the jam with a circle of greaseproof paper and set aside to cool.

A thing of beauty is a joy forever.

John Keats

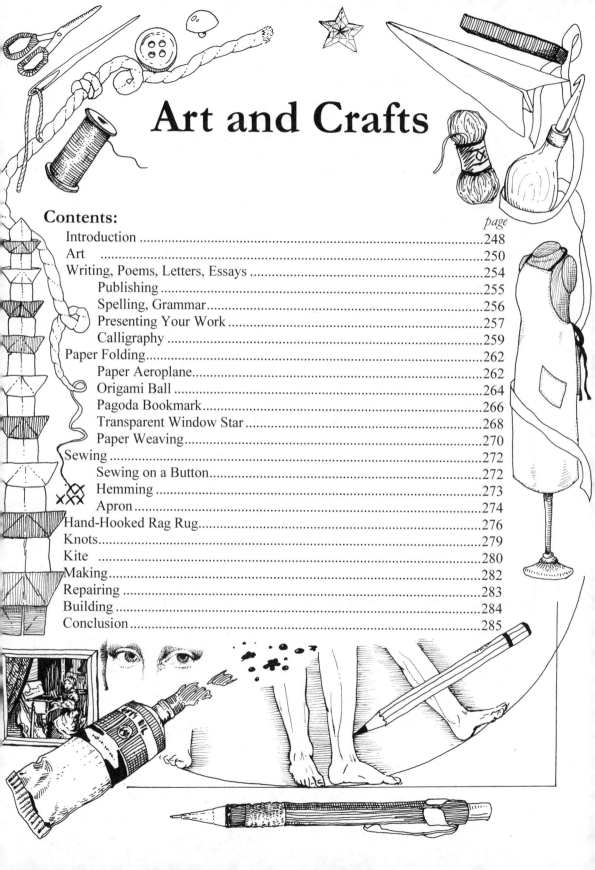

Art and Crafts

Contents:

Art and Crafts

In order to achieve a full and rounded education it is necessary to acquire both practical skills and academic knowledge. Unfortunately, this is not something that is being achieved by the current school-based system of education – schools are simply the wrong place to acquire practical skills that require personal commitment, practice, and freedom to complete projects in one's own time.

One fact that modern educators have failed to grasp is that real education involves acquiring a broad range of skills and abilities. It is undoubtedly true that a hundred years ago the majority of the population was hampered by the fact that they had a poor level of skill in reading and writing, and it was correct for that issue to be addressed – but it should not have been at the cost of losing the practical skills that had been developed over generations.

The ability to create something beautiful has always been one of the defining features of a human being, and the process of developing the requisite practical skills is one of the pleasures of life. Schools provide almost no opportunity for truly creative activity and it is therefore up to each person to make time in their own lives to redress this serious imbalance.

Learning a Craft

Learning a craft involves combining knowledge gained from other people, with your own unique abilities:

- **Books:** Books are a good place to start learning any new craft. They give you a chance to pick up the basic techniques and to discover whether or not it is an activity that you enjoy.

- **Courses:** Once you have acquired a basic knowledge of a craft, going on a course can provide an inexpensive way of learning more about it. You can learn as much from the other students as from the teacher.

- **Private Lessons:** If you identify a craftsperson from whom you particularly wish to learn, private lessons are the most efficient method.

- **Apprenticeship:** An apprenticeship carries working with a particular craftsperson a stage further. You work for them in their business and, in exchange, they instruct you in all they have learnt.

- **Working on Your Own:** In order to become really accomplished in any craft, you have to spend time working at it by yourself. Really good work is an expression of your personal creativity, and you cannot develop this if you are always under someone else's eye.

- **Experimenting:** You have to experiment and be prepared to make mistakes.

- **Selling Crafts:** If you try selling your work, you will get a true idea of what people really think of it.

- **Time and Enjoyment:** It takes years to develop creative skills to the full and you will not dedicate the required time to your craft unless you enjoy what you do.

What are Crafts?

- **Cooking and Gardening:** Knowing how to grow and cook food are the two most important practical skills. Cooking and gardening have been given separate sections in this book.

- **Art:** Art and crafts are intimately connected. It is fundamental to human nature to want to make whatever one does beautiful, and art, in all its forms – drawing, painting, modelling, etc. – helps one to develop an appreciation of beauty and the ability to create beautiful things. Once acquired, this skill can be transferred to everything to which you turn your hand.

- **Writing:** Writing has been included in the crafts section to counteract the idea that it is a functional activity, useful only for passing tests and exams.

- **Textiles:** Spinning and weaving have long been associated with civilised life and, prior to the Industrial Revolution, most people were engaged, to a greater or lesser extent, in the production of cloth or the making of clothes. Spinning, weaving and needlework are traditional crafts that give an insight into the way in which essential items are created from simple raw materials.

- **Woodwork:** Wood is the most versatile of all materials and can be used to make anything from furniture to houses.

- **Building:** Building is another basic craft that has been employed for thousands of years. Modern techniques involve using mass-produced building materials, but traditional skills are still in as great a demand as ever.

- **Mechanics:** Surprisingly perhaps, repairing and servicing machines calls for the same skills as traditional crafts. You have to be able to work sensitively, to use your powers of reasoning to locate a problem, and then to find a practical solution. Even though there are manuals, making machines work often comes down to the understanding that you yourself are able to bring to the problem.

- **Traditional Crafts:** There are many traditional crafts such as basket-making, candle-making, working with leather, pottery, etc., and the more experience you have of them, the better the all-round craftsperson you will be.

There is no reason why a self-motivated young person, who is neither subject to the restrictions of school nor obliged to go out to work every day, should not be able to explore all or most of the above areas over the course of their teenage years.

Crafts and Parenting

The most important activity that anyone undertakes in life is that of being a parent – but it is a role for which people are poorly prepared. Children need to be fed, clothed, housed, and have somewhere to play as well as needing an intelligent adult with whom they can talk and who is capable of answering their questions. Thus, if they are to be given a chance to become good parents themselves, young people must have opportunities to gain both practical skills and knowledge from books.

Art

When people are given a chance to plan out a course of study for themselves, art is always one of the first things to which they turn. It is, therefore, remarkable that it plays such a small role in the education programme provided by modern schools.

Somehow, the idea has arisen that certain people are 'good' at art and that they are the only people who should be encouraged to paint or draw. This is an unfortunate misconception. Art does not derive its value from other people considering it to be good, but rather from the fact that it is a means of expression. It is the principal means by which people are able to express their feeling for beauty, and as such is as important an aspect of life as the ability to express ideas and arguments through words.

Just as we don't say "Someone else is better at speaking than I am, so I will remain silent all my life," we should not say, "Someone else is more artistic than I am, so I will never paint or draw or create anything myself".

> "Damals war nichts heilig, als das schöne."
>
> "In days of yore nothing was sacred but the beautiful."
>
> *Schiller*

This has significant implications for society in general. If people leave the education system without an appreciation of beauty, then they cannot be expected to create beautiful things during their working lives. This must be at least part of the reason why modern societies have succeeded in destroying so many of the beautiful things that they have inherited from previous generations – the traditional countryside has been devastated by modern agricultural methods, and many urban areas are bleak beyond description.

It is sometimes said that it is the power of economics that has led to people creating such an unpleasant environment, but this reasoning is flawed. There have been other civilisations in the past that have generated enormous wealth and which have relied upon profit and trade to maintain their economies, but they have still been able to create things of beauty – churches, palaces, public spaces, works of art, gardens, and a flourishing countryside – which they have been able to pass down to posterity.

Another argument is that science and industry are responsible for all the ugliness in the world but this is also illogical, machines only make the things that they are programmed to make – if they make cheap, ugly things, it is because people have designed them to do so and, more

IT'S MEANT TO BE ART

You're joking, you're joking! *Anything* but art!!!

importantly, because people have demonstrated a willingness to buy them.

If the will were there, machines could be used to make things of beauty. Over the millennia, people have used every conceivable thing to aid them in their quest to create works of art: there is no reason to suppose that technology could not be used in the same way.

Thus, the problem is not one of economics nor of technology but is due rather to a lack of artistic appreciation in the population as a whole. One way to change this could be through education. If people are allowed to develop their own artistic potential, they not only create beautiful things themselves, but they also demand the same standard from others, and in this way act as a catalyst for change.

An Education in Art

The younger you are when you start to take art seriously, the better. The ideal is to start to draw before you learn to read and write and to maintain your artistic skills through daily practice from then onwards. There is no need to despair, however, if this has not been your personal experience – you will simply have to dedicate a little time to acquiring the basic techniques. If your early work does not match up to your aspirations, do not be discouraged – artistic skills, like everything else, improve with practice.

- **Practice:** Get in the habit of doing some drawing every day; it can be anything you want – cartoons, sketches, people, flowers, buildings, or whatever takes your fancy. The important thing is to awaken your own artistic potential. Young children start to draw on their own before they try to copy other people's work, and this is a good method to follow yourself. In that way you are able to incorporate things that you learn into your work without sacrificing your individual style.
- **No Judging:** There is a paradox involved in the study of art: on the one hand, it goes without saying that some works of art are better than others, but on the other hand, you gain nothing by judging your own work and comparing it to that of other people. You should do creative things because you want to – the simple fact that you are doing them makes them worthwhile. You have to suspend your judgement about how good or bad your work is and concentrate upon the enjoyment that it gives you.
- **An Appreciation of Good Art:** Even though you should not worry about whether your own work is good or bad, you should be able to appreciate the work of

great artists – study their pictures carefully and see if you can understand how they have achieved their effects; try to copy them, and try to understand in what way your work differs from the original.

- **Art and Lesson Work:** If you are studying at home, instead of filling exercise books with writing, you can use illustrations to record your work.

- **Good-Quality Materials:** It is important to have a range of good-quality materials at your disposal. You do not have to buy everything at once, but when you do buy something, make sure that it is of good quality – if necessary go to a specialist art shop:

    - **Paper:** The paper that you use makes a great deal of difference to how your pictures will look. Thick, slightly textured papers are best for coloured drawings.

        - **Crayons:** A good quality set of coloured crayons is essential.

            - **Pencils:** Graphite pencils are a very versatile drawing medium: have a range of pencils for different types of drawing.

                - **Pens:** Pens can be used for both writing and drawing. Your writing can be an extension of your artistic work, and if this is the case, using different coloured pens, calligraphy pens and pens with different-shaped nibs can enhance the overall appearance of what you do. You can also have pens that are specifically used for drawing – fine-tipped black pens, and dip pens, for example.

                - **Brushes:** In order to paint successfully you will need a range of different-sized brushes. The most expensive brushes are not necessarily the best; some brushes made with synthetic fibres are at least as good as their more expensive, traditional counterparts.

                - **Watercolours, Oil Paints:** There is no substitute for proper paints – it is generally safest to stick to the well-known brands or to a brand recommended by your local art shop. Paints are expensive but they last a long time.

- **Art and Crafts:** Art is not simply about painting and drawing. One of the main reasons for doing art is that it has an impact on your ability to do other things. This is most noticeable in the field of crafts. Once you develop a feeling for how to create beautiful pictures, you should find that this is useful in helping you to complete craft projects successfully. In addition, many craft projects themselves demand a degree of artistic ability: this applies in such varied fields as the painting and glazing of pots, the decoration of fabrics, and the painting of houses.

- **Range of Activities:** The wider the range of artistic activities you undertake, the better. Great artists of the past were renowned for their versatility – they painted, they drew, they sculpted, they cast bronze figures, they experimented with different media, and in some celebrated cases, such as Leonardo da Vinci, they were also involved in science, mathematics, engineering and architecture.

- **Art Books:** Art books are a major resource for anyone teaching themselves to paint and draw. There are numerous manuals available, that explain the basic techniques for working with different media – oil painting, watercolours, pencil drawing, etc. – and there are also countless publications that reproduce works of art that are in museums and private collections. These books provide ideal material for copying, and can often be obtained relatively cheaply second-hand or from discount book stores.

- **Courses and Teachers:** Most towns have a thriving culture of privately and publicly-funded art courses; they are usually well subscribed and provide an opportunity to learn from a practising artist and to meet and share ideas with other students of the subject. Over a period of time, it is possible to attend a number of courses which enable you to learn different techniques from a variety of different teachers.

Still life of a glass and spoon

Recommended Books:
Rendering in Pen and Ink, Arthur L. Guptill
The Notebooks of Leonardo da Vinci, Volumes I and II, Dover Fine Art Books

Writing

Writing is included in the arts and crafts section because it is, fundamentally, a creative activity. It is highly regrettable that schools, whose initial purpose was simply to teach people *how* to write, should have made writing into a mundane activity, used for tests and exams, with the result that instead of being enthused about writing, many people leave school with no idea of the possibilities that being able to write open up to them. Ideally, people should be left to decide for themselves what to write and when to write. Like painting and drawing, writing is an expression of one's individuality and it is not appropriate for other people to make you write anything, especially not things that do not reflect your own thoughts and feelings.

It is at least partly due to the activity of schools that the standard of writing has declined – anyone who has read the books highlighted in the literature section will have been struck by the quality of their writing and how unfavourably most modern works compare to them – and it is by studying outside of school that you will have the best chance of developing your own style of writing and learn to express yourself using the written word.

Writing Poetry

Even though writing poetry may seem to be a more demanding task than writing prose, many people's first attempts at writing are in verse. Writing poems makes you focus upon one word at a time whilst never forgetting what the poem as a whole is trying to express. It involves creating a mood or a feeling through the interweaving of words, it is closely allied to the world of music, and it is the ideal way of developing your skill as a writer – no matter what sort of material you may wish to write in the future.

> Only be willing to search for poetry,
> and there will be poetry;
> My soul, a tiny speck, is my tutor.
> Evening sun and fragrant grass are
> common things,
> But, with understanding, they can
> become glorious verse.
>
> *Yüan Mei (1716-98)*

What is the advantage of being able to write?

Writing is not only a highly-prized, practical skill that enables you to manage your own affairs and communicate with other people, it can also be a source of pleasure and enjoyment. In addition to the relatively few published authors who make a living through writing, there are many other people who write letters, articles, manuscripts, plays, poems, novels, etc., simply for the sense of satisfaction that it gives them. Writing and speaking are closely allied skills: the more comfortable you are expressing your thoughts on paper, the more articulate you will become in speech, and vice versa. People who can write well are in demand in every area of employment, and it is just as valuable a skill now as it was in the past.

Letter-Writing

Letter-writing is a traditional skill that is falling into disuse. Many people thought that e-mails would be able to take the place of letters but, instead, they have generated their own style of writing, which, at its best, is capable of conveying the maximum amount of information with the minimum number of words, but cannot play the same role as a good letter. Writing a letter, over a period of time, on a piece of paper, gives you a chance to express something that you would never have an opportunity to do in simple conversation: by then sending it through the post, you are giving your correspondent a tangible item that, in all probability, they will keep for many years.

Writing Essays

When you have read about something, discussed it and thought about it, it is natural to want to write your own account of it. This is the origin of essay-writing and there is no reason why a modern student should not be as enthusiastic about it as the great essayists of the past. As with art, the main purpose of an essay is to allow you to create something that you yourself consider worthwhile. Writing an essay – whether it is just a few lines or dozens of pages long – helps you to clarify your thoughts and to see a subject more clearly than can be done by simply thinking about it.

As with all creative activities, part of the motivation for writing is to share something with other people; not so that they can give it a grade or a mark out of ten, but so that they gain an insight into something that you consider important, interesting or entertaining. You have to judge for yourself whether your work has achieved the desired effect, and, if not, how it can be improved so that it does. You are not trying to appeal to a teacher's idea of what constitutes a good piece of work, but rather you are trying to produce something that you yourself consider to be good and which wins the respect of people you care about.

Publishing There is no longer any reason why your work should be confined to a small circle of people. It has never been easier to publish material and distribute it amongst family, friends, and the wider world. For example, a computer, a word-processing programme, and a printer allow you to produce a good-quality copy of your work which can easily be photocopied and distributed amongst the people you know. Furthermore, by becoming familiar with a programme that enables you to create a web site, it is possible to publish your work on the internet where it can be accessed by anyone with a computer. These are opportunities that did not exist in the past and they allow you to build up experience, receive feedback from readers, and determine how committed you are to writing; they can lead to your work being published in conventional media such as books, magazines, and newspapers, and provide a practical route to becoming a professional writer without your ever having to go to college or work for someone else.

Spelling

Spelling mistakes detract from what you have written. Inevitably, people only see the mistakes, assume that you are uneducated, and ignore the point that you are trying to make. It is, therefore, important to remove spelling mistakes from your finished work. Spelling is undoubtedly easier for some people than for others but even if you find spelling difficult, it should be possible for you to eradicate mistakes.

- Work with a dictionary beside you and look up words that you are not sure about.
- Write out your work in pencil, and get someone to check it before going over it in ink.
- Make a note of words that you consistently get wrong, and make an effort to learn them.

Computer spell-checks are useful but they have to be used in association with the above points because there are mistakes which they do not detect.

Grammar

Grammar is concerned with the structure of language – nouns, adjectives, adverbs, verbs, tenses, prepositions, pronouns, clauses, etc., etc. At one time English grammar was taught in schools in the belief that it would improve people's ability to write, but English does not follow rules of grammar in the same way as the classical languages (Latin and Greek) or other modern European languages, and teaching it proved counter-productive.

Nevertheless, there is a great difference between a well-written piece of English prose and a poorly written piece of work. A writer has to develop a feel for good grammar and studying grammar is only a small part of that process.

- **Read Good Books:** The best way to improve the standard of your writing is to read good books. You may, temporarily, find that your work mimics the style of your favourite author but, providing you read widely, you will eventually develop your own style.
- **Copying:** Copy out passages and poems that you particularly enjoy. You will find that by copying the work, you start to notice details about the punctuation and the arrangement of words that you would not see if you were simply reading it.
- **Talking:** If you want to be able to express yourself on paper, it helps if you can express yourself through speech. Intelligent conversation is the ideal way to improve your language skills.
- **Practice and Self-Criticism:** You are the person best qualified to know if your work has succeeded in expressing what you want to express. Make an effort to read it and re-read it over and over again to see if there is any way in which it can be improved. (Reading it aloud to others will enable you to see any flaws straight away.)
- **Grammar Books:** When you start to apply yourself to writing, books on grammar become interesting – you may not want to read them from start to finish, but it is useful to be able to look up specific points or read about specific topics.

Presenting Your Work

Your studies can allow you to practise your writing and artistic skills. After reading round a subject, you can build up an illustrated account that reflects your own ideas and understanding. For example:

1. Sketch out the illustrations and the heading in pencil.
2. Write the text in pencil and check it for spelling and grammar.
3. Complete the illustrations in colour.

Contd. overleaf

A page need not contain a lot of writing, it can be mainly pictures.

4. Select a decorative alphabet *(see pages 260, 261)* and write out the heading, using a calligraphy pen, if desired.
5. Go over the pencil writing in ink – you can use a simple style of calligraphy *(see page 259)*, or your best handwriting.
6. Decorate the borders of the page.

There is no harm in taking a few days over a single page of work, the important thing is to make it as good as possible.

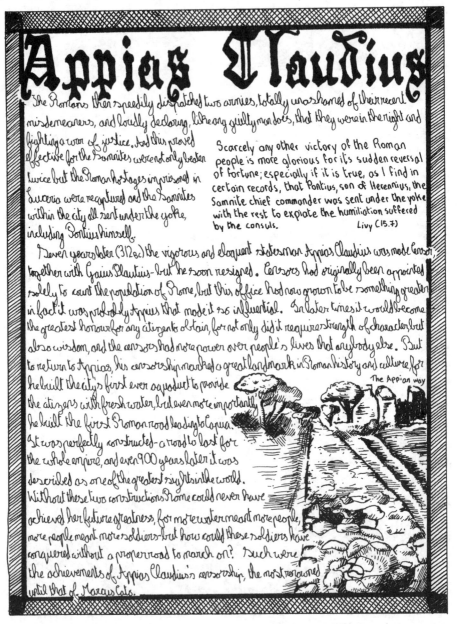

Written work gives you a chance to produce your own account of history.

Calligraphy

Calligraphy provides a way in which art and writing can be combined. Prior to the advent of the printing press, the presentation of a piece of writing was considered to be just as important as its content.

The Italic Aphabet

a b c d e f g h i j k l m

n o p q r s t u v w x y z

A B C D E F G H I J K L

M N O P Q R S T U V

W X Y Z

The Cancellaresca Alphabet
This elegant alphabet originated in the Vatican chancellery.

abcdefghijklm
nopqrstuvwxy z

ABCDEFG
HIKMNO
PQRSTVV
WXYZ

The Gothic Alphabet

a b c d e f g h i j k l m
n o p q r s t u v w x
y z

A B C D E F G H
I K L M N O P
Q R S T U V W
X Y Z

Advantages of Taking Care in the Presentation of Your Work

There are many advantages to applying a traditional, artistic approach to the written work that you do to accompany your studies. It encourages you to think carefully about each word that you write; it encourages you to plan the layout of each page; it enables you to combine illustrations and text; and it allows you to develop your skill as a calligrapher. Skills that are acquired in learning how to present work in this way can be directly transferred to working with graphics and layout on a computer – and should enable you to do this more successfully than someone who does not have the background of being able to do things by hand, on paper.

Paper Folding

Paper folding is an ideal way to learn about crafts: materials are plentiful, there is an unlimited number of things that you can make, and even simple projects require accurate folding and measuring if they are to be successful.

Paper Plane

You will need:
A piece of paper 8″ by 6″ (21 cm x 15 cm).

Method:
1. Fold the paper along the dotted line. Unfold. *(Diagram 1)*

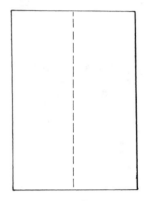

Diagram 1

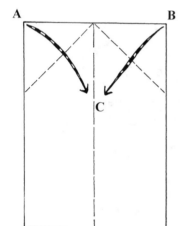

Diagram 2

2. Bring corners A and B to centre line C. *(Diagram 2)*

3. Fold on dotted line (approximately ¾″ (2 cm) below flaps). *(Diagram 3)*

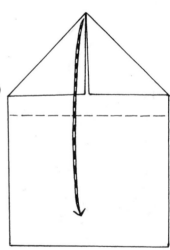

Diagram 3

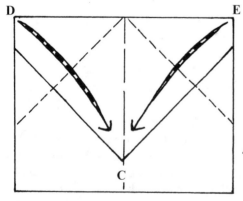

Diagram 4

4. Bring corners D and E to centre line C. *(Diagram 4)*

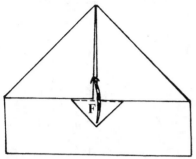

Diagram 5

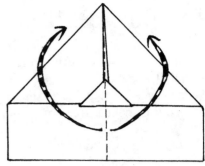

Diagram 6

5. Fold triangle F on dotted line.
   (Diagram 5)

6. Fold back on dotted line.
   (Diagram 6)

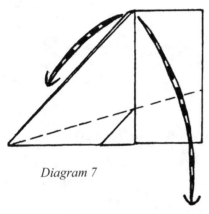

Diagram 7

7. Fold top layer along dotted line.
   Turn over and repeat on other
   side.
   (Diagram 7)

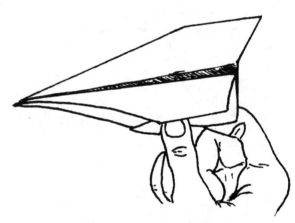

8. The plane is now ready to fly.

Paper Planes
Making paper planes is an enjoyable and educational activity. It is possible to find designs for different sorts of planes on the internet and in books, and by experimenting with different designs you can discover many of the principles of flight.
By adding flaps to the wings, or by incorporating a tail into the design, it is possible to replicate the techniques used in the production of aircraft and to gain a good practical understanding of aerodynamics.

Origami Ball

This origami design is particularly fascinating because it transforms a flat square of paper into an air-filled ball.

When made from coloured paper it makes an attractive Christmas tree ornament.

You will need:

1 square of paper, preferably coloured,
    6″ x 6″ (16 cm x 16 cm)
1 matchstick
A length of thread

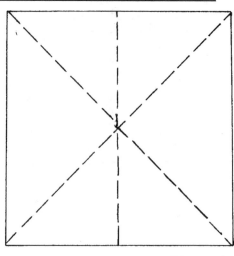

Diagram 1

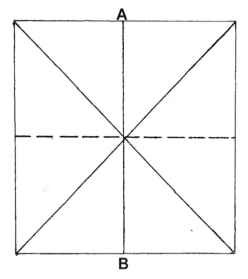

Method:

1. Fold along the dotted lines. Unfold. *(Diagram 1)*

2. Fold on dotted line, bringing A to B. *(Diagram 2)*

3. Push triangles C and D inside folded paper. *(Diagram 3 and 4)*

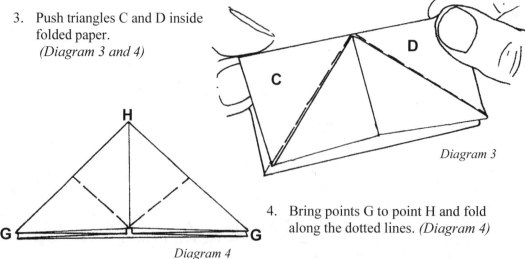

Diagram 3

4. Bring points G to point H and fold along the dotted lines. *(Diagram 4)*

Diagram 4

 Easy   *Medium*    *Advanced*

5. Bring points I to centre line J, along the dotted lines. *(Diagram 5)*

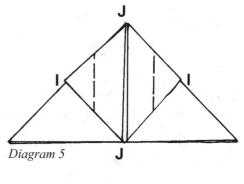

Diagram 5

Diagram 6a

6. Tuck flaps K and L into the two pockets M and N. The flaps must fit inside entirely and will need to be pushed and creased. *(Diagrams 6a & 6b)*

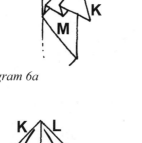

Diagram 6b

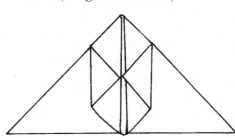

Diagram 7

7. Turn over and repeat directions 4, 5, and 6. *(Diagram 7)*

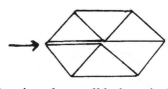

Diagram 8

8. Blow into the small hole at the base. *(Diagram 8)*
    The ball should blow up as in *diagram 9.*

9. Tie a length of thread around the middle of a matchstick and insert it lengthways into the paper ball. *(Diagram 9)*

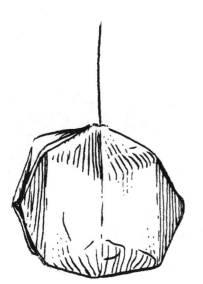

Diagram 9

Pagoda Bookmark

This paper pagoda makes an elegant bookmark as well as an interesting ornament.

For a satisfactory result the pieces of paper must be exactly square and the folds precise.

When using coloured paper, fold the coloured side inward at step 2.

You will need:

9 squares of paper of sides:

3½", 3¼", 3", 2¾", 2½", 2¼", 2", 1¾", 1½" respectively.

Method:

Starting with the largest of the nine squares, follow steps 1 to 4 of the Origami Ball *(page 264)*.

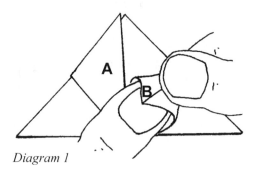

Diagram 1

1. Insert right thumb into triangle B and flatten into a square. *(Diagram 1)* Repeat on triangle A.

2. Bring points C to points D and fold along the dotted line. *(Diagram 2)*

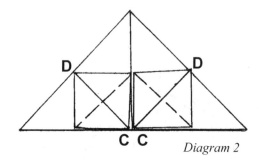

Diagram 2

3. Fold edge EE (top layer) underneath itself to inside. Repeat with edge FF. *(Diagram 3)*

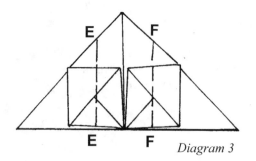

Diagram 3

---

266    Easy   Medium   Advanced

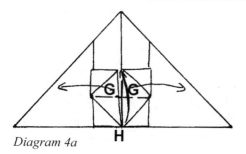

Diagram 4a

4. Take hold of triangles G and pull outwards.
   At the same time bring up point H and fold on dotted line.
   (Diagrams 4a, 4b and 4c)

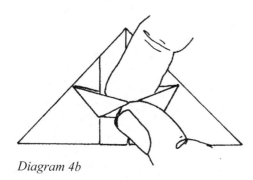

Diagram 4b

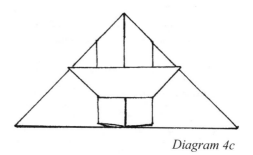

Diagram 4c

5. Turn over and repeat stages 1, 2, 3 and 4. This completes the first flight of the pagoda. *(Diagram 5)*

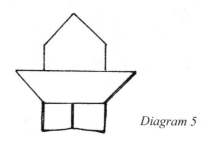

Diagram 5

6. Repeat with the other eight squares of paper.
   Attach the flights together by slipping the two legs of the smaller flight down into the grooves at the top of the larger flight beneath, and so on. *(Diagram 6)*

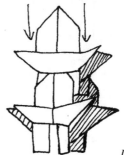

Diagram 6

Transparent Eight-Pointed Window Star

Window stars made from tissue paper or coloured waxed paper are a traditional German craft.

You will need:
1 sheet tissue paper 15" x 5" (38.3 cm x 12.6 cm) - this is one eighth of a standard-sized sheet of tissue paper.

Sharp, non-serrated knife

Stick of paper glue

Method:
1. Carefully fold and cut the tissue paper as shown in *diagram 1*.

Note: To get a clean edge to your paper: after you have made a fold, run your fingernail carefully along the crease to sharpen the fold and then slit along it with a sharp knife.

2. You will now have eight pieces each measuring 3¾" x 2½" (9.5 cm x 6.3 cm).

A   **B**

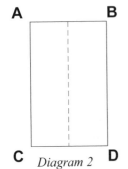

C *Diagram 2* **D**

3. Take one of the pieces and fold along the dotted line, bringing A to B and C to D. Open out. *(Diagram 2)*

Diagram 1

4. Fold corners A, B, C and D onto the central crease as shown in *diagram 3*.

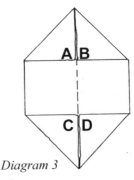

A B

C D

Diagram 3

     Easy   *Medium*   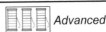 *Advanced*

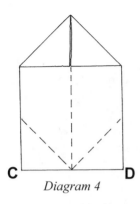

Diagram 4

5. Open out the corners C and D as shown in *diagram 4.*

6. Fold corners C and D onto the crease marks as shown in *diagram 5.*

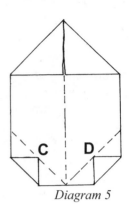

Diagram 5

7. Fold each of these corners over again as shown in *diagram 6.*

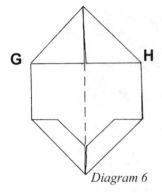

Diagram 6

8. Fold points G and H into the centre as shown in *diagram 7.*

9. Repeat with the other seven pieces.

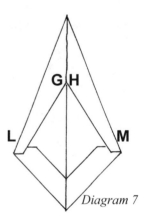

Diagram 7

Sticking the pieces together

1. Lightly touch the paper glue under points G, H, L and M and press gently. *(Diagram 7)*

Note: Tissue paper is very fragile and glue should be applied lightly.

2. Turn the piece over and stroke the glue stick over the bottom right-hand corner.
3. Repeat steps 1 and 2 with the second piece, and overlap the second piece onto the glued area of the first piece. *(Diagram 8)*
4. One by one glue and overlap the remaining pieces, pressing gently onto the glued area of the piece beneath.
5. Tuck the final piece under the first piece, thereby completing the star.

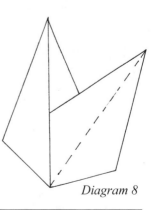

Diagram 8

Paper-Woven Basket

Working with paper can provide a practical experience of the principles of weaving. It is sufficiently rigid to be woven without a loom, allowing you to make mats and decorations out of strips of different-coloured paper.

A more ambitious project is this paper-woven basket. It is quite tricky and may take a couple of hours to complete, but the finished product is strong and can be used to hold pot-pourri, fir cones, lavender, knick-knacks, nuts, etc.

You will need:
Thick paper or thin card
(3 sheets of varying colours if desired)
Scissors
Pencils
Ruler

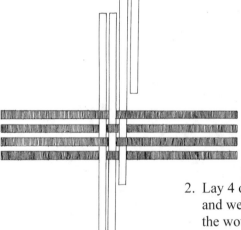

Diagram 1

Method:
1. Cut 8 long strips from the paper or card: 32 cm by 2 cm.

2. Lay 4 of the strips side by side on a flat surface and weave in the remaining four. Make sure that the woven square is as tight as possible and that it is exactly in the middle of the strips. *(Diagram 1)*

▯ *Easy*   ▯▯ *Medium*   ▯▯▯ *Advanced*

3. Fold all the ends up to make the side
    spokes of the basket.
    (Diagram 2)

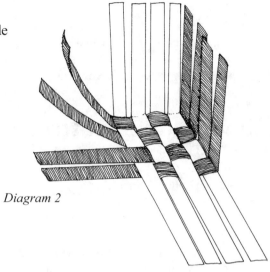

Diagram 2

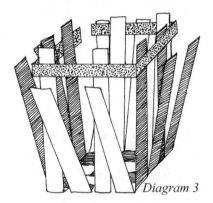

Diagram 3

4. Now cut 4 more strips 34 cm by 2 cm and
    weave them in and out of the upright
    spokes. Start weaving each new strip at a
    different corner.
    (Diagram 3)
    To make the upright weaving easier, you
    can fold each strip into quarters and place
    them like squares over the spokes one at a
    time.

5. When all 4 strips have been woven in, fold
    down the ends of the upright spokes and
    tuck them into, or fold them under, the
    weaving beneath, on the outside of the
    basket. *(Diagram 4)*

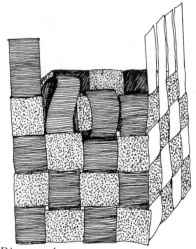

Diagram 4

6. A handle can now be added. Cut another
    long strip, 32 cm by 2 cm, and insert one
    end into the second square on one side of
    the basket and the other end into the third
    square on the opposite side of the basket.
    Fold round the ends until the handle is se-
    cure. *(Diagram 5)*

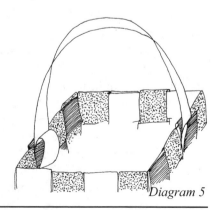

Diagram 5

Sewing

Sewing gives a practical insight into the structure and use of textiles. Everyone can master simple skills such as sewing on a button or sewing up a hem, and if you find that you enjoy sewing, you can progress to making clothes for yourself and for other people.

Sewing on a Button

You will need:
A button
18" (½ m) matching cotton thread
A needle

Method:

1. Thread the needle with the cotton and sew three small stitches on top of each other on the reverse side of the garment, where the old button used to be. This is to hold the thread in place.

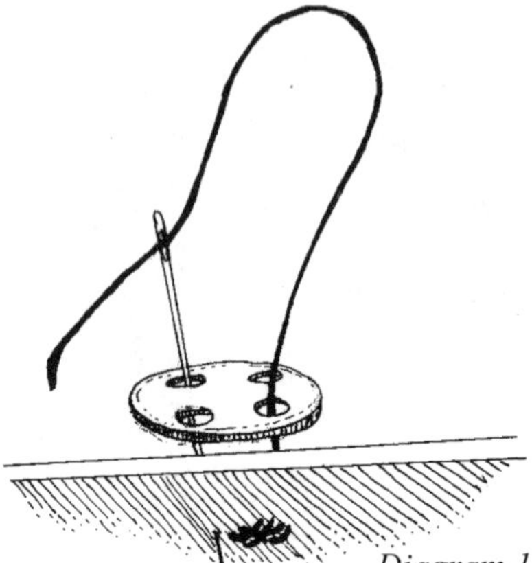

Diagram 1

2. Push the needle through to the right side of the garment and through one of the holes in the button. Pass the needle back through an adjacent hole and bring it out on the underside of the fabric. *(Diagram 1)*

3. Repeat this several times until the button feels secure.

4. Finish off with three stitches on the back of the garment, and cut the thread.

Buttons can have 2 or 4 holes. Those with 4 holes can be sewn on in different patterns. Always imitate the other buttons on the garment.

Textiles

Textiles have always been one of the most significant manufactured products: samples of woven linen fabric have been found in Switzerland dating back to 8000 BC, the cotton industry is known to have been well established in India by 3500 BC (and not much later than that in Peru), stories date the production of silk in China to at least 2700 BC, and wool production was central to both the ancient Greek and Roman civilisations in the Mediterranean.

All of these ancient civilisations used simple, hand-made tools to spin yarn and weave fabric. It is not difficult to buy or make replicas of these tools and to use them to make fabrics in your own home.

  Easy   *Medium*   *Advanced*

Hemming

The lower hem on dresses, and many other garments, frequently comes undone, and can easily be sewn up by hand using hemming stitch.

You will need:

A sewing needle

3 ft (1 m) thread, matching both the colour and the weight of the fabric e.g. use a cotton thread for heavier-weight cottons and linens, and a polyester thread for more lightweight fabrics

Note: If you cannot match the colour exactly, use a thread that is slightly darker than the material.

Method:

1. Thread the needle with the length of thread.

2. Fold the material as in *diagram 1*.

3. Sew three small stitches on the turned-up edge of the hem, to secure the thread.

4. As shown in *diagram 1*, catch up one or two threads of the garment fabric and then bring the needle up through the fold of the hem edge.

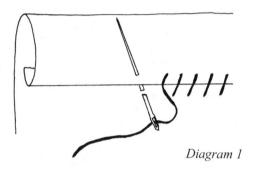

Diagram 1

5. Repeat along the length of the hem. If you run out of thread, fasten off, again with three small stitches into the folded hem, and continue as before.

6. Finish off with 3 small stitches.

If you work carefully, your stitches will not show on the right side of the material.

Textiles continued...

People's relationship to textiles changed during the Industrial Revolution when production became mechanised. The British Empire was organised in such a way as to make it possible to transport raw materials from around the world to British mills and then to export the finished product back to the various parts of the Empire. This may have appeared to be a liberating development at the time – freeing millions of people from working at hand-operated spinning wheels and looms in their homes – but it had the effect of introducing the world to the idea of becoming dependent on industrially-produced products. This process was taken a step further when synthetic textiles were developed in the 1930s and 1940s.

Apron

You will need:
> 1 m (39″) of 1 m (39″) wide material – medium to heavy weight cotton or linen mix
> 2.3 m (2½ yds) of 2 cm wide cotton tape for neck and ties
> 2 sheets of broadsheet newspaper
> Adhesive tape
> Ruler
> Marker pen
> Sharp scissors
> Pins
> An iron
> Reel of sewing thread in matching or contrasting colour
> A needle

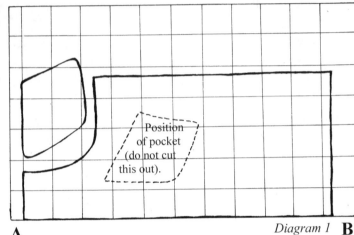

Position of pocket (do not cut this out).

A   *Diagram 1* **B**

Method:

1. Tape together the two sheets of newspaper along their long sides.
2. Rule a grid of 10 cm (4″) squares on the newspaper.
3. Using *diagram 1*, with a marker pen (or felt tip pen), copy the design for the apron and pocket onto your squared paper. 1 cm (3/8″) on the diagram represents 10 cm (4″) on your squared paper.
4. Cut out these patterns.
5. Fold your material in half and place the apron pattern on it so that the pattern edge AB is on a fold of the material.
6. Pin the pattern on and cut it out.
7. Place the pocket pattern on a single thickness of material. Pin and cut out.
8. Remove pins and open out the apron.
9. Turn under 1 cm (½″) of material all the way round the edge of the apron. Fold again to form a hem 1 cm (½″) wide. *(Diagram 2)*
10. Press this hem with a medium-hot iron and then pin it all the way round.

Diagram 2

> Note: You may find it difficult to turn under the hem on the curve of the apron. If you stretch the material slightly as you work, it will be easier.

  Easy   Medium   Advanced

11. Sew it down using backstitch. *(Diagram 3)*

12. Cut the tape into 1 length of 70 cm (28″) for the neck, and 2 lengths of 80 cm (32″) for the ties.

13. To fasten the neck tape turn under ½ cm (⅜″) of one end of the tape and sew securely onto the reverse side of the top of the apron, so that the turned under piece of the tape is hidden. Repeat with the other end. *(Diagram 4)*

14. To fasten the side ties lay 3 cm (1¼″) of the tape on one of the corners of the apron, and fasten securely with backstitch. Repeat with the other length of tape on the other corner. *(Enlarged picture, diagram 4)*

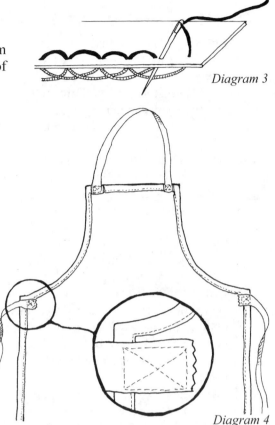

Diagram 3

Diagram 4

Pocket:

1. Turn under 1 cm (½″) of material all round the edge of the pocket, then turn under again, as before, to form a hem. Press with an iron.

2. Sew the hem along the side that will be the top of the pocket, using backstitch.

> Note: It is a good idea to try the apron on at this stage and to make sure that the pocket is in the correct position for the height of the person. (If the apron hangs too low, tie a knot in the neck tape.)

3. Position the pocket on the apron front. *(Diagram 1)*

4. Sew the pocket in position along the two sides and the bottom, using backstitch.

Hand-Hooked Rag Rug

Rag rug making is a traditional craft that people have done for hundreds of years. It requires very few tools and once the basic technique is learnt, there are no limits to the variety of things you can make – cushions, tea cosies, wall hangings, chair pads, blankets, etc.

This pattern is for a wall hanging, as it is advisable to start with something small.

These instructions are for right-handed people and need to be reversed if you work with your left hand.

You will need:

- 25″ x 25″ (64 cm x 64 cm) square piece of hessian or sacking cloth
- A water-resistent marker pen
- A wooden frame – an artist's stretcher, or embroidery frame
- Old pieces of material. For this flower design, you will need black cloth for the outline, various shades of pink for the flower, two yellows for the centre, and a large piece of blue cloth for the background. These colours can be varied according to what material you have.
- Scissors
- A hook *(diagram 1)*, this can be purchased from a specialist supplier. *(See page 335)*
- 8 foot (2.5 m) strip of 2″ (5 cm) wide carpet braid, cut into four 2 foot (64 cm) strips
- Needle and strong thread.
- 4 pieces of matching ribbon 1½″ (4 cm) wide 4″ (10 cm) long

Diagram 1: Hook

Note 1: A wide variety of materials can be used in rag rug making: sheets, blankets, jumpers, dresses and even ribbons, leather and even plastic bags.

Method:

1. First of all, work out your design and practise drawing it several times on a piece of paper.

2. Draw a square 4″ (10 cm) in from the edges of the sacking cloth and then fold the material in quarters, to find the central point. Sketch out your design, on the cloth, using a soft pencil. Make sure that it is centred in the middle of the material. When you are satisfied with your drawing, go over it with the marker pen. *(Diagram 2)*

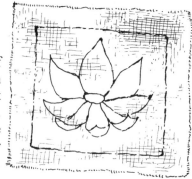

Diagram 2

  Easy *Medium*  *Advanced*

3. Fix the material to the frame with drawing pins or a staple gun, trying to keep the cloth as taught as possible. You can now begin to hook the rag rug.

4. Cut out a strip of black material ¼″ to ⅜″ (6 to 10 mm) wide, and at least 6″ (15 cm) long. Always cut straight along the line of the fabric, never diagonally.

Diagram 3

5. Hold the hook in your hand as if you were going to write with it, keeping the angle of the hook upwards, then push it firmly through the hessian from front to back. *(Diagram 3)*

> Make the hole big or your hook will catch on the threads as you bring it back. When you make the next hole, the first one will close up.

Diagram 4

6. Hold the strip of material you are going to use in your left hand and catch it up with the hook. *(Diagram 4)*

7. Bring the end to the front and leave 1″ (25 mm) above the fabric.

8. Working from right to left, move about two threads away and push the hook into the fabric.

9. Catch up the next bit of material and pull it through to the front to make a loop ½″ (12 mm) tall.

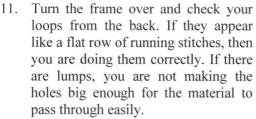

10. Work across the fabric in slight curves until you finish the strip of material. Leave the end as before, 1″ (25 mm) above the fabric. *(Diagram 5)*

Diagram 5

11. Turn the frame over and check your loops from the back. If they appear like a flat row of running stitches, then you are doing them correctly. If there are lumps, you are not making the holes big enough for the material to pass through easily.

> *Note 2:* Always work in the same direction, or you will find that each loop pulls out the previous loop. Do not be tempted to run a strip from one area to another under the fabric, as you will be sure to catch it up later – it is much easier to just snip off the material and start again.

12. When you start a new strip pull its end through the same hole as the end of the last strip, then proceed as before. However, do not worry if you cannot make the joins in this way, as it is not always possible. The ends can be trimmed as you go along.

13. Proceed in this way, first with the outlines, then with the filling in, until the pattern is complete.

14. Once you have finished, take out the staples or drawing pins and remove the wall hanging from the frame.

Binding the Rug

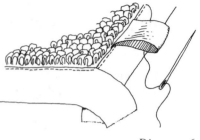

1. Trim round the raw edges of the fabric to leave a border of about 2″ (5 cm) all round.
2. Cut diagonally across the 4 corners ½″ (1 cm) away from the weaving.
3. On the front of the rug, stitch the carpet braid to the base fabric on three of the sides, as close to the weaving as possible, *(diagram 6)*. Use backstitch *(see page 275)*.

Diagram 6

4. As you sew what will be the top edge of your rug, place the pieces of ribbon, folded in half, at intervals along it and stitch them in, leaving the loop sticking out.
5. Turn the rug over and trim away excess braid at the corners.
6. Fold the braid down onto the wrong side and backstitch it to the reverse side of the rug, leaving the corners until last.
7. At the corners trim the braid carefully. Fold the pieces down and stitch them together *(diagram 7)*. The corners should not be bulky.

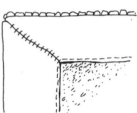

Diagram 7

You have now finished your rug!

Spinning and Weaving

If you are interested in clothes, textiles, carpets, etc., you will probably enjoy finding out more about traditional methods of production. The very best-quality textiles and carpets are still made by hand.

Traditional methods of spinning and weaving are still practised in many parts of the world and it is not difficult to obtain books that describe techniques used in different countries. Craft groups and societies that practise hand spinning and hand weaving are widespread and are able to offer practical help and support.

Prior to the introduction of the spinning wheel from India, in the fourteen or fifteen hundreds, spinning was done by hand; thread was drawn from a bundle of wool or fibre wrapped round one stick, called a distaff, onto another stick, called a spindle. Weaving is slightly more complicated because some sort of frame is required to hold the material taut as it is being woven, but the whole process of producing finished cloth from simple raw materials is well within the scope of everyone. It is also possible to experiment with dyeing the fabric, maybe even using natural vegetable dyes produced in your own garden.

Carding wool in Medieval England

   Easy Medium  Advanced

Knots

Knowing how to tie a few different knots is a very useful skill. Study each knot carefully and practise tying it several times to ensure that you remember it correctly.

Reef Knot

The reef knot is the standard knot used for joining two pieces of string together. Providing that it is arranged as shown in the diagram, it will not slip.

Lark's head Hitch

Useful for securing a ring to a rope or piece of string.

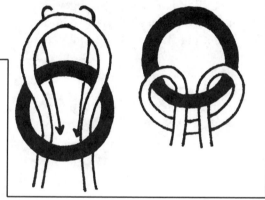

Clove Hitch

The clove hitch is the ideal knot to use if you want to attach something to a post or rail. It was traditionally used for mooring boats. It is quick to tie and easy to undo.

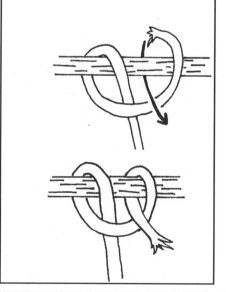

Bowline

The bowline is the simplest non-slip knot that allows you to make a loop.

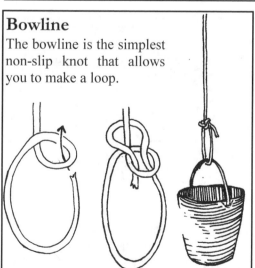

Kite

This kite is easy to make, exceptionally stable, and will fly in the lightest breeze.

You will need:
Sheets of newspaper
Sheet of plastic 100 cm x 90 cm
Two 90 cm pieces of 6 mm dowel
Parcel tape
A metal or plastic ring (1 – 2 cm diameter)
Thick tear-resistant tape
Kite string on a reel

Method:

1. Tape sheets of newspaper together to make a rectangle 100 cm by 90 cm. Fold it in half and make a template as shown in *diagram 1*. Cut out the shaded areas.
   Take care to make the template as accurate as possible. If it is not symmetrical, the kite will not fly.

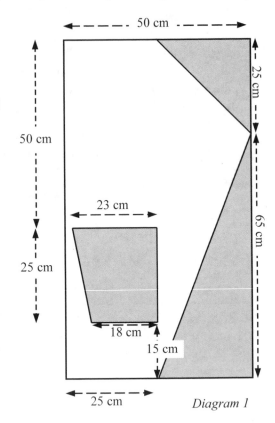

Diagram 1

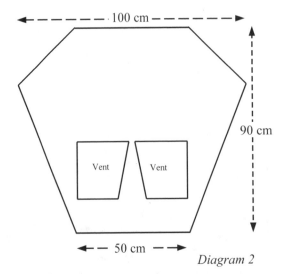

Diagram 2

2. Unfold the template, tape it onto the plastic sheet and cut out the kite as shown in *diagram 2*.

Note: The vents allow air to flow through the kite and give it stability in high winds.

  Easy Medium Advanced

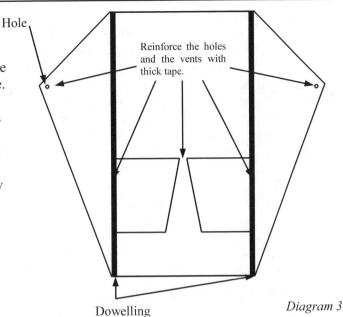

Hole

Reinforce the holes
and the vents with
thick tape.

3. Fix the dowelling in place
with strips of parcel tape.
Use plenty of tape to en-
sure that the dowelling is
well secured.
Make holes for attaching
the string.
Reinforce any potentially
weak point with several
layers of tear-resistant
tape. *(Diagram 3)*

Dowelling

Diagram 3

4. Cut 1½ metres of kite string off the reel.
Attach one end to each of the holes in the kite
using a bowline *(page 279)*.
This forms the bridle of the kite.

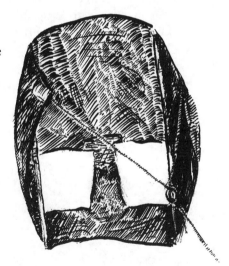

5. Position the ring in the centre of the bridle
using a lark's head hitch *(page 279)*.

6. Attach the flying string to the ring, with a
bowline, and the kite is ready to fly.

Kite-making provides practical experience of the skills used in engineering and the principles
of aerodynamics.
There are many designs and many different materials that you can use.
Information and ideas are readily available on the internet and in books:
e.g. **Kites**, David Pelham, The Overlook Press

Making Things

Making things has traditionally been an important part of human life. People measure the degree of civilisation that a society has achieved by the quality of the pottery, the jewellery, the implements, the weapons, and the toys that it has left behind, and it is strange that so few people are now actively involved in making things, either for business or for pleasure. Subjects such as woodwork, metalwork, and pottery are given a low priority in schools, and most people finish their schooling with a firm belief that they cannot make the things that they will need in life. Consequently, they have no choice but to buy everything that they want, and in this way are more or less robbed of their independence. Home-based education provides an environment conducive to the creative process:

- **Making things requires personal commitment.** Something that is a pleasure when you decide to do it for yourself, becomes tedious when you are doing it because someone has told you to do so.
- **The creation of each item has its own rhythm.** When you are making something, you often need to work at it for several hours per day until it is completed; sometimes you lose your inspiration and have to put it to one side for a while; sometimes you have to stop work if you are tired, etc. In short, you cannot squeeze the creative process into a particular time slot allocated to it by a rigid timetable. If you are involved in making something quite demanding, you may need to drop all other work until it is finished – and when it is finished, give yourself a break from making things.
- **You need your own space.** When you are making things you need your own space and your own tools.
- **You need to be able to work in a pleasant atmosphere.** No one can do their best work if they are trying to work in a chaotic atmosphere.

While it is not possible to make everything that is now considered useful or essential (making a computer, a car or an aeroplane out of basic raw materials would be quite a daunting task), it is still possible to design and build many of the items that people have become accustomed to buying from shops. You can start with simple projects that require only the most basic tools and build up from there according to your

personal interests and requirements – woodwork, woodcarving, making wooden toys, furniture, metalwork, jewellery, ceramics, basket weaving, working with glass, etc, are all activities that can be done in the home.

Things that you make yourself can often be more beautiful, better suited to your needs, and less expensive than comparable manufactured items and, in addition, the process of making them is itself rewarding and provides you with an opportunity to develop your creative skills. In every respect, it is much better to make things than to buy them.

Mending Things

Every modern home is full of all sorts of electrical and mechanical items, which are prone to wear out or break down. For many people, this is a source of extra stress, but it can also be seen as an opportunity to develop your skills.

Repair charges are increasingly prohibitive and it is now commonplace to replace an item simply because one of its components no longer works. This means that you have little to lose by dismantling any machines or appliances that break down. At the very least, you will develop an understanding of how they have been put together, and it is quite likely that you will be able to identify the broken component, order a replacement, install it, and get the appliance working again.

Skills that are developed in basic craft work are surprisingly useful when it comes to mending even quite complex items. Once you start to examine a piece of machinery, you quickly realise that the mind that invented it and put it together does not differ significantly from the mind that invented the first machines a few hundred years ago – things are generally arranged in a logical and systematic manner, and even though individual components (such as parts of a computer) may be very complex, the way that they have been put together is quite straightforward.

Tips:

- Before replacing any item – even shoes, clothes, tools, etc. – consider that you might be able to repair it instead.
- Before tackling modern, electrical items, experiment by trying to repair pieces of equipment that use older technologies, such as bicycles, clocks or clockwork toys.
- When repairing electrical items, always disconnect them from the supply. Some things (televisions for example) retain an electrical charge for a while after they are disconnected – always respect instructions such as 'do not remove this cover'.
- Try to work out how the item has been assembled, and reverse the process in order to disassemble it. If you find yourself having to force an item to the point of damaging it, take a break and return to it when you are calm.
- Do some research: for example, learn how an internal combustion engine works and read the manual carefully before working on the engine of a car.
- Make sure that you look after things: read the manual and follow the instructions for servicing the item. In this way you will extend its life span and will also be more knowledgeable about how it works and more able to repair it if it does break down.

Mending things is a little more complicated than I remembered

So many wires!

Building

Building is another skill that at one time was part of everyday life but which is now considered beyond the scope of the average person.

Until recently, people made their own houses using materials that were plentiful in their own locality. This gave rise to the distinctive styles of architecture that are associated with different areas – where stones were abundant, people built with stones; where clay was available, people either baked bricks or built earth houses; whenever possible slate was used for roofing, otherwise roofs were thatched, tiled, or covered with shingles. Houses built in this way lacked the sophistication of modern buildings – they did not have plumbing, central heating or electricity – but they achieved a harmony with their surroundings that makes them the ideal to which many people still aspire: few people in the UK, for example, would turn down the opportunity to live in a thatched cottage in the countryside, built out of local stone, with roses and honeysuckle growing round the door.

Nowadays, builders are hemmed in by red tape and regulations and have little chance to express their creative skills, but the basic techniques that they use have remained largely unchanged over the years. Any building-related skills that you are able to pick up will almost undoubtedly come in useful at some point in the future, enabling you to work on your own home and possibly providing a flexible source of employment. Ways to pick up building skills include:

- **Doing simple jobs such as painting and decorating.** Each decorating job tends to be fairly small and self contained, and therefore gives you a chance to learn from your mistakes and to experiment with new ideas without disrupting the whole household.

- **Taking responsibility for repair and maintenance jobs.** Simple jobs such as unblocking gutters and sinks, replacing broken panes of glass, replacing light bulbs, oiling door hinges, hanging pictures, etc. help you to become familiar with the way in which your house has been put together.

- **Experimenting with using cement and plaster.** Modern building relies heavily on the use of cement. Cement is a limestone-based product that is used to knit together inert material such as sand and gravel to make mortar and concrete. You can develop an understanding of its properties by doing simple jobs in the garden – making concrete steps, building a wall, making concrete paths, etc. Plaster is useful for finishing off interior walls. It is usually made from gypsum.

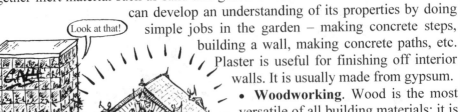

- **Woodworking**. Wood is the most versatile of all building materials: it is perfect for structural elements such as beams and it is also ideal for doors, windows and flooring; it is even possible to make the walls and roof out of wood as well. Any experience that you gain in working with wood will be useful in building.

Building a House

When we moved to France in the early 1990s, we had little money, but a great deal of time on our hands. Instead of buying a house, we decided to purchase a plot of land upon which we could build, as and when materials became available.

Over the next few years, we reused stones from a ruined house, retrieved oak beams from a disused hay store and collected second-hand windows and doors. We also purchased new materials – bags of cement, sand from a local quarry, slates, etc. – and over the course of five years built a house in which we could live. This experience allowed us to acquire a range of building skills – masonry, carpentry, concreting, tiling, slating, wiring, plumbing, plastering, painting, etc. – in addition to designing the house and negotiating the planning process, and I would say without hesitation that it taught me more than any other project in which I have been involved: it leaves university degrees far, far behind as an educational experience.

Not only did I learn practical skills but I also learnt something about what is required to successfully convert an idea into reality. In addition, we now have a house which, even though it is constructed by amateurs, has won the respect of everyone who has visited it. The response that I have received has left me with the impression that many people are deeply unhappy with the current system, which gives them virtually no opportunity to build their own houses. Acquiring building skills as part of your education means that you are at least giving yourself a chance to defeat the system and perhaps one day build a house for yourself, as people have done for thousands of years in the past.

Conclusion

Crafts is, essentially, the area in which the education you have received is put to some use. A person with an immense amount of book learning, but no practical skills, lacks the ability to do anything with their knowledge, and someone with practical skills but no learning is unlikely to be innovative or creative. A good craftsperson can take knowledge that they have gained from various sources and use it to create things of beauty and originality. This can apply to the making of clothes, the building of houses, designing publications, traditional crafts such as basket-making, modern crafts such as the design and maintenance of machinery, and also, in a more subtle way, to other areas of life. Craft work teaches people to take responsibility for something and to work on it until it is as good as it can possibly be. This is an admirable approach to have and is likely to lead to success in whatever you undertake.

धीरे धीरे रे मना, धीरे सब कुछ होय।
माली सींचे सौ घड़ा, ऋतु आये फल होय ।।

Oh slowly, slowly comes understanding,
Everything happens slowly.
The gardener emptied a hundred jars of water,
But only with the season came the fruit.

A Hindi saying

Academic Subjects

Contents:

Introduction

Until the advent of compulsory schooling, there was a fairly clear consensus about what was meant by education: it consisted, above all, of a knowledge of Latin and Greek and a certain familiarity with classical texts; added to this, scholars were expected to know something about history, politics, and philosophy; they would have been able to read at least one or two modern languages apart from their mother tongue, and to have read and be able to quote from major works of literature; they were expected to have travelled, to have an appreciation of music and a knowledge of natural history; and really good scholars would also have had a degree of competency in mathematics – especially geometry, but perhaps also algebra. This sort of scholarship was gradually discredited as it became apparent that so-called 'scholars' were no wiser than other people; they were simply using their learning to install themselves in positions that allowed them to live a life of ease.

Consequently, when, in the twentieth century, secondary education began to be provided at public expense, there was little consensus between different sections of society over what should be included in the curriculum. Traditional scholars maintained that Latin, Greek, etc., constituted the only proper form of education, but this view was opposed by business people who considered such knowledge out of date and thought that a modern education should be centred around science, technology, and ideas that would be useful in practical employment.

Initially, state-funded secondary schools followed the traditional model (probably because it would not have been possible to find teachers trained to teach any other material), but they have gradually moved to a curriculum in which virtually nothing would be recognisable to someone who attended school one hundred years ago.

A moment's reflection will tell anyone that this is an undesirable situation; knowledge that has been built up over thousands of years may at times have been badly presented but, in general, if it has been examined and re-examined by generation after generation, it is likely to have some value – or it could not have survived for so long. Our school system has discarded virtually all this knowledge and now revises and reviews its curriculum every few years. New subjects are introduced, old subjects are rewritten, and everything is in a state of flux. The reasons for this are bound up with politics, finance, and employment, and in the frenzy of the debate over what should and what should not be taught, people lose sight of the effect that this has on the students themselves: parents are not familiar with the material that their children are learning, just as their parents were not familiar with what they learnt when they were at school. The implication of this is that the material that today's students are being taught will have been forgotten by the time their children go to school, or, to put it another way, most of the things that people have learnt at school over the past fifty years have been of a transitory nature and are of no long-term use.

Given that that is the case, the current school curriculum is unlikely to yield useful ideas to someone who is interested in learning things of lasting value: the discerning student is now forced to devise their own curriculum and to decide for themselves what they wish to learn and how they propose to study it.

The past three sections of the book have focussed upon practical activities – gardening, cooking, and crafts – because the acquisition of practical skills ought to be an essential part of everyone's education. These practical skills only come into their own, however, when they are combined with a good understanding of the world, and a lively interest in the world of knowledge, and this comes from academic studies.

The sections on history and literature at the beginning of the book provide the basis upon which further academic studies can be built, and go over the sort of work that could be covered in the early stages of 'secondary' education.

The following section outlines how other subjects, such as geography, modern languages, and music can be incorporated into this work and discusses the best ways of dealing with mathematics, science and technology. When studying these subjects, it is important not to fall into the trap of imagining that you have a particular goal in view, or that you are rushing to complete an area of study by a particular date. Providing you develop the habit of only studying things that interest you, there is no reason why you should not continue to enjoy these subjects for the rest of your life.

My spade is made of iron, so it can work hard soil, but this soil is a nice soft loam rich in humus and could be worked with bronze tools

You know, the word soil comes from Anglo French which may come from Latin *solium* meaning "seat". Which I think might come from the Latin word *solum* meaning "ground"

How Academic Knowledge Became Discredited

It is not difficult to understand the process by which academic knowledge has become discredited: there was once a time in which the only people who studied books were those who found them interesting and these people acquired knowledge that made them useful to the smooth running of society; they could communicate with people from other countries, they could keep written records of transactions, they had an understanding of politics, diplomacy, and military strategy, they could administer laws and they had knowledge useful in surveying and the design of buildings.

Not surprisingly, countries were eager to maintain a supply of these educated people and many parents were eager for their children to enter their ranks. Unfortunately, instead of waiting for educated people to present themselves, or gently encouraging learning in the population as a whole, it was thought expedient to force learning upon a few 'privileged' children, whether they wanted it or not, by sending them to elite private schools.

The effect of this was to make some of the finest achievements of our culture (Latin and Greek grammar, geometry, algebra, Shakespeare, etc.) the object of loathing to schoolboys who were forced to learn about them at school and helped to create the impression that academic studies are fiendishly difficult.

Even more seriously, students who graduated from these schools took over the positions that had traditionally been held by educated people, and when they proved unable to display either wisdom or virtue, people lost faith in the value of academic knowledge itself.

Geography

Geography is perhaps the most intrinsically interesting of all the 'academic' subjects because it deals with the lives being led by people all over the world. This makes it a good starting point for anyone who does not like writing but who does want to spend some time doing work in books. Drawing maps provides an ideal introduction to the subject and is excellent training in the art of supplying the maximum amount of information in the simplest way.

Drawing Maps

If you want your maps to be accurate, it is advisable to adopt a precise, technical approach to copying the basic outline, and the position of major landmarks. The following method involves copying a map square by square, and although it may seem time-consuming, it does, in fact, enable you to draw accurate maps of any size, relatively quickly.

Diagram 1

1. Cut a piece of tracing paper slightly larger than the size of the page from which you are copying the map.

2. Use paper clips to fix your tracing paper over the map that you are copying. *(Diagram 1)*

3. Mark out a square or rectangle, on the tracing paper, round the area of the map that you want to copy.

4. On the tracing paper, divide this area into squares. Use a ruler to ensure that all the squares are the same size, if necessary extend the area marked on the tracing paper to accommodate an exact number of squares – the more detailed you want the map to be, the smaller you should make the squares.

Note: You can make your copy larger or smaller than the original by making the squares on your paper larger or smaller than those that you have marked on the tracing paper.

5. Mark out a square or rectangle on the page, or piece of paper, on which you want to draw the map. Divide it into the same number of squares as you have marked on the tracing paper.

6. Copy the map square by square, using a sharp HB pencil. *(Diagram 2)*

7. Go over your outline with a fine black pen.

8. When the ink is dry, rub out the pencil marks.

9. Colour in your map, add place names and any other writing.

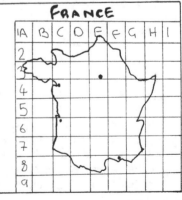

Diagram 2

Maps can be used to convey all sorts of different information:

- **National and State Boundaries:** You can draw maps of the world, region by region, marking on national boundaries.
- **Capital Cities:** Maps can be used to show capital cities and major centres of population; this gives an insight into both politics and economics.
- **Rivers and Mountains:** River valleys are traditional places of human settlement: they are characterised by rich soils, mild climates and good transportation. Rivers often provide boundaries between countries, as do large mountain ranges. The courses taken by rivers are determined by the presence of mountain ranges. Marking rivers and mountains on maps gives an insight into why and how countries have been formed.
- **Volcanoes and Earthquakes:** Maps show that earthquakes and volcanoes tend to occur most frequently in specific zones, supporting the idea that the Earth's surface is made up of 'tectonic plates' that are moving relative to each other.
- **Ancient Civilisations and Military Campaigns:** Maps are the clearest way of showing the extent of ancient civilisations. They also show how campaigns of conquest, migration, and exploration have tended to follow certain geographical routes.
- **Climate:** The climate zones of the earth – polar, temperate, tropical, etc. – are best understood through maps, and maps are also a good way of indicating the presence of deserts, forests, jungles, etc., and how they are formed by local weather patterns.

Bhutan

Nepal

India

Sri Lanka

291

Human Geography

The subject of geography is traditionally divided into human geography, which covers every aspect of human life – where people live, what they live on, political boundaries, trade, etc. – and physical geography, which is concerned with the structure of the Earth. In practice there is a considerable overlap between these two branches, because physical geography has always had a significant effect on human affairs, and especially in recent years, human activity has had a significant effect upon the landscape.

The study of human geography requires you to take an active interest in the things that are going on around you. This can involve reading books and magazines, studying atlases, consulting the internet, talking to people, and reflecting on the state of affairs, in your own locality, in your country, and in the world at large.

There are various issues around which the study of geography revolves:

- **Population Growth and Distribution:** The world population is much larger now than at any time in recorded history. Most of the world's population is still centred in the same areas as in the past – in particular the river valleys and coastal regions of India and China – but a few regions, most noticeably North America, are now providing a home to a much larger population than ever before. Some areas, such as the deserts of Southern California and the Florida swamps, which were at one time considered uninhabitable, are now covered with cities containing millions of people. The need to support these populations is a major factor in world affairs.

Flags

Drawing flags is a good way of gaining a knowledge of cultures and customs around the world, whilst keeping the emphasis on artistic work. Flags used by different countries reflect their culture and recent history: there is a family of flags based upon the colours of Islam; there are flags that contain the colours of African unity, there are many flags inspired by the French tricolour, which has come to symbolise republican government; there are flags based on those of previous colonial rulers; and there is the famous Stars and Stripes of the United States. Drawing flags in conjunction with maps helps to clarify the current state of political affairs and alliances.

- **World Agriculture:** From prehistoric times human populations have been dependent on a few basic cereals – rice in the East, wheat in the Middle East and Europe; maize in the Americas; sorghum in Africa; etc. – and the ability to produce enough of these crops is still critical to survival. In recent years the production of cash crops – coffee, tea, cotton, cocoa, bananas, etc., has made the situation more complicated. Understanding which countries are producing which crops, and to whom they are selling them, helps you to unravel the complexities of modern economics: cocoa from West Africa goes to Europe; coffee from Brazil goes to the USA; tea from India still goes to Britain, etc. It is also interesting to know which countries are self-sufficient in food and which are not.

- **Mineral Resources:** In the past, a nation's wealth was determined by its ability to produce food, but now mineral resources, especially oil, also play a significant role. The industrialised countries of Europe and the United States have more or less exhausted their own resources, and in order to maintain their standing in the world require a plentiful supply of crude oil, natural gas, coal, phosphates and mineral ores from other less 'developed' countries. This trade has a profound effect upon the lives of millions of people around the world.

- **Wealth and Power:** Wealth and power is now concentrated in the hands of a few industrialised countries: there is a correlation between wealth, industrial production, military power, and consumption – but it is still difficult to understand why some countries are rich and others poor, or why some are strong and others weak. A study of human geography helps to make the picture clearer, especially when it is combined with a knowledge of history and a study of human nature.

Political Leaders

Knowing something about political leaders provides another source of insight into world politics. Instead of writing about them, you can try drawing them – many politicians and rulers have distinctive features, and it is interesting to speculate on the extent to which their features have been formed by the stresses and strains of office or whether they reflect character traits that drive a person to seek the supreme position of power in their country.

Jacques Chirac, France

293

Physical Geography

Physical geography is concerned with the structure of the planet itself. The subject provides a young person with a chance to experience the difference between understanding and explanations. People have always had to live with the physical characteristics of the planet – mountain ranges, rivers, volcanoes, earthquakes, storms, droughts, etc. – and have always sought to explain them. In the past, these explanations tended to be religious in nature, whereas now they are scientific. These explanations only become really interesting when you have had a chance to experience the original phenomenon yourself and, in most cases, it is experience rather than explanations that really deepens your understanding of the physical world.

The Local Landscape

Simply observing your local landscape can give you an insight into the principles of physical geography. Before people established a new settlement they would have had to determine how easily it could be defended, whether it had a plentiful supply of water, whether the surrounding land could support them, whether it was free from flooding, and how convenient it was for travel. By walking round your area, you should be able to work out why people originally chose to live there and the reasons why development has spread since then.

Geology

It is interesting to make a collection of rocks that you find when walking near your home, visiting the coast, or when you go on holiday. It should be possible for you to work out which sort of rock is most prevalent in the area in which you live – limestone, chalk, granite, etc. – and how this has affected local building and industry. If you visit disused quarries, abandoned mines, or cliffs that are being eroded on the coast, you may also be able to find rarer geological samples such as crystals and fossils. (Extreme care should be exercised in visiting any such areas; do not explore holes in the ground, walk close to the edge of cliffs, or take any chances with an incoming tide; do not go unaccompanied; and do some research about the place that you are visiting to ensure that it is safe.)

Travel

In many ways travel is the best teacher of geography, because it allows you to experience at first hand the differences and the similarities between the different people and places of the world.

- **Travel as Opposed to Tourism:** Ideally, travel should involve an element of chance: you should be able to change your plans from day to day, make use of local facilities, and be forced to speak the local language. It may sometimes put you in a situation in which you don't know where your next meal is coming from or where you are going to spend the night, but it is these uncertainties that help you to appreciate the area through which you are travelling.

- **Where to Travel:** Travel does not necessarily involve visiting other countries or spending a lot of money. Walking and cycling trips starting from your home, or with a short train ride, can take you to places that you would never normally see when driving around in a car. Youth hostels and campsites offer reasonably-priced accommodation. As you gain experience, you can extend your travels.

- **What to Avoid:** There are now established routes and trails that are detailed in travel guides and which are followed by thousands of people. If possible these should be avoided.

- **How to Travel:** Travel is most enjoyable when you are with other people. Family holidays have a bad reputation, but if members of a family get on with each other when they are at home and are in the habit of working and studying together, travel only strengthens the bonds between them. Travelling with people who are able to share your enjoyment, and with whom you can reminisce afterwards makes the whole experience more rewarding.

- **Safety:** Travel has never been a risk-free exercise, particularly for young people travelling without their families. It therefore makes sense to follow simple rules of safety when away from home: if possible do not travel alone, travel with someone who you know well, do not display ostentatious signs of wealth, do not carry too much money with you or things that you cannot afford to lose, and keep in contact so that friends and relatives know where you are.

When personal observations are taken in conjunction with reading about climate, volcanoes, earthquakes, and weather patterns, the Earth starts to feel more like a living entity than an inanimate object. It is a finely-balanced system that somehow manages to maintain an environment that supports life. The more one understands it, the more respect one is bound to feel for it, and the less one wants to interfere.

Languages

The study of languages is an indispensable part of any real education. The benefits that learning a language confer include:

- **Being Able to Speak to People from Different Countries:** The obvious advantage of learning a language is that it enables you to speak to people from different countries.

- **Your Intellectual Abilities are Improved:** No one really understands the nature of intellectual thought, but, logically, it cannot exist before someone learns to speak a language. It is, therefore, not surprising that being able to speak a second or third language enhances your intellectual abilities.

- **You Become Better at Your Own Language:** When you study another language, you inevitably compare the vocabulary and the grammar of the new language to that of your own and you start to become more conscious of the language that you use from day to day.

- **Once You Learn One Language, it is Easier to Learn Another:** When you speak only one language, all foreign languages can fill you with dread, but once you have learnt one new language the idea of learning others starts to appear rather in the light of an interesting challenge than something to be feared.

- **You Can Read Books in Their Original Language:** Once you start to read books in their original language, you will become reluctant ever to read translations again.

- **You Become a More Tolerant Person:** When you can see life from someone else's perspective you become more tolerant, and this makes every aspect of life more pleasant both for yourself and for the people you know.

Well met, मैं bin Judith

Bonjour, εἰμι Craig

Jambo, sono Anaxagoras

For all these reasons, the ability to speak and read foreign languages has long been one of the defining features of an educated person.

How to Study Languages

Modern learning aids include books, cassettes, CDs, CD ROMS, night school classes, private tuition, and correspondence courses. All these have their value but there is another, traditional method of language study which has largely fallen into disuse, and which may provide a more appropriate starting point. This involves learning a language through its literature.

In this method, the most important consideration is the selection of the text. If you have no prior knowledge of a language, select a simple text, perhaps something that is read to children, but make a point of selecting the best literature that the language has to offer – whether it is children's or adult literature. If possible, obtain an edition of the text that has the original language on one side of the page and the English translation on the other. In addition to the text itself, you will need a good dictionary and, if the dictionary does not have a grammar section, a book that explains something about the grammar of the language.

Selecting a Language

It may be advisable to begin with a modern language because there are more texts to choose from, and you may have an opportunity to speak it on your travels. Spanish is the most widely spoken, and therefore most useful Western language after English, but both German and French have a rich literary tradition, which makes them rewarding languages to study. You could also consider learning Italian, Portuguese, or Dutch, or look further afield to a language such as Swahili; you could even be really ambitious and study a language that has a different alphabet, such as Arabic, Hindi, or Chinese.

Reading Texts

Different people read new languages in different ways: one suggestion is to read a text one paragraph at a time. The first read-through should give you an idea of its meaning and, if necessary, you can then read it a second time, looking up words you do not understand, in a dictionary. When you come across a particularly difficult passage, you can translate it word by word, on paper, and then try to make sense of what you have written.

Speaking and Pronunciation

Being able to read a language does not necessarily help you to speak it well – it is all too easy to develop the habit of mispronouncing words in your head whilst you are reading. This can be corrected by studying the pronunciation of the various letters (this is included in some dictionaries), looking up the pronunciation of words that you are not sure about (dictionaries contain phonetic spellings), making an effort to listen to the language being spoken by native speakers (radio stations, satellite television channels and the internet make this a relatively easy exercise), and speaking the language yourself (if no other opportunities present themselves, this could involve private lessons with someone who comes from the country whose language you are studying).

German: Sneewittchen, the Brothers Grimm

German has a rich tradition of fairy stories and myths. They are traditionally told to children but when you have a chance to read them in the original, you can see why they are also enjoyed by adults. This extract is from the classic fairy story, "Sneewittchen" (Little Snow White).

Es war einmal mitten im Winter und die Schneeflocken fielen wie Federn vom Himmel herab, da saß eine Königin an einem Fenster, das einen Rahmen von schwarzem Ebenholz hatte, und nähte. Und wie sie so nähte und nach dem Schnee aufblickte, stach sie sich mit der Nadel in den Finger und es fielen drei Tropfen Blut in den Schnee. Und weil das Rote im weißen Schnee so schön aussah, dachte sie bei sich: Hätt ich ein Kind so weiß wie Schnee, so rot wie Blut und so schwarz wie das Holz an dem Rahmen.

Bald darauf bekam sie ein Töchterlein, das war so weiß wie Schnee, so rot wie Blut und so schwarzhaarig wie Ebenholz und ward darum das Sneewittchen (Schneeweißchen) genannt. Und wie das Kind geboren war, starb die Königin.

Über ein Jahr nahm sich der König eine andere Gemahlin.

Es war eine schöne Frau, aber sie war stolz und übermütig und konnte nicht leiden, dass sie an Schönheit von jemand sollte übertroffen werden. Sie hatte einen wunderbaren Spiegel, wenn sie vor den trat und sich darin beschaute, sprach sie:

»Spieglein, Spieglein an der Wand,
wer ist die Schönste im ganzen Land?«,

so antwortete der Spiegel:

»Frau Königin, Ihr seid die Schönste im Land. «

Da war sie zufrieden, denn sie wusste, dass der Spiegel die Wahrheit sagte.

Sneewittchen aber wuchs heran und wurde immer schöner und als es sieben Jahre alt war, war es so schön wie der klare Tag und schöner als die Königin selbst. Als dieser einmal ihren Spiegel fragte:

»Spieglein, Spieglein an der Wand,
wer ist die Schönste im ganzen Land?«,

so antwortete er:

»Frau Königin, Ihr seid die Schönste hier,
aber Sneewittchen ist tausendmal schöner als Ihr.«

Da erschrak die Königin und ward gelb und grün vor Neid.

Glossary (Where necessary the infinitive of the verb is in brackets.)

der Schnee – the snow	aussehen – to appear, to look	trat (treten) – stepped
wie – like	bei sich – to herself	beschaute (beschauen) – to look
der Himmel – the sky, heaven	bald – soon	die Wand – the wall
das Fenster – the window	bekam (bekommen) – had, got	ganzen – whole, entire
der Rahmen – the frame	genannt (nennen) – named	zufrieden – satisfied
das Ebenholz – the ebony	starb (sterben) – died	denn – because
nähen – to sew	nahm (nehmen) – took	wuchs (wachsen) – grew
wie – as	die Gemahlin – the wife	wurde (werden) – became
aufblicken – to look up	leiden – to bear, tolerate	als – when, than
der Tropfen – the drop	jemand – anybody	fragte (fragen) – asked
weil – because	sollte (sollen) – should	erschrak (erschrecken) – (was) shocked
schön – beautiful, pretty	werden – to become	der Neid - the envy

Once in the middle of winter (literally "it was once the middle of winter"), when the snowflakes fell like feathers down from the sky, there sat a queen by a window, that had a frame of black ebony, and sewed. And as she sewed thus and looked up at the snow, she pricked her finger with the needle and there fell three drops of blood into the snow. And because the red in the white snow looked so pretty, she thought to herself, "Would that I had a child as white as snow, as red as blood and as black as the wood of the (window) frame."

Soon after that she had a little daughter, who was as white as snow, as red as blood and as black-haired as ebony, and was therefore called Little Snow White. And when the child was born the queen died.

After a year the king took to himself another wife. She was a beautiful woman, but she was proud and haughty and could not bear that anyone should surpass her in beauty (literally "that she in beauty by anybody should surpass become"). She had a wonderful mirror, (and) when she stepped before it and looked at herself therein, and said:

> "Mirror, mirror on the wall,
> Who is the fairest in the entire land?"

-the mirror answered thus:

> "Lady Queen, you are the fairest in the land."

Then she was satisfied, because she knew that the mirror spoke the truth.

Little Snow White, however, grew up and became ever more beautiful and when she was seven years old, she was as beautiful as the clear day and fairer than the Queen herself. When she (the Queen) one day asked her mirror:

> "Mirror, mirror on the wall,
> Who is the fairest in the entire land?"

-it answered thus:

> "Lady Queen, you are the fairest here,
> But Little Snow White is a thousand times fairer
> than you."

Then the Queen was shocked and became yellow and green with envy.

Little Snow White

French: Le Comte de Monte-Cristo, Alexandre Dumas

Alexandre Dumas is probably France's most popular writer. In this extract from "The Count of Monte Cristo" the hero, Edmond Dantès has been falsely accused of treason, and imprisoned in the Château d'If. After fourteen years of captivity his fellow prisoner, the Abbé Faria, falls ill and dies and Edmond is able to substitute himself for the dead man's corpse. In this way he hopes to escape confinement:

On transporta le prétendu mort du lit sur la civière. Edmond se raidissait pour mieux jouer son rôle de trépassé. On le posa sur la civière ; et le cortège, éclairé par l'homme au falot, qui marchait devant, monta l'escalier.

Les porteurs firent une vingtaine de pas, puis ils s'arrêtèrent et déposèrent la civière sur le sol. Un des porteurs s'éloigna, et Dantès entendit ses souliers retentir sur les dalles.

« Que cherche-t-il donc ? se demanda Dantès. Une bêche sans doute. »

Une exclamation de satisfaction indiqua que le fossoyeur avait trouvé ce qu'il cherchait.

« Enfin, dit l'autre, ce n'est pas sans peine.

— Oui, répondit-il, mais il n'aura rien perdu pour attendre. »

A ces mots, il se rapprocha d'Edmond, qui entendit déposer près de lui un corps lourd et retentissant ; au même moment, une corde entoura ses pieds d'une vive et douloureuse pression.

« Eh bien, le nœud est-il fait ? demanda celui des fossoyeurs qui était resté inactif.

— Et bien fait, dit l'autre ; je t'en réponds.

— En ce cas, en route. »

Et la civière soulevée reprit son chemin.

On fit cinquante pas à peu près, puis on s'arrêta pour ouvrir une porte, puis on se remit en route. Le bruit des flots se brisant contre les rochers sur lesquels est bâti le château arrivait plus distinctement à l'oreille de Dantès à mesure que l'on avança.

« Mauvais temps ! dit un des porteurs, il ne fera pas bon d'être en mer cette nuit.

— Oui, l'abbé court grand risque d'être mouillé », dit l'autre — et ils éclatèrent de rire.

On fit encore quatre ou cinq pas en montant toujours, puis Dantès sentit qu'on le prenait par la tête et par les pieds et qu'on le balançait.

« Une, dirent les fossoyeurs.

— Deux.

— Trois ! »

En même temps, Dantès se sentit lancé, en effet, dans un vide énorme, traversant les airs comme un oiseau blessé, tombant, tombant toujours avec une épouvante qui lui glaçait le cœur. Quoique tiré en bas par quelque chose de pesant qui précipitait son vol rapide, il lui sembla que cette chute durait un siècle. Enfin, avec un bruit épouvantable, il entra comme une flèche dans une eau glacée qui lui fit pousser un cri, étouffé à l'instant même par l'immersion.

Dantès avait été lancé dans la mer, au fond de laquelle l'entraînait un boulet de trente-six attaché à ses pieds.

La mer est le cimetière du château d'If.

Glossary (Where necessary the infinitive of the verb is in brackets.)

la civière – the stretcher	retentir – to ring out, to resound	le bruit – the noise
se raidissait – stiffened (himself)	la dalle – paving stone	le flot – the wave
le trépassé – the deceased	une bêche – a spade	se brisant (se briser) – breaking (themselves)
le falot – the torch	le fossoyeur – the gravedigger	
un pas – a step	la peine – trouble	bâti (bâtir) – built
s'éloigna (s'éloigner) – went off	douloureuse – painful	à mesure – as
entendit (entendre) - heard	le nœud – the knot	mouillé – wetted

They carried the supposed corpse from the bed to the stretcher. Edmond stiffened himself the better to play his part of a dead man. He was placed on the stretcher and the procession, lit by the man with the torch, who walked in front, ascended the stairs.

The bearers took twenty steps, then they stopped and set the stretcher down on the ground.

One of the bearers went off, and Dantès heard his shoes ringing on the paving stones.

"What are they looking for?" Dantès asked himself. "A spade no doubt."

An exclamation of satisfaction indicated that the gravedigger had found what he was looking for.

"At last," said the other, "and not without trouble."

"Yes," he replied, "but it won't have lost anything by waiting."

With these words he approached Edmond, who heard a heavy resounding object being placed beside him; at the same moment, a rope encircled his feet, with an acute, painful pressure.

"Very well: the knot – has it been tied?" asked the gravedigger who had remained inactive.

"And well-tied," said the other, "I can answer for that."

"In that case let's be on our way."

And the lifted stretcher continued on its way.

They took about fifty steps then they stopped to open a door, then they continued on their way. The noise of waves breaking against the rocks on which the chateau is built came more distinctly to the ear of Dantès, as they advanced.

"Bad weather!" said one of the bearers, "it wouldn't be nice to be in the sea on this night."

"Yes, the abbé runs a great risk of getting wet," said the other – and they burst out laughing.

They took four or five steps more, ascending all the time, then Dantès felt that they were taking him by the head and by the feet and that they were swinging him to and fro.

"One," said the gravediggers.

"Two."

"Three!"

At the same time Dantès felt himself thrown, in effect, into an enormous void, traversing the air like a wounded bird, falling, always falling, with a fear that froze his heart. Despite being pulled below, by something heavy that precipitated his rapid flight, it seemed to him that that fall lasted a century. Finally, with a terrifying noise, he entered like an arrow into the icy water, which made him give a cry, stifled the same moment by the immersion.

Dantès had been thrown into the sea, to the bottom of which he was dragged by a thirty-six pound shot, attached to his feet.

The sea is the cemetery of the Château d'If.

éclater de rire – to burst out laughing	pesant – heavy
balancer – to swing	la chute – the fall
lancé (lancer) – thrown	une flèche – an arrow
blessé – wounded	pousser un cri – to give a cry
l'épouvante – the fear	étouffé (étouffer) – stifled
glaçait (glacer) – froze	au fond – at the bottom
quoique – although	entraînait (entraîner) – dragged
en bas – below	un boulet – a shot (cannon ball)

French *contd*: Le Bourgeois Gentilhomme, Molière

'The Bourgeois Gentleman' is one of the wittiest and most entertaining plays in French literature. It tells the story of Monsieur Jourdain, a tradesman who has made a great deal of money and now wants to acquire an education and become a gentleman.

In this extract he is asking his master of Philosophy to help him write a love letter to a beautiful young *marquise* (marchioness).

Monsieur Jourdain. – Je suis amoureux d'une personne de grande qualité, et je souhaiterais que vous m'aidassiez à lui écrire quelque chose dans un petit billet que je veux laisser tomber à ses pieds.

Maître de Philosophie. – Fort bien.

Monsieur Jourdain. – Cela sera galant, oui.

Maître de Philosophie. – Sans doute. Sont-ce des vers que vous lui voulez écrire ?

Monsieur Jourdain. – Non, non, point de vers.

Maître de Philosophie. – Vous ne voulez que de la prose ?

Monsieur Jourdain. – Non, je ne veux ni prose ni vers.

Maître de Philosophie. – Il faut bien que ce soit l'un, ou l'autre.

Monsieur Jourdain. – Pourquoi ?

Maître de Philosophie. – Par la raison, Monsieur, qu'il n'y a pour s'exprimer que la prose, ou les vers.

Monsieur Jourdain. – Il n'y a que la prose ou les vers ?

Maître de Philosophie. – Non, Monsieur : tout ce qui n'est point prose est vers ; et tout ce qui n'est point vers est prose.

Monsieur Jourdain. – Et comme l'on parle, qu'est-ce que c'est donc que cela ?

Maître de Philosophie. – De la prose.

Monsieur Jourdain. – Quoi ? quand je dis: « Nicole, apportez moi mes pantoufles, et me donnez mon bonnet de nuit », c'est de la prose ?

Maître de Philosophie. – Oui, Monsieur.

Monsieur Jourdain. – Par ma foi ! il y a plus de quarante ans que je dis de la prose sans que j'en susse rien, et je vous suis le plus obligé du monde de m'avoir appris cela.

Glossary (Where necessary the infinitive of the verb is in brackets.)

je souhaiterais (souhaiter) – I would like	le pantoufle – the slipper
vous aidassiez (aider) – you would help	le bonnet de nuit – the nightcap
laisser tomber – to let fall, drop	par ma foi – by my faith
point – not	je susse (savoir) – I knew
ne…que – only	appris (apprendre) – taught
s'exprimer – to express oneself	

Monsieur Jourdain – I am in love with a lady of quality, and I would like you to help me write her something in a little note that I want to drop at her feet.

Master of Philosophy – Very well.

Monsieur Jourdain – That will be gallant, won't it?

Master of Philosophy – Without doubt. Is it verse that you wish to write to her?

Monsieur Jourdain – No, no, not verse.

Master of Philosophy – You only want prose?

Monsieur Jourdain – No, I want neither prose nor verse.

Master of Philosophy – It is absolutely necessary that it be one or the other.

Monsieur Jourdain – Why?

Master of Philosophy – By reason, Monsieur, of there being no way of expressing one-self but prose or verse.

Monsieur Jourdain – Is there nothing but prose or verse?

Master of Philosophy – No, Monsieur; all that is not prose is verse, and all that is not verse is prose.

Monsieur Jourdain – And what one speaks – what then is that?

Master of Philosophy – That is prose.

Monsieur Jourdain – What? When I say "Nicole, bring me my slippers and give me my night cap", is that prose?

Master of Philosophy – Yes, Monsieur.

Monsieur Jourdain – By my faith! for over forty years I have been speaking prose without knowing it, and I am infinitely obliged to you for having taught me that.

Monsieur Jourdain, the 'Bourgeois Gentilhomme'.

Latin and Greek

Latin and Greek provide the classic example of how schools have achieved the precise opposite of what they were intended to do. There has never been any doubt that Greek literature is the pearl in the crown of Western learning and culture. The works of Homer represent literary perfection, and Plato's books on the life of Socrates raise issues of morality, politics, religion, education, and the nature of good and bad, in such a clear and thought-provoking way that it is hard to conceive they will ever be bettered. Added to these are great historical works such as those of Thucydides and Herodotus, plays, poems, myths and legends, scientific treatises and classical mathematical texts. What is more, much of the work produced during the time of the Roman

Homer, the blind poet who composed The Iliad and The Odyssey.

emperors, including the gospels of the New Testament, was originally written in Greek.

Latin literature cannot match the Greek for quality, but it was the language spoken throughout the Roman Empire, and an enormous number of writings have survived from that time. A student of Latin is able to read the works of Julius Cæsar, Titus Livy, Horace, Virgil, Pliny, and Marcus Aurelius in the original. Moreover, it is the language from which French, Spanish, Italian, and Portuguese are directly descended and a knowledge of Latin makes it easier to learn and understand these languages.

The Renaissance in Europe demonstrated the benefits that accrued from people in all walks of life (as opposed to simply a few clerics) being fluent in Latin and Greek; when scholars had a chance to compare their current knowledge with that contained in ancient manuscripts every branch of the arts and sciences was rejuvenated. Painters used Greek mathematics to bring a sense of perspective to their pictures, astronomers used Greek ideas to challenge the belief that the Earth was at the centre of the universe, and political leaders found inspiration in Greek and Roman history to challenge the existing modes of government.

All this served to convince people that education had to involve a thorough knowledge of Latin and Greek – no matter what career an individual may be destined

"Carpe diem, quam minimum credula postero."

"Seize the present day, trusting the morrow as little as may be."

Horace

to follow – and, in an effort to achieve this, they founded schools in which boys were rigorously instructed in Greek and Latin grammar from the age of eleven onwards.

With the benefit of hindsight, we can see that this effort was inevitably destined to fail. The principal result of this coercion was to make successive generations dislike Latin and Greek more and more. Even for the minority that did become proficient, the reason for doing so was seldom because they appreciated or understood the texts, it was simply a way to get good marks at school.

Thus instead of creating a society in which everyone has a reasonable knowledge of the ancient languages upon which our civilisation is based, schools have achieved the opposite: even though most people receive over twelve years of compulsory schooling, they are unlikely ever to study Latin or Greek, and may even be ignorant of the fact that the great works of literature were originally written in these languages.

Disastrous though this may be for society as a whole, it has advantages for the individual student. The fact that people are no longer taught Latin and Greek at school means that they no longer learn to dislike them and, consequently, they are free to discover for themselves the benefits that can be gained from studying these ancient languages.

It is important to remember that the great mistake of the past was to teach Latin and Greek to people when they were too young. There is no reason why a young schoolchild should be interested either in ancient grammar, or in the subject matter of ancient texts. It is far better for young people to concentrate on subjects that are of more immediate use, to study one or two modern languages so that they can develop a feel for how languages work, and to become familiar with good translations of ancient authors. They can learn Greek and Latin when they have an independent interest in the texts themselves and have decided that they want to study a classical language. Education should not finish when someone reaches the school or university leaving age, and it is far better for people to leave full-time education still looking forward to learning new things in the future than for teachers to try to cram everything into the time available, whether their students are interested or not.

Πολλὰ τὰ δεινὰ κοὐδὲν ἀνθρώπου δεινότερον πέλει.

"Wonders are many, and nothing is more wonderful than man."
Sophocles

Latin and Greek Books

Centuries of scholarship have gone into the study of Latin and Greek with the result that there is a wide range of books available to modern students. Second-hand book shops often contain dictionaries, grammar books, texts in the original, and translations, at reasonable prices.

The Harvard University Press publishes the Loeb Classical Library, a series of bilingual books which display the original text with an English translation, on facing pages. It comprises all the major works of Greek and Latin literature.

Science

Science is in danger of suffering the same fate as Latin and Greek. In their enthusiasm to make sure that everyone learns science, schools are teaching it to children at younger and younger ages, but the only visible result of this policy is that the understanding of science continues to decline. Even people who did well at school experience a sense of panic when faced with the prospect of having to teach their own children science, and this is a sure sign that they gained very little understanding from the science that they studied.

The reasons for this are quite complicated. Part of the problem is the link that is made between science and technology: the modern economy is dependent upon technology and it is considered essential that the education system should produce people conversant with every aspect of technological development. This *is* important, but experience shows that you do not have to study the theory of science in order to understand how machines work. Technology can be studied as a subject independent of science and insofar as some scientific understanding is required to design, operate, or repair particular machines or to work with particular technologies, the appropriate knowledge can be picked up as and when it is needed. This is not a revolutionary suggestion – it is the approach that has been used by engineers since the first machines were invented, and is essentially how the majority of technicians and engineers still work today.

> "Human subtlety will never devise an invention more beautiful, more simple or more direct than does Nature, because in her inventions, nothing is lacking and nothing is superfluous."
>
> *Leonardo da Vinci*

The Importance of Science

However, science is not only taught because it is considered useful. There is a widely-held belief that scientific thought has succeeded in answering all the questions that people have asked since the beginning of time: questions such as, 'What is the origin of the universe?', 'What is life?', 'Is there a God?', 'Is their life after death?', 'What are the stars?', 'What is the sun?', 'What is the world made of?', etc.

It is therefore important that science teaching should be successful: if science really has answered all these questions, then as many people as possible should be given the opportunity to partake of this knowledge for themselves. If, on the other hand, scientists are making exaggerated claims about the depth of their understanding, people need to investigate the work that has been done and expose its flaws.

A society in which everyone thought that science had all the answers, but in which hardly anyone had studied it in depth, would be no different from the Middle Ages, when everyone thought that the Church was preaching the absolute truth, but hardly anyone had read the Bible or the Greek texts upon which this truth was supposed to be based.

Successful Science Teaching

There are two aspects to science: observation and explanations; it is a process in which the student observes natural phenomena, and then studies the theories that have been put forward to explain them. One of the major problems facing science teaching today is that people are not given enough opportunities to make their observations: many young people do not have sufficient contact with Nature, they spend too much time sitting in classrooms, watching television, and being indoors; they do not have sufficient experience of the natural world, and, consequently, are in no position to understand it. This cannot be compensated for by doing extra science in the classroom, in fact that is only likely to make matters worse.

The first step to successful science teaching is to let a young person have as wide and varied an experience of Nature as they possibly can; only when they have had a chance to develop their innate understanding of the laws that govern the natural world should they start to study scientific theories and ideas in earnest. They will then be able to evaluate these ideas for themselves and decide whether they should be accepted or rejected. This brings them closer to what science is really about – the cut and thrust of intellectual debate, logical argument and the search for truth – instead of being taught to repeat other people's ideas without ever having had a real chance to evaluate or understand them.

"If a man does not ask himself, 'What am I to make of this?' 'What am I to make of that?' – there is nothing whatever I can make of him."

Confucius, The Analects

Experiments and Play

Over the years, scientists have developed their ideas by performing carefully-controlled experiments, which has led people to believe that in order to teach science to children, you have to make *them* do scientific experiments. This represents a misunderstanding of the way in which people learn. People, and especially children, learn through play. All play is a form of experimentation and it is far more sophisticated than the experiments that can be set up in a science lesson. Being allowed to play and investigate their environment, in an unregulated way, is the most important training for a young scientist. If this is happening, it is relatively unimportant whether or not they perform the scientific experiments that are part of a conventional science course. They will have plenty of time in the future to familiarise themselves with other people's methods and ideas.

A Sensible Science Curriculum

Here are some suggestions on how to approach the subject of science:

- **Play:** As mentioned on the previous page, if you spend time outside, simply enjoying yourself, you will automatically learn an enormous amount about the natural world.

- **Talking and Discussion:** Science is sometimes presented as a set of definitive answers, which makes people frightened to discuss scientific questions for fear of appearing foolish. However, providing your ideas are based upon your own observations, they will always be perfectly valid. Discussing them with other people gives you a chance to learn from their ideas and clarify your own thoughts.

- **Gardening:** The garden is the perfect science teacher. It teaches you about plants, animals, the seasons, the weather, the balance of Nature, life, death, water, the power of the sun, illness and disease, crops, trees, and a myriad other things. If you are a thoughtful gardener, your gardening will also lead you to read books and to ask questions and will enable you to gain a theoretical as well as a practical understanding of the world around you.

- **Walking:** Walking provides another way of being in touch with Nature, and, in addition, walking with someone else furnishes an ideal opportunity for talking and discussion.

- **Painting and Drawing:** In order to paint something well, you have to study it very carefully and this gives you an unparalleled insight into its structure and the way that it works. Keeping an artistic record of the flowers in your garden, or the trees in your neighbourhood, is an excellent scientific exercise. Drawing the human body is a good way of learning about human anatomy.

- **Study of Wildlife:** No matter what aspect of wildlife you are interested in – birds, insects, mammals, reptiles, amphibians, flowers, or trees – it will further your understanding of science. It will teach you about the diversity of Nature and the delicate balance that has to be maintained in order for life to survive.

  > "Tongues in trees,
  > books in the running brooks,
  > sermons in stones,
  > and good in everything."
  > *William Shakespeare*

- **Plant a Tree:** Planting a tree is a good long-term scientific project, especially if you can plant a tree that is naturally dominant in the area in which you live. You are able to see for yourself how vulnerable the tree is when it is small but that, as it gradually grows in size, it starts to provide shelter and food for an increasing number of birds and insects, until it eventually becomes the lynchpin around which the local ecosystem revolves.

- **Make a Wildlife Sanctuary:** A similar project is to protect a piece of waste ground – it does not need to be very big, it could be part of your garden – and leave it untouched for several years. To watch it being colonised by mosses, grasses, wild flowers, brambles, nettles, shrubs and eventually trees and to see the proliferation of insects, frogs, toads, small mammals (such as mice, voles, etc.), and birds that are attracted to it, is a revelation.

- **Cooking:** Cooking gives an insight into another aspect of science. When cooking, you are experimenting with the effect that heat has on substances and the effect of mixing different things together. This is essentially what is involved in the study of chemistry. Cooking does not cover exactly the same ground as chemistry – for example it does not involve working with toxic substances – but it does provide an excellent practical introduction to the subject.

- **The Night Sky:** Studying the night sky, perhaps with the aid of a telescope, teaches you about the stars and the planets and gives you a feeling for the vastness of space. It encourages you to find out more about the science of astronomy and the theory of gravity, and how ideas and theories about the nature of the universe have evolved over a period of time.

- **Science Past and Present:** One of the best ways of developing an understanding of modern science is to study its origins and, in particular, the lives of the most famous scientists: for example current views on astronomy date back to the Renaissance and the work of Copernicus, Kepler, and Isaac Newton; genetics owes its origins to the work of Gregor Mendel and the theory of evolution to Charles Darwin, both of whom lived in the 1800s; the generation of electricity was pioneered by Michael Faraday, also in the 1800s; and radioactivity was studied by Marie and Pierre Curie, who worked at the beginning of the twentieth century.

- **Books:** Once you become interested in the lives of scientists, it is only a small step to studying their work, and the books that they wrote. It is also interesting to read counter-arguments and to find out about the disputes that arose when new scientific ideas were put forward. Modern books, written to popularise science, can also be interesting – particularly those aimed at an adult audience and which are not designed to get students through specific exams. School and college science books tend to be the least interesting things to do with the subject and should, if possible, be avoided.

- **Magazines:** If you are worried that your science education has been incomplete, a subscription to a science magazine can be a good investment. Do, however, be prepared for a shock: science magazines now tend to be dominated by stories about genetic engineering and drug production. They paint a picture of an industry dominated by big business and national interest, and seem far removed from the ideal of scientists impartially searching for truth.

Science as a Philosophy

The subject of science rests upon the assumption that the human brain is capable of understanding and explaining everything, including itself, through a process of logic. This is an assumption which can itself never be proven by logic and shows that, in essence, science is not a practical subject, but a philosophical one. This is something that has to be kept firmly in mind when scientific theories are presented as though they were facts.

> "I don't know what I may seem to the world. But to myself I seem only like a boy playing on the seashore and diverting myself in now and then finding a smoother pebble or prettier shell than ordinary, whilst the great ocean of truth lay all undiscovered before me."
>
> *Last words of Sir Isaac Newton*

Science and Specialisation

One of the difficulties that faces the student is the extreme level of specialisation that now exists within the study and practice of science – not only do physicists not understand the work of biologists, but botanists do not understand the work of zoologists; someone who specialises in working on one area of the body does not know anything about the work of someone who works upon another; someone who works upon one particular cell may know nothing about the work of someone who works upon a different cell; and someone who works on one molecule within the cell may know nothing about the work being done upon another molecule. This degree of specialisation goes against gaining any sort of overall understanding of life and the working of the universe, and would indicate that although people trained to work in this way are given the designation of 'scientists' they are in fact technicians. They are fulfilling a role that is deemed necessary for the efficient running of the economy, but their studies do not equip them to understand the consequences of what they are doing or the direction in which they are going.

Science and the Individual

The fact that science education is now principally designed to train people to fulfil specialised jobs raises important questions for the individual. It is unwise to assume that there are other people, in positions of authority, who are able to take an overview of the whole situation and ensure that scientific ideas are used safely and appropriately. It is quite likely that scientific ideas are being used inappropriately, perhaps due to their being only partially understood, and that, as a result, people are being put at risk. This should provide further motivation to study science seriously – and to a higher standard than it is at present covered in the school curriculum.

For example, modern medical techniques make use of the most advanced scientific ideas. Up until a few years ago, people could have been excused for thinking this to be a wholly good thing but it has now become apparent that all these techniques carry a level of risk. In some cases it is better to have no treatment than the treatment on offer, sometimes traditional therapies can be more effective than modern methods, and there could be times when making use of modern medical science will save your life. There may be occasions where this is too important an issue to be left to other people to decide for you, and the better the understanding you have of science, the more likely you are to make the right decision.

> "It is a miracle that curiosity survives formal education."
> *Albert Einstein*

Many similar considerations apply to agriculture and the environment. Prior to the Industrial Revolution and the advent of modern science there *were* no environmental problems. Science and industry are responsible for the environmental difficulties that we face, and it is not logical to assume that people who have specialised exclusively in science will be able to resolve them. Conversely, if people do not take the trouble to understand the technicalities of such things as energy production, agriculture, and the use of chemicals, they will not be in a position to recognise what does represent good environmental practice, and what does not.

Conclusion

In many ways the development of modern science has failed to live up to its early promise; it has made the world a more dangerous place, without having done much to really improve the standard of living for ordinary people. However, it is clear from a study of human history that it is not possible to turn back the clock: science is not something that can be undiscovered, and the challenge that faces the next generation is to learn how to use scientific knowledge wisely. It is therefore immensely important that the subject should be taught well.

Ideally, people should be able to become familiar with the natural phenomena that science seeks to explain, while they are young. When they are older they can study scientific books and ideas, in the way that they ought to be studied; that is to say, with a degree of reflection and a thorough understanding of all the mathematics and reasoning that has gone into each theory. They will then be able to integrate their scientific knowledge into everything else that they have learnt, and, hopefully, will emerge with a truly balanced education.

Technology

Fortunately, the study of technology raises none of the difficult issues posed by the study of science. Irrespective of whether you like machines or not, it makes sense to know how they work, and to know how to make use of those which allow you to do things that you want to do, i.e. study technology.

Much of the work covered by the modern education curriculum under the heading of science, is really intended to improve people's ability to understand machines: almost all forms of employment involve the use of some sort of machinery, and the demand for people who are competent in the use of modern technology is increasing all the time. There is a growing suspicion amongst educators and employers that there is something about our current education system and its reliance upon schools that makes it unable to provide young people with the technological skills that they will require in the modern workplace, and, ironically, there is a real possibility that it is the inability of schools to train people in the use of modern technology that will drive people back to more traditional forms of education.

Home-based learning offers certain inherent advantages:

- **Flexibility:** If you are taking a machine to pieces, or are trying to do something on a computer, it is often inconvenient to stop at a particular time. Sometimes you have to work on it continuously until you have completed the task you have set yourself.

- **Rewards:** At home, as in the workplace, success is its own reward; if you succeed in mending the vacuum cleaner, you can clean your room, if you succeed in getting your computer to work, you can get on the internet, etc. This is much better than success being based on how well you do in an exam.

- **Responsibility:** Everyone feels responsible for things in their own home, and it is natural for them to look after them properly, to make sure that they understand how they work, and to extract the maximum use out of them.

- **Up to Date:** The way in which the education system is run makes it permanently behind the times: teachers are trained, courses are written, exams are set, and qualifications are awarded – all of this takes several years, and by the time the system has been set in place, modern technology has moved on.

My soup-spoon invention – the latest technology!

Over the past few years it has become apparent that school-children understand modern technology better than their teachers. This can only be because they learn more about technology when they are at home than when they are at school. If they spent less time at school, they would become even more skilled in the use of technology.

History of Technology

The world of machines can appear quite daunting, especially to someone who has no experience of working with them. The fact is, however, that a few hundred years ago people were still working almost exclusively with hand-operated, handmade equipment. The development of technology has taken place over a very short period of time and even though the complexity of machines has steadily increased, there has not been a major change in the thought processes that give rise to them. Consequently, modern, high-tech machines are essentially built according to the same principles as early mechanical devices; that is to say, they consist of a range of components connected together in such a way as to achieve the desired result.

You can retrace the process by which technology has evolved by working on various different machines in your home, for example:

- **Garden Tools:** Some thought should be given to garden tools, since they represent the technology that first allowed people to start shaping their own environment. In particular, it is the use of iron tools that allows people to break up the soil and grow crops instead of being dependent on hunting and gathering. Simple tools such as spades, rakes, hoes, axes, etc. remain the benchmark for the appropriate use of technology.
- **Woodworking Tools:** Woodworking tools such as chisels, saws, planes, etc. are slightly more sophisticated than garden tools and require more maintenance; they need to be kept sharp, and treated with care.
- **Bicycle Mechanics:** Modern bicycles still work on simple principles, even though the precision of their engineering has increased over the years. It is possible to maintain and repair your bike with the aid of a basic tool kit and the application of common sense.

Investigation and experimentation are two ways of discovering how things work, but this can be aided by help from other people and by studying books, manuals, and magazines.

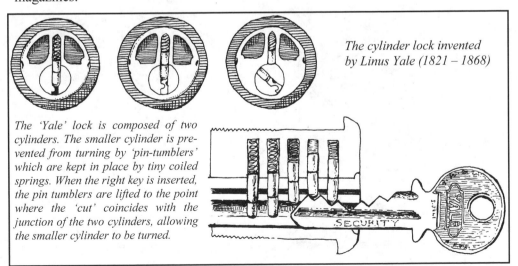

The cylinder lock invented by Linus Yale (1821 – 1868)

The 'Yale' lock is composed of two cylinders. The smaller cylinder is prevented from turning by 'pin-tumblers' which are kept in place by tiny coiled springs. When the right key is inserted, the pin tumblers are lifted to the point where the 'cut' coincides with the junction of the two cylinders, allowing the smaller cylinder to be turned.

Electrical Equipment

When people started to make use of electricity, the nature of machines changed. Instead of components being connected to each other by cogs and chains, they were linked by wires; however, this does not mean that skills gained by working on mechanical machines cannot be applied to electrical items. It is still important to work in a methodical manner, and to remember every step you take.

Common sense is the biggest asset when working on electrical equipment – it is not necessary to have understood everything about the theory of electricity or how each component works. The important thing is to find out how the different parts of a machine are connected together (this is done by tracing the course of the wires), and then to determine the function of each component; for example, in a washing machine it is fairly easy to identify the motor that turns the drum, the pump that pumps out the water, and the switch, or circuit board, that switches the different components on or off, etc. If a machine is not functioning properly, a process of logical deduction will probably enable you to find out which part is responsible. So long as it is not a complex electronic component, you may be able to dismantle and repair it, and at the very least will gain an understanding of how it has been put together.

The more hands-on experience of this sort that you have, the easier you will find it to understand electrical items and technical information about electricity.

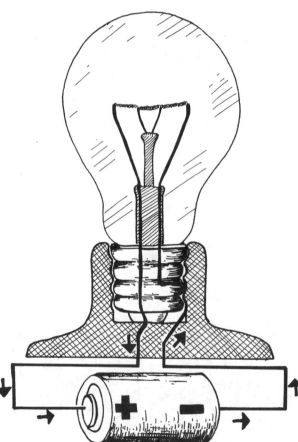

The Incandescent Light Bulb invented by Thomas Edison (1847 – 1931)

Electric current flows through a thin tungsten wire filament, which causes it to heat up to about 3000°C (5400°F), at which temperature it emits a bright light. The bulb is filled with an inert gas to prevent the filament from burning out.

The invention of the light bulb has revolutionised people's lives, because it means that they no longer have to regulate their days according to the rising and setting of the sun.

Computers

Computer technology has been developing at a breathtaking pace over the past few decades, causing successive revolutions in the way that people work and live. The process is not under the control of any single government or corporation and no one knows what the next development is going to be – or even whether there will be another development.

Changes driven by advances in computer technology can develop considerable momentum before established businesses and regulators notice that they are happening. One of the greatest effects of computer technology has been to change the nature of employment: nearly all office work now involves the use of a computer, and repetitive jobs are increasingly disappearing from the factory floor as computer-operated machines take over routine tasks. At the same time as making traditional forms of employment redundant, computers are generating whole new industries: for example, computer games, which hardly existed a few years ago, now represent a multi-billion dollar business, and the internet has had a huge impact upon every aspect of the economy.

These factors make everyone agree that it is not enough for young people to be trained to use today's computers; they must be prepared to adapt to advances in technology, and to learn how to use them, long after they have left school.

Here are some suggestions as to how the subject can be approached in the home:

- **Remember that the Computer is a Machine:** It is important to remember that a computer is simply a machine. Even though some of its components may be very complex, the way in which it is put together is very simple. Most have been designed in such a way as to allow you to add extra components as and when you need them, and it is a good idea to become familiar with the inside of your computer (this applies mainly to desktop computers; it is more difficult to work on portable computers because all the components have been miniaturised).

  Take off the outer cover and try to identify the various parts – the hard drive, the CD drive, the memory cards, the sound card, the modem, etc.; the manual may help you to identify which is which. This helps you to demystify your computer and gives you some confidence that you may be able to repair it if it goes wrong (with modern machines 'repair' generally means replacing the malfunctioning component).

- **Use a Computer to do Something Useful:** The best way to learn about any piece of technology is to use it – theoretical studies can come later. Use a computer to edit a picture, design publications, or publish a website: in short something that you want to do and which the computer makes possible. It is easier to negotiate the frustrations that are an inherent part of learning to use a computer, when you have a particular goal in mind.

- **Don't Start Too Young:** Contrary to what is sometimes suggested, starting to work on computers when you are very young does not give you an advantage over other people: computers are relatively unstimulating when compared to other things that you can play with when you are a child, and spending too much time on them is likely to retard, rather than advance, someone's overall education. Learning about the world at large will be of use to you when you come to use a computer, but learning about a computer will not be of much use in understanding the world at large.

- **Don't Be Afraid of Computer Programming:** Writing your own programmes is not particularly difficult. There are many books on the subject and plenty of information on the internet. Learning something about computer programming helps you to understand how commercial programmes work: all programmes are operating under the same constraints and tend to follow the same patterns. Once you become familiar with the logic behind the way programmes are written, it becomes easier to get the most out of the software that you have on your machine.

- **Get in the Habit of Solving Your Own Problems:** It is all too easy to become dependent on other people to solve problems that you encounter with your computer. Computers seem to be able to generate a never-ending stream of error messages resulting from conflicts between programmes, shortage of memory, 'corruption' of files, the incompatibility of components, etc., not to mention the problems that occur within a programme because you have failed to understand how to use it properly. If you are relying on someone else to sort out each of these difficulties, you will always be in fear of your computer. You have to take responsibility for making it work yourself: read the manuals, study the help menus, and consult other people, but make sure that you are the one in control of your machine.

Help! Anaxagoras! The computer has frozen! And it is humming at me!!

Base and ignoble cad! How dare you frighten a lady so— you shall be spared this once, but if I ever catch you at the same tricks again...

Technology, Employment, and Leisure

The greater the understanding you have of the workings of modern technology, the more opportunities for employment will be open to you, whether or not you have the relevant qualifications. It is important to bear in mind, however, that while it is a matter of common prudence for everyone to become as competent as possible in the use of the machines by which they are surrounded, individuals are still responsible for the use to which that knowledge is put. It cannot be right to work for an enterprise unless you approve of what it is doing; in fact, the greater the level of skill you bring to a job, the more responsibility you bear for its consequences. If everyone who made the effort to understand modern technology also tried to ensure that it was used only for beneficial purposes, the world would be a safer and better place in which to live.

One aspect of modern technology that has to be guarded against is the way in which it can absorb more and more of your time and thoughts. It is always best to maintain a balance between different areas of your life, and if you find yourself becoming obsessive about your computer, force yourself to take a break, lend it to someone else, or put it back in its box. You can then do something that will help to put everything back into perspective, such as spending time in your garden, going for some long walks, or talking to real people.

Over-reliance on Technology

As a final note on technology, it is possible that we are becoming over-reliant upon machines. People who live in cities are dependent on complex technology for many of the essentials of life such as food, water, clothing, housing, transport, heating, and communication. History shows that this sort of arrangement does not have a very good track record and common sense would suggest that it would be advisable to move towards a lifestyle that only relies upon technology for those things that are not essential.

Music

Music is an intrinsic part of life in every society around the world: wherever you go, people sing, dance, and play musical instruments. In fact, musical instruments represent a branch of technology which, judging by the care taken over making them, must, in the past, have been more highly valued than any other.

A strange feature of the modern education system is that it allows large numbers of people to grow up without acquiring the ability to play a musical instrument – in fact, this is one of the strangest of all the paradoxes of the school system: playing music is something that is common to all people, all over the world, and even people brought up on the slave plantations of the New World acquired the ability to play musical instruments, despite the fact that they were kept at work from sunrise to sunset from the age of eight or nine-years-old.

"Let the character be formed by the poets; established by the laws of right behaviour; and perfected by music."

Confucius, The Analects

Learning to Play an Instrument

Fortunately, most people have the opportunity to learn to play an instrument at home, and for many people this is their principal experience of home-based, self-education.

Each instrument has its own characteristics and it takes time and regular practice to get the most out of it. When learning to play a musical instrument you come to understand something about the process of learning: often the more you practise a tune one day, the worse you will play it, but when you try the same tune the following day, you will play it perfectly; some days you will play everything badly, other days you will play everything well; sometimes you will play something brilliantly until you think to yourself, 'I'm doing really well,' and then everything will go wrong.

When you start learning to play an instrument, you have an idea of how you would like to be able to play it; you listen to the sound that you are actually making and it makes you despair; you keep practising and one day you realise that you are creating the music that you wanted to make when you started out – but now you want to play even better.

Learning to play an instrument teaches you that learning is not a purely mental activity – the head does play its part but at some point something else takes over: you feel what you want to do and somehow you do it – it involves your head, your heart and your hands working together.

Some Practical Points:

- **Making Time:** It takes time to learn to play an instrument, and you cannot make that time if your life is governed by other people telling you what to do: you have to have the freedom to organise at least some of your day in the way that suits you best. If school or other commitments make regular practice impossible, it is probably best to delay learning an instrument until you can give it the time that it requires.

- **Music Lessons:** It is easier to learn music from a good teacher than to teach yourself from a book, but a bad teacher can remove all pleasure from any subject, especially music. If you decide to have a teacher, you must choose carefully; a good teacher will not want to push you through exams, but will teach you to master your instrument, correct your mistakes, enjoy your successes, inspire you to do better and will become your friend.

- **Reading Music:** Written music is simply a tool that enables you to get more pleasure from your instrument. Musical notation represents an enormous intellectual achievement on the part of musicians over many centuries, and although it can appear rather daunting at first, when taken one step at a time its underlying logic becomes clear.
  If you want to learn how to read music, avoid taking short cuts – it is easy to ignore the music and to play tunes from memory at the beginning, but you will be caught out later when the pieces that you are playing become more complicated.

"The man that hath not music in himself,
Nor is not moved with concord of sweet sounds,
Is fit for treasons, stratagems, and spoils."
William Shakespeare

Mathematics

Mathematics has been left to the end of the book because it is the subject that poses the most difficulties for people at school. It is my belief that these difficulties occur, not because some people are inherently bad at mathematics, but because there is a fundamental flaw in the way that the subject is dealt with by the modern education system. Ancient civilisations (such as the Greek and Egyptian) were very clear that there were two distinct sides to mathematics – the practical and the theoretical – and they did not mix them. Children and young people concentrated upon practical aspects of the subject and it was only when they had acquired a thorough grounding in the way that numbers are used in everyday life that a few of them studied the theoretical side. When this method is followed, people do not have difficulties with mathematics, but gradually acquire all the knowledge that they need of the subject in a painless and effortless way.

Anaxagoras, did you know that young children learn mathematics these days?

Young children… what times are we in?!?!

Schools are faced with the difficulty that their pupils are not involved in practical activities, or rather that the practical activities in which their pupils *are* involved have to be fitted in outside school hours and vary from person to person within the same class. This makes it impossible for the mathematics teacher to draw upon examples that are relevant to everyone in a particular group. Even when an attempt is made to keep the lessons focussed upon practical mathematics, it does not coincide with the practical experience of the various individuals in the class, and makes no more sense to them than the most abstruse mathematical theory.

All these difficulties are avoided when learning is centred around the home, and when people take more responsibility for their own education – almost every activity that they are involved in uses one or another aspect of mathematics and, over a number of years, they will pick up a sound, practical knowledge of the subject, automatically designed to meet the needs of modern life.

The efficiency of this method is demonstrated by the fact that people all round the world, irrespective of how much education they have had and whether or not they are able to do sums on paper, are able to use numbers very efficiently to count, to keep a track of their finances, to conduct business, to play games, to measure, to build, and whatever else they need to do.

This is incredible, this is beyond belief! These children must be hyper – hyper – hyper intelligent! Mathematics, the great philosophy of life and the universe…children?!?!! Let me see them!!!

Practical Mathematics

- **Counting:** Fortunately most people learn to count long before they go to school. (Counting provides the perfect example of the conflict between the practical and the theoretical aspects of mathematics: there is no theoretical explanation for how counting works and if people had to learn to count using theoretical principles, counting would cease to be possible. However, people experience a need to count and they therefore do it without worrying about the philosophical repercussions. This simple example should serve to highlight the danger of introducing theories and explanations too early in mathematics teaching.)

- **Arithmetic:** Simple arithmetic arises automatically out of counting. Once you have learnt to count, it is only a small step to adding quantities together and subtracting one amount from another; and from there to multiplying and dividing. These calculations can be done either in the head or on paper. As with counting, there do not need to be any theoretical explanations: everyone recognises that things can be added, subtracted, multiplied and divided, and is grateful to learn any techniques that help them to reach the correct answer.

- **Gardening:** Mathematics deals not only with numbers but also with the definition of space (the subject of geometry), and this is an area that is addressed in a very practical way in the garden: vegetable beds are laid out, rows are marked out, and plants are spaced so as to make the most efficient use of the land they occupy. The gardener also has to take into account that different plants grow at different rates, that the movement of the sun makes some parts of the garden more suitable for some plants than for others, and that the garden will change of its own accord over a period of time. The garden also teaches about the return that you can get for different types of investment – each gardener works out how many seed potatoes they have to have in order to get the potato crop they require, and in the same way how many carrot seeds, how many lettuce seeds, how many peas, how many beans, etc., they have to dry and store for the following year.

- **Cooking:** Cooking calls for the use of weights and measures: the imperial system (pounds and ounces) makes use of fractions, and the metric system (kilograms, grams, etc.) makes use of decimals. Cooking can demand quite a high level of mathematical skill – you sometimes have to convert from one system of measurement to another, double or halve the ingredients in a recipe, or make use of ratios when cooking things such as rice and grains – but people do not stop cooking because they cannot understand the mathematics involved. If you make a mistake in your calculations it may ruin the meal, and you then have to work out what you did wrong and make sure that you do not make the same mistake again. That is the way that mathematics *should* be learnt.

- **Crafts:** Craft projects tend to call for a more conscious application of mathematical principles than gardening and cooking. Their success often depends on great accuracy in measuring, and precision in the way that things are cut out and folded, or shaped to a particular size.
- **Building:** Building requires all the skills employed in other crafts and also makes use of some mathematical principles – such as Pythagoras's theorem and trigonometry – which are difficult to understand when taken out of context.

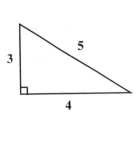

Pythagoras's Theorem: Pythagoras's theorem relates to the properties of right-angled triangles. If the sum of the squares on the two shortest sides is equal to the square on the longest side, then the triangle is right-angled. The simplest example of this is provided by a triangle in which the two shortest sides are respectively 3 and 4 units long, and the longest side is 5 units long. 3 squared is 9, 4 squared is 16; 9 plus 16 is 25, which is 5 squared. ($3^2 + 4^2 = 5^2$), and the angle between the two shortest sides must therefore be a right angle. This fact is made use of extensively by builders and craftspeople who want to make sure that their work is square.

- **Modern Technology**: Computers are machines that have been designed to perform mathematical computations very rapidly. It is by performing these computations that they are able to display text, edit pictures, send messages, record music, store data, and all the other things that they are able to do. The more time that you spend working with a computer, the more familiar you become with the mathematical principles that govern its operation – simply by getting it to work at all you are having to follow a process dictated by the mathematics built into the computer, and the more familiar you become with the operation of particular programmes the greater will be your intuitive understanding of the principles that make the computer work. In this way, even though you may not take the trouble to try to understand the details of computer technology, your computer may bring you close to the point where practical and theoretical mathematics touch: the computer appears to be capable of creating a 'virtual reality' through its calculations, which coincides with the idea that the material universe is the product of energy being operated upon by mathematical principles.
- **Music:** Music and mathematics are closely allied: they are both slightly mysterious and seem to be based on principles that transcend ideas and theories.
- **Money:** Traditionally, businessmen were second only to philosophers in their knowledge of mathematics, and this is because money is the ideal medium for learning about every aspect of mathematical calculation. Money is an artificial, man-made concept, governed solely by the laws of mathematics. Furthermore, whether rightly or wrongly, money is a subject in which almost everyone is passionately interested. The implications of this are clear: you only have to give a young person responsibility for managing money, or the opportunity to make money and their skills in calculation will increase from day to day. (The fact that

our society currently prevents many young people from taking responsibility for money matters is probably one of the main reasons why mathematical skills are in decline.) Using money teaches you to understand the decimal system, improves your skills in adding, subtracting, multiplying and dividing, makes the concept of minus numbers very easy to understand, and frequently involves using percentages.

Specific examples of areas that develop mathematical skills are: managing the housekeeping budget, checking that bills and bank statements are correct, keeping a record of cheques and credit card payments, calculating interest earned and interest owing, working out which types of bank accounts are most advantageous to your circumstances, ensuring that you are in receipt of any benefits to which you are entitled, completing the tax return, keeping a record of tax paid, monitoring insurance payments and making sure that you have the most appropriate cover, being responsible for foreign exchange conversions if you go abroad, and keeping overall accounts. It is hard to imagine that anyone involved in this sort of work (and it is all material with which most families now have to deal) could ever consider themselves to be underachieving in mathematics.

- **Games:** There is another practical method of becoming familiar with the underlying principles of mathematics and that is playing games. Cards, dice, chess, and draughts are just a few of the many games based on the laws of chance and logic and, as with other areas of study, you will come to understand these laws much better by playing with them than by reading about them in books.

4-2-1 *421 is based on a game that was popular throughout the Roman Empire and is still played on the Continent.*

A game for 2 players
Uses: 3 dice   21 counters
Aim: To be the first to get rid of all one's counters

Descending value of throws:
421	8 counters
111	7 counters
666	6 counters
611	6 counters
555	5 counters
511	5 counters
Etc. to	
222	2 counters
211	2 counters
654, 543, 432, 321	2 counters
665, 664, 663 ... 224, 223, 221	1 counter

First Phase: Players take it in turns to throw all three dice. After each has thrown, the player with the lower value score takes the number of counters corresponding to their opponent's throw. Play continues in this way until all 21 counters have been distributed.

Second Phase: The player with the most counters starts. They have a maximum of 3 throws; they can stop after one throw, or re-throw 1, 2, or all 3 dice. The same applies after the second throw. The other player may not have more throws than the first player, but may have less. The player with the higher value score, after both players have thrown, gives the corresponding number of counters to their opponent. If both scores are the same, players have an additional throw, and the player with the higher score gives to the other player the number of counters corresponding to the original score. Play continues in this way, with the players taking it in turn to throw first, until one player has no counters left.

Awale

The Aim: To finish the game with more stones than your opponent.

Awale or Mancala is traditionally played on a special board, which consists of two sets of six hollows arranged opposite each other and 48 seeds or 'stones' – four per hollow *(see diagram 1)*. It can, however, be played on or with anything else that serves the same purpose.

Player A

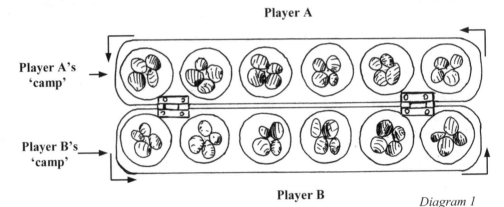

Player A's 'camp'

Player B's 'camp'

Player B

Diagram 1

The Rules:

- Player A starts by removing all the stones from any one hollow in his camp. He then proceeds in an anticlockwise direction, depositing one stone in each hollow as he passes over it, until all the stones are used up. If necessary, stones are deposited in player B's camp.

- Player B then has his turn – he also redistributes the stones from one of his hollows in an anticlockwise direction.

- Moves are carried on in this way, but sometimes the opportunity arises to make a capture.

Different versions of Awale are played in different parts of Africa; the Masai play a version of the game in which each camp has nine hollows. The game is widely used to teach children the principles of mathematics.

Capturing:

- A player may only capture stones that are in his opponent's camp.
- A player may only make a capture if, when he has added his final stone to one of his opponent's hollows, the number of stones in it has been brought up to 2 or 3. Captured stones are removed from the board and kept in a pile in front of the player who has won them.
- If the hollow in which the player places his final stone is empty, or, after the addition of his stone, contains more than 3 stones, he cannot make a capture.
- If, on the other hand, the stones in this hollow can be captured, the player may also capture the stones in the hollow to the right of it, and continue to capture all the stones in his opponent's hollows – moving in a clockwise direction – *provided they contain 2 or 3 stones. (Diagram 2)*
- If the player comes to an empty hollow, or one containing over 3 or only 1 stone, he cannot go on, and his turn ends.

Player A

The 6 stones just moved by player B are shown in black.

The shaded hollows are those that can be emptied of stones.

Player B thus captures 8 stones after this move.

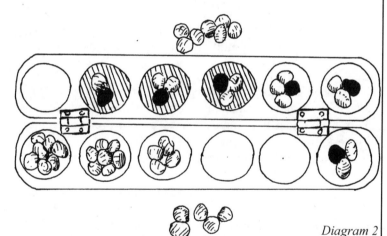

Diagram 2

Player B

Finishing the Game:

- Eventually there will not be many stones left, and it is quite possible that, when it is his turn, one of the players will have no stones in his camp. He must miss his turn and the other player must immediately replenish the empty camp with at least one stone. If he cannot do so, all his stones become the property of the other player and the game is over.
- Sometimes the game reaches a kind of stalemate with five or six stones still left on the board. The game then ends by the agreement of both players and the winner is the person who has captured the most stones.

Theoretical Mathematics

Just as trying to teach young people about the theory of mathematics (decimal places, algebra, graphs, etc.) can prevent them from becoming proficient at practical mathematics, not giving them the time to learn practical mathematics prevents them from ever being able to fully understand the theory of mathematics. This is most graphically illustrated by the idea of irrational numbers.

Irrational Numbers

The Square Root of Two ($\sqrt{2}$):
Pythagoras's theorem states that in a right-angled triangle the sum of the squares on the two shorter squares is equal to the square on the longest side.
The simplest right-angled triangle is one in which the two shortest sides each have a length of one.

One squared is one ($1 \times 1 = 1$) and therefore the sum of the squares on the two short sides is one plus one, which is two. ($1^2 + 1^2 = 2$)

The length of the longest side is therefore equal to a number that when multiplied by itself makes two i.e. the square root of two ($\sqrt{2}$).

It has been proved that there is no number which when multiplied by itself makes exactly two, and the square root of two is therefore known as an irrational number. This means that it is impossible to give a precise number for the length of the longest side of the triangle.
It is possible to work out approximations for the value of the $\sqrt{2}$, for example:
1.41421356237309504880168877242097 x
1.41421356237309504880168877242097 =
1.9999999999999999999999999999901
In most practical applications, it is sufficient to use 1.41 as an approximate value for $\sqrt{2}$ ($1.41 \times 1.41 = 1.9881$). This is found to be sufficiently accurate in building and engineering work, but it does not help mathematicians to resolve the difficulty of having a specific length to which they are unable to apply a specific number.
In ancient Greece the fact that $\sqrt{2}$ is an irrational number is believed to have been kept a closely-guarded secret by the Pythagoreans. When it was revealed by one of their members, his subsequent death in a shipwreck was attributed to the anger of the gods. Later Greek mathematicians decided that if some distances could not be defined, all numbers should be excluded from the study of geometry, and they kept the subjects of arithmetic and geometry completely separate.

Because people are taught about such things as $\sqrt{2}$ and π (π, pi, is the Greek letter used to denote the number that defines the ratio between the diameter and the circumference of a circle; it too is irrational) before they have had a chance to do any practical work with area, circles, triangles, ratios, squares, square roots, etc., they have no chance of understanding the significance of the fact that these numbers are irrational. Students realise that they do not understand the ideas that are being presented to them, but they do not grasp that that is the whole point of the exercise – these are numbers that *cannot* be understood – and they imagine that some fault exists with themselves.

Mathematics is the foundation upon which the whole of modern science is built; it underpins every transaction that takes place in the world of commerce, makes possible the organisation of human societies, is fundamental to the art of building and is at the centre of every branch of engineering. Becoming involved in any of these areas gives someone a chance to test out the efficiency and reliability of mathematical methods. Once someone has tested out the practical use of mathematics, they are ready, if they so wish, to turn their minds to its theoretical foundations; only then will they be able to appreciate how strange it is that the subject, which on the surface appears to be the most logical of all branches of knowledge, is in fact built upon a series of paradoxes and irrational ideas.

This is probably why, in the ancient world, people who were destined to become rulers of their country were urged to study the theory of mathematics after completing their secondary education. It is the surest way to learn that even when you know yourself to be in the right, you may still be wrong, and even when you are sure that something is definitely true, it may still be untrue. These are lessons that our modern education system signally fails to instil into its graduates – and, consequently, the world is a far more dangerous place than it need be.

Numbers

The peculiar thing about numbers is that everyone uses them (even very small children) but no one (not even university professors) knows what they are.

There is a purely abstract side to numbers – 1, 2, 3, 4, etc. – which people intuitively understand. Children learn to apply this abstract understanding to physical objects – one finger, two fingers, three fingers, etc. The problem is that no two fingers are exactly the same. Thus there are not really two fingers; there is one finger, and another finger which is slightly different from the first finger, etc. It is the same way with everything that people try to count: for example, you can have a stick, and then break it in half, which means that you now have two sticks – the number of sticks has doubled even though the total amount of wood remains the same. (Alternatively, you may choose to say that you now have two half sticks, by which token your original stick perhaps should not have been considered to be a stick but simply a part of the whole tree, the tree a part of the forest, etc.)

The difficulty in defining numbers has been one of the traditional preoccupations of mathematicians and, in the past, has helped to prevent them from taking themselves, and their subject, too seriously.

Timetable and Curriculum

People who have only experienced school-based education understandably find it difficult to envisage how learning can be organised outside of a school-type environment. The greater part of their anxiety is usually due to the fact that they cannot believe that young people have their own, independent motivation to study – it is assumed that, left to their own devices, young people will laze around, contract bad habits, and spoil their chances of ever 'making anything of themselves' – and that some sort of coercive environment is therefore essential. Parents and other adults who hold this belief are unwittingly depriving their children of any chance of making a success of their education: it does not matter what age you are, as soon as someone tells you that you have to read a book, sit at a desk, listen to a lecture, or, in fact, do anything at all, that instantly becomes the thing that you least want to do. This means that you have to be very flexible about the timetable and the curriculum that you adopt.

Obviously how you work, and what you work on, will vary over the course of time:

- **Playing:** Never underestimate the importance of play: it is the most effective learning technique we have. It is often assumed that children lose interest in playing when they are of school age, but this is far from being the case. Children are using their time very productively when they are playing, even up to the age of fifteen or sixteen years old. Perhaps it is easier for children to play when they have brothers and sisters of varying ages at home, but the essence of play is that it has no rules and is solely under the control of the person who is playing. If a child is happy playing, their parent should not worry about trying to make them do lessons.

- **Recovering from School:** Don't expect someone to recover from school over-night. Some children, even though they themselves chose to leave school, want to continue using their school books for a long time afterwards (perhaps so that they have a sense of doing 'proper' work), whereas other children refuse to look at any sort of book for months after leaving school. Whatever the case, you have to respect what the child wants. You must be prepared to change your routine from day to day until they have had a chance to rediscover their own equilibrium.

- **Structured Lessons:** The idea of structured lessons, in the school sense of the word, does not make sense in the home: if a parent *is* capable of 'teaching' a particular subject, the only effect of their so doing would be to put a severe strain on family relationships – no one likes being lectured in their own home. However, this does not mean that parents and children should not work together in a fairly formal setting. Home-based education gives parents and children the chance to sit down together, to get some books out, read them, do some writing and drawing, discuss what they are doing, and talk over life in general. This can be one of the most pleasurable and rewarding aspects of being a parent and, conveniently, it does, more or less fall within the accepted definition of 'lessons'. Mornings are the best time for this sort of activity, because everyone is at their most alert and wide awake.

- **Afternoons:** If you do your bookwork in the morning, then you can do your practical activities in the afternoon.
- **Holidays:** You may well find that your 'educational' routine provides a structure for extremely enjoyable days, but even so it is probably a good idea to follow the term times of local schools.

These are the sort of activities that you might try to fit into each week:

- **'Lessons':** An hour or two each morning, working from books, drawing, writing, discussing, etc.
- **Reading Aloud:** One member of the family can read a chapter of a book aloud each day to the rest of the family.
- **Playing:** People should never be so busy that they don't have time to play.
- **Games:** Half an hour or more a day playing card games, dice games, board games is not only educational in itself but is also conducive to discussion.
- **Painting:** One morning per week spent painting.
- **Music:** Once you decide to learn a musical instrument, practise at least fifteen minutes per day.
- **Gardening:** A good gardener needs to spend some time in their garden every day.
- **Cooking:** If you enjoy cooking, then you will probably want to cook at least one or two meals per week.
- **Crafts:** When you have a craft project in progress, you will probably want to spend a few hours per day working on it until it is finished.
- **Computer:** Computers consume a lot of time, especially when you are learning how to use them. To get the most out of the time spent working at a computer it is probably best to limit yourself to one or two hours per day.
- **Walking:** Going for a daily walk, especially if there is not much to do in the garden, is good exercise and provides some time for reflection and seeing the world.
- **Languages:** It takes persistent effort to become proficient at a language and it will require at least half an hour per day, or a morning per week, once you decide to tackle it seriously.
- **Reading:** If you are doing all the above, you will probably have a pile of books that you want to read, related to the work that you are doing in 'lessons' or to other activities. You could easily want to spend an hour a day reading.

This is simply a list of suggestions – different people do different things – but one fact that does stand out is that, even with the best will in the world, there are hardly enough hours in the day for someone to do all the things that they need to do in order to get a complete and fully-rounded education. When seven or eight hours of daily school attendance is added into the equation, it is not surprising that education suffers.

Qualifications

The modern school and university system derives its legitimacy from the fact that it awards qualifications. The argument being put forward by this book is that qualifications do not accurately represent the level of someone's education, and that a young person is much better advised to pursue education rather than qualifications.

Once you have acquired an education, qualifications should not pose a problem – it is a well-established maxim that the greater can take in the lesser, but the lesser cannot take in the greater. Most modern education systems provide people with various opportunities to re-enter them at every level, and this is particularly true after you have reached the compulsory school leaving age: there are night school classes, correspondence courses, and college courses, (both private and state funded) that will train anyone to pass the exams necessary to gain admittance to university, in whatever subject is required.

> "Any sort of training which aims at acquiring wealth or bodily strength is not worthy to be called education at all."
>
> Plato

Ask yourself 'Why do I want a Qualification?'

The problem encountered by students who are used to studying at home, without reference to examinations and qualifications, is not that the examinations are too difficult, but that they seem pointless. Someone who has developed the habit of reading round a subject, taking the trouble to understand it from different angles and has perhaps made use of it in practical situations, can find it difficult to adapt to a system in which the only object is to repeat to the examiner the things that the examiner wants to hear.

The reason why students find themselves in this situation is often because they have failed to ask themselves why they want a qualification. Schoolchildren are constantly told that exams are important, and some of this conditioning inevitably permeates through to people who do not go to school; they assume that their path must, at some point, converge with people who do go to school, and that the time will come when they must stop the work that they are doing, however rewarding it might be, and sit some exams so that they can get qualifications, and go to university, etc.

These assumptions deserve to be questioned. Whilst it is true that the path of a home-taught pupil must, at some point, converge with that of the school-taught pupil, it does not follow that the home-taught pupil has to enter the school/university system. Someone learning at home is already part of the real world, they may even have contacts and projects that they can develop into a business or into a means of employment; the schoolchild, on the other hand, is in a situation that is removed from society at large and they have no choice but to leave it sooner or later. Joining them in this predicament may not be the wisest course of action for the home-taught student.

The question they should ask themselves is whether the qualifications that they stand to gain by doing a course, re-entering school, going to university, etc., will be of specific use to them in helping them to do the things that they want to do. If the answer to the question is 'yes' then they will probably be able to pass over the peculiarities of the examination system without too much concern, but if the answer is 'no', studying for a qualification may not prove to be a worthwhile experience.

Taking a Pragmatic Approach

If you do decide to try to get a qualification, it is advisable to take a fairly pragmatic approach:

- Do some research to determine the minimum qualifications required at each stage of the path that you intend to follow – don't get drawn into doing unnecessary courses by people who have a vested interest.
- Obey the rules. In order to get a qualification you are generally expected to obey certain rules – handing in assignments on time, attending courses, behaving with a reasonable level of decorum, etc. – there is no point in joining the course if you don't intend to obey these rules.
- Study the syllabus and past exam papers, and take note of hints and tips given by teachers and lecturers. Qualifications are simply about giving the answers that the examiners want to receive. The more research you do into the way the examiners think, the more able you will be to do this.
- Focus on the work in the syllabus and forget about other things for a while.
- Work out a concentrated programme of study for the two months leading up to the exam – in this way your knowledge of the required material will be at its peak on the day of the examination.
- Practise sitting exams in order to develop your exam technique. This involves learning how to present the maximum number of points for which you can be awarded marks, in the shortest possible time.
- If you don't succeed at your first attempt, work out where you went wrong and try again.

Most importantly of all, don't think that you are stupid if you fail the exam and, what is more difficult, don't feel particularly proud if you pass it. In either event, you should not allow the experience to distract you from the process of self-education, which will, hopefully, continue to be a source of real enjoyment for the rest of your life.

Work and Employment

There are two ways in which your education should prepare you for work. Firstly, it should provide you with sufficient understanding of yourself, and of the world, to enable you to select the form of employment that is most appropriate to your own interests and abilities. Secondly, it should equip you with the knowledge and skills that will enable you to operate in your chosen profession with distinction.

Both of these criteria are best met by the process of self-education: if, throughout your education, you have had a chance to make up your own mind as to how you want to spend your time, which activities you consider worthwhile, and, most importantly of all, have had time to reflect upon what you want to achieve in your life and which values you consider the most important, then you are in a position to make a sound choice about what sort of job you want to do. Unfortunately, many young people are denied this chance for reflection and find themselves being hurried from school, to university, and into work before they have really had a chance to get to know themselves.

Once you have chosen a particular field, the qualities that are required for success are exactly the same as those cultivated by self-education – if you are in the habit of taking responsibility, making sure that you understand what you are doing, have a range of skills, are meticulous in your work, and have made a wise choice in your mode of employment, then you cannot help but do well. The more varied and wide-ranging your education, the more likely you are to make a wise choice about what sort of work you want to do, and the greater the range of skills you will bring to it. In fact, there is no reason why your employment should not evolve directly out of your education, as you spend more time doing the things that you enjoy and in which you become increasingly skilled. This is a fairly traditional way of finding employment and it still works well, even in today's complex conditions.

Many people find themselves doing jobs that they do not enjoy, and working for businesses of which they do not approve. This is disastrous both on a personal level and for society as a whole; the work you do should be a reflection of everything that you have learnt over the course of your education, and, ideally, is something that you value as your personal, unique contribution to the society in which you live.

> Tzŭ Lu asked:
> "What qualities must one possess to be entitled to be called an educated man?"
> "He who is earnest in spirit, persuasive in speech, and withal of gracious bearing," said the Master, "may be called an educated man; - earnest in spirit and persuasive of speech with his friends, and of gracious bearing towards others."
>
> *Confucius, The Analects*

Conclusion

The purpose of this book has been to highlight the virtues of an education that has not been qualified (or compromised) by examinations and qualifications. I started from the premise that learning for learning's sake is the ideal upon which real education is based – and that such an education is as valuable today as it has been at any time in the past. I still believe this to be the case, and, furthermore, in the course of writing the book I have found that the essence of a good education is even simpler than I had imagined.

The practical skills that we all need in order to operate successfully in the world can be most easily acquired at home. This is true for traditional activities such as cooking and housekeeping, and also for the most technologically advanced skills such as designing websites or computer programming.

Modern technology, combined with the availability of books, now provides everyone with access to almost any sort of material, ranging from copies of classical texts, to the most up-to-date scientific papers. This means that it is no longer necessary to leave home in order to pursue the more academic aspects of education, and also that people are now free to study those things that interest them, in their own time, and in their own way. History shows this to be by far the most efficient method of study, and as more people make use of it I am sure that we shall gradually see education reassume its traditional place in society – respected for what it is, rather than for what it can bestow.

Conversion Tables

Weights

ounces (oz)	grams (gm)
⅓	10
½	15
1	25
1½	40
2	50
2½	65
3	75
4	125
5	150
6	175
7	200
8	225
9	250
10	300
11	325
12	350
13	375
14	400
15	425
16 or 1 lb	450
2 lbs	900
2 lbs	1000 or 1 kg

Note: It is difficult to make accurate conversions between the metric and imperial systems of weights and measures. It is always advisable to follow either one system or the other throughout a particular recipe.

Measures

teaspoons	ml
½	2½
1	5
2	10
3	15
tablespoons	
1	15
2	30
3	45
fl oz / pints	
4 fl oz	120
5 fl oz / ¼ pint	150
6 fl oz	175
8 fl oz	240
10 fl oz / ½ pint	300
15 fl oz / ¾ pint	450
20 fl oz / 1 pint	600
1¾ pints	1 litre

Oven Temperature

Gas Mark	°C	°F
1		
2	120	250
3	160	325
4	180	350
5	190	375
6	200	400
7	220	425
8	230	450

Useful Addresses

Education Otherwise, P.O. Box 7420, London N9 9SG
   A UK support group for home-educating families. www.education-otherwise.org

Centre for Alternative Technology, Machynlleth, Powys, SY20 9AZ
   Useful source of information on building, gardening, crafts, etc. Has an excellent bookshop and mail order catalogue. www.cat.org.uk

Chase Organics, Riverdene Business Park, Molesey Road, Hersham, Surrey KT12 4RG
   Supplier of seeds and products for organic gardeners. Shop and mail order catalogue.
   www.chaseorganics.co.uk

Iriss of Penzance, 66 Chapel Street, Penzance, Cornwall TR18 4AD
   Craft supplies, including hooks and material for rag rug making.
    www.rugkit.co.uk

FUN Books
   Specialist supplier of home-education books. Will supply to people around the world by mail order.
   Dept. W, 1688 Belhaven Woods Court, Pasadena MD 21122-3727
   www.fun-books.com

Homeschool Today! Australian home school books.
   B. Paine, PO Box 371, Yankalilla, SA5203
   http://homeschoolaustralia.beverleypaine.com

Index of Recommended Books

Arranged alphabetically, by author.

Index

Also From Nezert Books

The UK's top selling guide to home education. This highly-acclaimed book offers a new insight into how traditional methods can be used to provide today's children with modern skills.

One-to-One
A Practical Guide to Learning at Home
Age 0-11
Gareth Lewis
320 Pages
Fully Illustrated

- **Reading** - practical advice on how to make reading enjoyable for children of all reading abilities.
- **Writing** - how to teach a child to produce perfect handwriting in a few weeks.
- **Arithmetic** - a painless introduction to the world of mathematics.
- **Gardening** - detailed advice on creating and caring for a small vegetable plot.
- **Cooking** - well-balanced, tried and tested recipes for children to follow with their parents.
- **Crafts** - detailed instructions for making high-quality crafts.

£12.50

---

500 Adding-Up Sums
500 Taking-Away Sums
500 Multiplication Sums
500 Division Sums

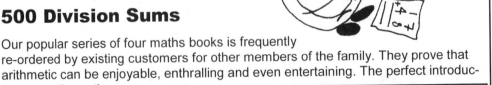

Our popular series of four maths books is frequently re-ordered by existing customers for other members of the family. They prove that arithmetic can be enjoyable, enthralling and even entertaining. The perfect introduction to mathematics.
Suitable for all ages.

Special Offer:
Set of four (RRP £4.50 per title) **£12.50**

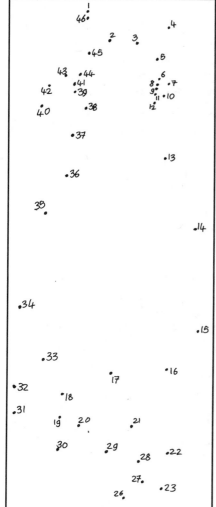

Dot to Dot   Join the dots to make a picture.

Freedom in Education Magazine

Started in January 2003, the Freedom in Education Magazine is a monthly, independent journal that supports home education and new educational initiatives.

- Articles
- Cartoons
- Quizzes and Puzzles
- Recipes and Gardening tips
- News and Information
- Stories from History
- Mathematics
- Letters

For more information, visit our websites:

www.freedom-in-education.co.uk - a popular, comprehensive site, featuring articles that have attracted attention from around the world.

www.jamboree.freedom-in-education.co.uk - an internet site for parents and children, featuring original cartoons, recipes, crafts and much more.

Dot to Dot and Code taken from May 2003 issue
Freedom in Education Magazine

Code answer: Better to wear out than to rust out

Code
Here is the key for the code. It will help you to read the proverb below.
Solution above

a b c d e f g h i j k l m n o p q r s
t u v w x y z

Proverb:

Please photocopy the form below if you wish to place an order.

If you would like to be kept informed about future publications from Nezert Books please write to Nezert Books, Nezert, 22160 Duault, France.

For more information, visit our website: **www.nezertbooks.net**

Special Offer – Order Form

	Price	Quantity	Total
Freedom in Education Magazine (12 issues)	**£12.00**		
Set of Four—500 Adding-Up Sums, 500 Taking-Away Sums, 500 Multiplication Sums, 500 Division Sums.	**£12.50**		
One-to-One A Practical Guide to Learning at Home Age 0 - 11	**£12.50**		
Unqualified Education A practical Guide to Learning at Home Age 11 - 18	**£12.50**		
Postage and packing—postage and packing free for customers using this form. Please allow ten days for delivery.			**0.00**
Please return this form, with a cheque made payable to Nezert Books to: **Nezert Books, Nezert, 22160 Duault, France.**		**Total**	

Name: ....

Address: ....

....

....

E-mail (if you wish to be informed of despatch of order):

Telephone (optional):

Customers outside the UK, please contact us directly regarding prices and methods of payment. Please mention that you are enquiring about the Special Offer available to purchasers of Unqualified Education:

Nezert Books, Nezert, 22160 Duault, France

Tel: 0033 296 215597   E-mail: info@nezertbooks.net

For news and information about alternatives to school-based education:

www.freedom-in-education.co.uk